Reading *the* Renaissance

A Volume in the Series
STUDIES IN PRINT CULTURE AND THE HISTORY OF THE BOOK

Edited by
Greg Barnhisel, Joan Shelley Rubin, and Michael Winship

Reading *the* Renaissance

BLACK WOMEN'S LITERARY RECEPTION
AND TASTE IN CHICAGO, 1932–1953

MARY I. UNGER

University of Massachusetts Press
Amherst and Boston

Copyright © 2025 by University of Massachusetts Press
All rights reserved

ISBN 978-1-62534-858-6 (paper); 859-3 (hardcover)

Designed by Sally Nichols
Set in Adobe Jenson Pro
Printed and bound by Books International, Inc.

Cover design by adam b. bohannon
Photo by Esther Bubley, *Woman and young boy in waiting room, Union Station, Chicago, May 1948*.
© Esther Bubley Collection. Courtesy Newberry Library collection,
Chicago, Burlington & Quincy Railroad Company records.

Library of Congress Cataloging-in-Publication Data
A catalog record for this book is available from the Library of Congress.

British Library Cataloguing-in-Publication Data
A catalog record for this book is available from the British Library.

To the residents of Bronzeville—past, present, and future.

Contents

Illustrations ix
Preface xi

INTRODUCTION
Race, Gender, and Reading in the Black Chicago Renaissance
1

CHAPTER 1
"A Useful and Necessary Part"
Vivian Harsh's Community Reading
23

CHAPTER 2
Bad Girl Brooks
Refusing the Respectable Reader in Popular Poetry
53

CHAPTER 3
For My People
Bronzeville's Bookstores and the Making of Modern Black Readership
85

CHAPTER 4
"A Magazine for All Americans"
Negro Story's *Wartime Reading*
110

CHAPTER 5
The Book Circle
Black Women Readers and Middlebrow Taste in Bronzeville
138

CONCLUSION
Legacies of Black Women's Reading
163

Notes 173
Index 211

Illustrations

FIGURE 1. Edwin Rosskam, "Books on Display in Shoe Store Window, 47th Street, Chicago, Illinois," July 1941.   7

FIGURE 2. Map of the Hall Branch Library, undated.   31

FIGURE 3. "The Negro: A List of Books," ca. late 1930s.   35

FIGURE 4. Vivian Harsh's list of fifteen "colored assistants" in the Chicago Public Library system, April 28, 1925.   45

FIGURE 5. Dewey R. [Jones], "Defender Column Contributors Win High Honors," *Chicago Defender*, July 30, 1927.   64

FIGURE 6. "Honored," *Sunday Chicago Bee*, [September?] 23, 1945.   83

FIGURE 7. "Best Buys in Books," advertisement for Negro Digest Book Shop, *Ebony*, March 1947.   98

FIGURE 8. Advertisement for *Sunday Chicago Bee* Book Department, *Sunday Chicago Bee*, December 5, 1943.   101

FIGURE 9. Illustration by Elton Fax in *Negro Story* 1, no. 2 (July–August 1944).   121

FIGURE 10. Two-page spread from *Negro Story* 1, no. 2 (July–August 1944).   133

FIGURE 11. Members of the Book Circle, undated photograph.   141

FIGURE 12. The Book Circle letterhead and seal, undated.   143

Preface

Reading has once again become dangerous. As I write this in the spring of 2024, book bans are on the rise across the United States, targeting books some consider harmful to the American reading public. On March 14, 2024, the American Library Association (ALA) released a report showing that in 2023, public libraries across the country experienced a "92 percent increase in [the] number of titles targeted for censorship over the previous year." Specifically, the ALA documented "efforts to censor 4,240 unique book titles in schools and libraries," far surpassing the previous high of 2,571 in 2022. Moreover, their data show that "titles representing the voices and lived experiences of LGBTQIA+ and BIPOC individuals made up 47 percent of those targeted in censorship attempts." Indeed, books that "promote learning and empathy" are particularly under attack, notes ALA president Emily Drabinski, threatening the existence of stories that challenge the status quo. The director of the ALA's Office for Intellectual Freedom, Deborah Caldwell-Stone, echoes this concern: "Each demand to ban a book is a demand to deny each person's constitutionally protected right to choose and read books that raise important issues and lift up the voices of those who are often silenced."[1] Reading is thus framed as dangerous, as it has been in past eras, because of its power to produce an informed and empathetic citizenry.

The women of *Reading the Renaissance* knew this power of reading well. Rather than suppress it, however, they instead provided sanctuary for it, facilitating acts of reception in order to build new worlds. On the South Side of Chicago in the middle decades of the twentieth century, Vivian G. Harsh, Gwendolyn Brooks, Margaret Walker, Alice Browning, and Ora G. Morrow created infrastructures of reading for Black communities that introduced readers to a rich variety of print culture. At the center of this book, then, is the matter of the politics of access—the ability for democratic societies to value, preserve, and protect stories on the margins and to make them freely available to the general public. The five women featured here did so during a particularly fraught historical moment, navigating the meanings and practices of reading through two great crises in Jim Crow America: the Great Depression and World War II. For them, reading provided a means to see to the other side of history, to imagine a world past crisis. We similarly live between two worlds: between fascism and democracy, between genocide and refuge, between pandemic and wellness. Our test is theirs: to decide the fate of books and thus the future of the nation's democracy.

The local acts of reading and reception that Harsh, Brooks, Walker, Browning, and Morrow created on Chicago's South Side were profoundly intertwined with the national imaginary of democracy and books. Through their endeavors, they generated new reading publics, changed the habits of Black readers, and made reading more accessible and relevant on both the local and the national scale. Their expansion of democratic reading in turn enabled literary advancements, such as the first bestseller by a Black author and for Black readers. It also created a bridge between the Black clubwomen's movement of the nineteenth century and the radical Black feminism of the late twentieth century. Harsh sat at the center of this literary life at the Hall Branch Library, collecting and promoting Black literature and culture. A frequent patron of the Hall Branch herself, Brooks challenged the Black press as a young teenager. A decade later, Walker's poetry facilitated the rise of Black-owned bookstores, while Browning built the Black magazine publishing industry by hand, and Morrow convened a long-standing book club that provided patrons for both Bronzeville's library and local Black bookstores. Throughout this literary ecosystem, these women left behind evidence of the audiences they built and the reading practices they promoted. A generation later, their vision of an active reading public lives on in current infrastructures of reading across Chicago that preserve these ephemera for future readers and educators.

Indeed, *Reading the Renaissance* was born out of an encounter with the archive, namely, the collection that bears the name of Bronzeville's first librarian: the Vivian G. Harsh Collection of Afro-American History and Literature at the Carter G. Woodson Branch of the Chicago Public Library system on the city's South Side. I first visited this repository of Black literature and culture in the summer of 2013 as part of an institute funded by the National Endowment for the Humanities (NEH). Led by Liesl Olson, then director of Chicago studies at the Newberry Library, the institute introduced me to important cultural centers across the city, including the Harsh Collection, which I grew up not far from but not knowing in suburban Evanston. Over the course of a decade, these archives would tell me the story of the Black Chicago Renaissance through letters, meeting minutes, newspaper articles, ads, and personal journals—the material evidence of the long history of Black memory work in Chicago.[2]

I must therefore first thank the librarians, archivists, and staff of the numerous institutions that house the materials at the center of this volume. *Reading the Renaissance* would not exist without the care and labor of Beverly Cook, Tracy Drake, Raquel Flores-Clemons, and Jordan McKenna, among many others, at the Vivian G. Harsh Collection of Afro-American History and Literature. It would also not exist without the work of those of previous generations who first began collecting and preserving the stories of Bronzeville, namely, Timuel Black, Michael Flug, Donald Franklin Joyce, and Christopher Robert Reed. I also thank Christopher Reed for his correspondence regarding Black bookstores in Bronzeville. I am particularly indebted to the Mapping the Stacks initiative, led by Jacqueline Goldsby, which recovered and organized materials documenting Black Chicago. It is these intrepid archivists, historians, scholars, and activists who make it possible for people, including me, to study, learn from, and teach the Black Metropolis's literature, culture, and history.

My sincere thanks to Kheir Fakhreldin and staff at the Chicago State University Archives for their help with the Book Circle records and for permission to reprint images from this collection. Thank you to Eloys Long Goon, current member of the Book Circle, for graciously reaching out to share stories about the group. I am grateful, too, to Robert Campbell for correspondence about the S. & S. bookstore's recording studio. Over the course of the twelve years I worked on this project, I visited the Chicago History Museum many times; I am grateful to its terrific staff for their assistance in tracking down various collections and documents. I am also indebted to Jessica Becker, Genevieve Coyle, and Michael Lotstein at the Yale University Library for their help with the Yale University Press papers. I must also thank June Can and Rebecca Maguire at the Beinecke Rare Book and

Manuscript Library for assistance with the Langston Hughes papers, especially during the COVID-19 pandemic, and for being so gracious in providing digital copies of materials when I could not travel to conduct research onsite. Thank you to Johanna Russ at the Chicago Public Library, Special Collections Division, for help with the Carl Roden papers; to the Bronzeville Historical Society, particularly Sherry Williams; to the staff of the Wisconsin Historical Society, Madison, for their help with accessing *Sunday Chicago Bee* microfilm; and the staff of the Manuscripts, Archives, and Rare Books Division at the New York Public Library's Schomburg Center for Research in Black Culture for assistance with the Sadie P. Delaney papers. My thanks, too, to Blake Spitz at the Robert S. Cox Special Collections & University Archives Research Center (SCUA), University of Massachusetts Amherst, for guidance with letters in the vast collection of W. E. B. Du Bois papers. I thank the SCUA for permission to reprint from these letters. I am grateful to the Margaret Walker Center in Jackson, Mississippi, especially Angela D. Stewart, for assistance with Walker's journals and for permission to reprint excerpts from one of them. I must also extend my thanks to Benjamin Shepard for helping to work out the rights to reprint an image from *Ebony*. Special thanks to Ebony Media Group, LLC, for this permission. Finally, I thank Jean Bubley for her assistance in securing permission to reproduce a photograph by Esther Bubley on the cover of this book, and I am grateful to the Newberry Library for granting the right to do so. The Newberry Library has been central to my personal and professional growth; it is especially meaningful, therefore, to have one of its materials grace this cover.

This book is the product of two grants from the National Endowment for the Humanities. The first, mentioned earlier, provided the materials and inspiration that led to this project. I am grateful for conversations that summer of 2013, and over the intervening years since, with Liesl Olson, Jacqueline Goldsby, Olga Herrera, Jayne Marek, Kinohi Nishikawa, and Tyler Schmidt, which have informed this project and my thinking about the Black Chicago Renaissance. The second grant from the NEH, a 2017 Summer Stipend, provided the means to finish the final stages of research for the book. I am extremely grateful to the NEH for its support of the humanities in such precarious times.

Through the course of this project, I have found a number of kindred spirits in the Society for the Study of Midwestern Literature—namely, Sara Kosiba, Andy Oler, Jennifer J. Smith (also part of the NEH institute acknowledged earlier), and Ross K. Tangedal. My thanks to them for supporting this work in a number of ways, including organizing a panel at the 2022 American Literature Association annual meeting (in Chicago, no less) on Chicago and the American Midwest, and for graciously awarding me the 2020 David D. Anderson Award for my article on the Book Circle. My gratitude in particular goes to Terrion L. Williamson, who adjudicated the award that year. I am thankful for her support of my project, which has benefited tremendously from her groundbreaking work with the Black Midwest Initiative.

I have gained much from correspondence and conversations with other scholars I admire, including Melanie Chambliss, Richard Courage, Jaime Harker, Laura Helton, Kristin Matthews, Elizabeth Schlabach, and E. James West. I am grateful to Nate Marshall for a thoughtful conversation about Gwendolyn Brooks during his visit to Ripon College in the fall of 2017. I am indebted to Susan Tomlinson and Jennifer Tuttle at *Legacy: A Journal of American Women Writers* and to Amy Blair and James Machor at *Reception*. My thanks, too, to Paula Rabinowitz for her support of my work on Black women readers.

This project is also the product of a vibrant community at the University of Illinois at Urbana-Champaign that informed my study of American literature from 1998 to 2002 and then again from 2004 to 2012. I owe Dale Bauer the most and thank her deeply for her wisdom and encouragement; there is no better mentor. A close second, however, is Gordon Hutner, from whom I learned much while working on *American Literary History*. Thank you to Robert Dale Parker for his enthusiasm and support, and for continuing to influence my own students today by making literary theory accessible to undergraduates. I am grateful to William J. Maxwell for introducing me to American modernism while an undergraduate at Illinois and for inspiring me—via a comment on an essay about T. S. Eliot, no less—to seek out graduate studies. I am also thankful to many others in the Departments of English and Gender and Women's Studies at Illinois—especially Trish Loughran, Cris Mayo, Julia Saville, Siobhan Somerville, Julia Walker, and Emily Watts—who took me seriously, transformed my thinking, and urged me onward.

If this project is a product of my past riches at Illinois, then it is also a product of my subsequent wealth at Ripon College. I am grateful to the college for a sabbatical leave in 2018 that allowed me to begin writing the first pages of this book, for numerous travel grants that enabled me to present iterations of this project at conferences, and for other funding that made this book possible. Mostly, though, I must thank the English department—particularly Megan Gannon, David Graham, Doug Northrop, Ann Pleiss Morris, Tom Truesdell, and Robin Woods—for their daily material and emotional support. Thank you to this unflappable group for making West Hall a fun place to work and for their flexibility whenever life intervenes. I have also benefited in untold ways from friends and colleagues across the college (past and present), particularly Russ Blake, Sarah Frohardt-Lane, David Hutson, Barbara McGowan, Sarah McGowan, Andy Prellwitz, Jody Roy, and Andrea Young. Thank you, too, to my colleagues in Women's, Gender, and Sexuality Studies, especially Travis Nygard. I am also indebted to Brian Bockelman for boosting the humanities through various initiatives at the college. Lastly, I am forever grateful to Vida Vande Slunt.

Here in Oshkosh, I thank Jim and Gretchen Flood. I have benefited tremendously, as has my family, from their hospitality on the banks of Lake Winnebago—a land originally inhabited by the Menominee and Ho-Chunk Nations.

I wish to acknowledge, too, that this book would not have been possible without the care and labor of the staff at the University of Wisconsin-Oshkosh Children's Learning and Care Center and the Davis Childcare Center in Oshkosh. I am grateful in particular to Angie Soda and Lise Gehrke at Davis for providing a safe and enriching environment for my children. It is not enough to have a room of one's own in order to write, I have found; one must also have the time and headspace that comes with knowing your family's needs are being met while you are away. Thank you to the dedicated staff at Davis in particular for providing this critical element.

Some portions of the introduction and conclusion to *Reading the Renaissance* were published in earlier forms. I am grateful to Oxford University Press for permission to reprint passages adapted from "Black Women Readers," in *Oxford Research Encyclopedia of Literature*, edited by Paula Rabinowitz(April2020),http://dx.doi.org/10.1093/acrefore/9780190201098 .013.953. I am likewise grateful to the *Chicago Review of Books* for permission to reprint portions of chapter 3, which first appeared in "Selling the Black Chicago Renaissance," *Chicago Review of Books*, April 14, 2021, https://chireview ofbooks.com/2021/04/14/selling-the-black-chicago-renaissance-bronzevilles -black-owned-bookstores/. Finally, I am grateful to Penn State University

Press for permission to reprint portions of chapter 5 that first appeared as "The Book Circle: Black Women Readers and Middlebrow Taste in Chicago, 1943–1953," *Reception* 11 (2019): 4–20.

At the University of Massachusetts Press, Brian Halley has been a profoundly supportive editor; this book is better for his guidance and steady hand. I am so pleased to have *Reading the Renaissance* join the Studies in Print Culture and the History of the Book series, and I am grateful to the series editors, the University of Massachusetts Press editorial board, and two anonymous readers for their incisive and thoughtful comments, which have helped me sharpen the arguments of this book. I also thank Amanda Heller, Ben Kimball, and Sally Nichols for shepherding the project through the production process with their care and expertise.

I am the lucky beneficiary of many supportive family members and friends who have provided sustenance over the years. Thank you to Marlene Kluss and Jenni Lieberman for their decades-long friendships. Thank you to my furry co-authors, Linus, Charlie, and Kaia, for their company and comfort, especially during late-night writing sessions. Thank you to all of the Eatons, Huths, and Ungers. I am particularly grateful to Elizabeth Huth-Taylor and to my brother David as well as the rest of the Oak Park Ungers—Rachel, Rosemary, Michael, and Irene—for their unwavering support and love. Thank you to the Eatons—Annette, "Papa" Bill, Mike, and Simona—for their love and encouragement as well.

I am deeply grateful to my first and best teachers: my parents, Diane and Donald Unger, who taught me to love books and reading, and who remind me to laugh and learn as much as I can. They have sacrificed for and supported me more than anyone, and I owe whatever success I have achieved to their unwavering love. Thank you. I am especially grateful for the untold hours of child care and FaceTime conversations enthusiastically provided by Grandma and Bapa.

My biggest thanks go to my favorite Eatons. Andy and Danny have grown with this project, always reminding me to be curious, to keep trying, and, when in doubt, to have a dance party. Nothing makes me happier than being their mom. Finally, to my comrade, my coconspirator, my favorite colleague, Marc Eaton, who nourishes me, believes in me, protects my time, and who always inspires better thinking and doing: I could not have done this without you. Thank you.

Reading *the* Renaissance

INTRODUCTION

Race, Gender, and Reading in the Black Chicago Renaissance

On the evening of March 14, 1945, the social worker, activist, and writer Fern Gayden made her way to the Hall Branch Library at 4801 South Michigan Avenue in Bronzeville, a predominantly African American neighborhood on Chicago's South Side. Here, at eight o'clock, she would present a public review of *Black Boy*, Richard Wright's searing new memoir, at the monthly meeting of the library's Book Review and Lecture Forum. That Gayden would deliver the review was fitting, given her personal connection to Wright. Originally from Kansas, Gayden had moved to Chicago in 1927 at the age of twenty-three with the intent of becoming a lawyer. Instead, she became a social worker with a more than fifty-year career as well as a central figure in the Black Chicago Renaissance. Alongside Wright, Margaret Walker, and Frank Marshall Davis, Gayden was a member of the South Side Writers Group (founded by Wright in 1936) and co-editor of a short-lived yet influential literary magazine, *Negro Story* (1944–1946), with another Bronzeville resident, Alice Browning. Gayden's connections to Wright were especially tight; years earlier, she had served as his family's caseworker, assisting them in securing housing in the city.[1]

The evening of the fourteenth marked the end of an unusually mild March day in the city, no doubt raising Chicagoans' hopes for an early spring. As Gayden entered the main doors of the Italian Renaissance–style library, walked through the octagonal rotunda and past the circulation desk, down the pale green hallways lined with dark English oak, and back to the room where she was to give her review, she would have noticed the unusual presence of the Chicago Police Department. Officers had "packed the meeting," the Chicago sociologist Horace Cayton would later report, in an attempt to "pan" Wright's book publicly. Perhaps it was Wright's depiction of the white police officer who, the author recounts, "created a new fear in me" that so offended the Chicago police, mobilizing them to gather at the library's book club meeting en masse. Wright's accounts of racialized violence, especially his portrayal of "the 'white' man who had beaten the 'black' boy" and rendered him "too full of fear to cry now," were already causing *Black Boy* to arouse strong reactions across the country.[2]

Indeed, Cayton, a friend of Wright's, wrote to the author in April 1945, concerned about the book's reception. "Please write and let me know how Black Boy is getting along," he requested. "I watch the New York Times every week and see that it's jumping up into the best seller class." Five years earlier, Wright's *Native Son*, with its scorching portrait of Bigger Thomas, shot to the top of national bestseller lists, thanks to its inclusion as a Book-of-the-Month Club selection. By all accounts, in the early months of 1945, *Black Boy* (another BOTM Club selection) seemed on track to surpass Wright's earlier phenomenon, but Cayton worried about the public's reactions—especially in Chicago. "There's been a lot of discussion of [*Black Boy*] in Chicago," he noted before recounting, secondhand, the recent incident at the local library. What happened that evening—what Gayden said about Wright's book as well as how the police officers responded—has not been preserved. Nevertheless, whatever she did say quelled concerns about any disruption or even violence that might have erupted as a result of the police presence, and she completed her review without incident. Reporting to Wright afterward, Cayton assured him that, in the end, the forum apparently "went off rather well in spite of [the policemen's] presence."[3]

In its description of Bronzeville's Hall Branch Library as a site of engaged, even impassioned literary reception, the story of Gayden's public review speaks to the intimate relationship between readers and writers during the Black Chicago Renaissance from the 1930s through the 1950s. The fact that, in this instance, tensions between local police and Chicago's Black community simmered not in the streets but in the local library illustrates the importance of reading and reception as practices around which Black identity and community cohered for Bronzeville residents in the middle decades of the twentieth century. Moreover, that Gayden—a mostly unremembered figure of the Renaissance—led the public forum and tamed its riotous undertones reveals the centrality of Bronzeville's Black women as arbiters of cultural taste and literary reception in Chicago during the Renaissance. Indeed, neither Wright nor Cayton was present at the Hall Branch that evening to facilitate the book's discussion. (Wright departed Chicago in 1937.) In this way, Gayden exemplifies the many Black women in Bronzeville who grounded Chicago's literary life.

Reading the Renaissance constructs a history of the Black women, like Gayden, who read and reviewed, published and promoted, and collected and curated literature of the Black Chicago Renaissance. Based on extensive archival research, this project interprets how local figures such as Vivian G. Harsh, Gwendolyn Brooks, Margaret Walker, Alice Browning, Ora G. Morrow, and Gayden herself cultivated particular literary tastes through collective acts of reading and reception. It does so by reconstructing a network of readers, book clubs, literary magazines, civic programs, and book businesses that Black women in Bronzeville created, led, and transformed from the early 1930s through the early 1950s. While some of these women are remembered today—notably Brooks and Walker—many of them are not. From various backgrounds and professions, these women influenced the production of Black literature in Chicago as well as its readership and reception. While Wright served as a compass for young Black writers—both through his pen (writing "A Blueprint for Negro Writing") and through his physical presence in the city (forming the South Side Writers Group)—it was Black women on the ground in Bronzeville who circulated literature and literary values throughout the community over the course of nearly thirty years.

In book clubs, public forums, print reviews, little magazines, local programming, and other public venues, Black women debated the role of literature in racial uplift efforts, set literary standards, and acted as community gatekeepers for cultural production. Not only did these women help produce, distribute, review, and promote Black literature in Chicago at mid-century, but also they participated in the broader world of literary reception and tastemaking. This volume places close readings of Renaissance texts alongside letters, scrapbooks, meeting minutes, reviews, and other ephemeral evidence of local reading practices to show how Black women facilitated diverse strategies of reading while teaching community members how to engage a variety of print cultures. It thus considers Chicago's Black Renaissance not just as a movement that produced innovative literature but as one that also built a remarkable infrastructure of reading and reception practices directed by Black women.

In offering a cultural history of these women, their reading communities, and their reception practices, this book advances three arguments. First, Bronzeville's Black women readers innovated reading and reception practices—what, why, and how readers were supposed to read—while formulating new literary tastes and expectations. The women discussed here not only revamped the social use and meaning of reading from previous decades and traditions but also advanced new ideas about what type of literature to value, such as the middlebrow. Moreover, they changed the public identity of Black readers. During the Renaissance, much of the literary labor—editing, publishing, and promotion—was carried out by working women in the community, professionals in fields other than literature and publishing. While some, such as Harsh, Brooks, and Walker, were members of Black Chicago's literary world, many others such as Browning, Gayden, and the women of Morrow's Book Circle had their feet in other worlds; they were teachers, social workers, and other professionals in the community. The Renaissance thus fostered a literary environment in which Black readers assumed new identities, reading practices, reception values, and concepts of literariness in the public sphere.

Second, these reading and reception practices both benefited from and facilitated the growth of Black readership. The reading communities and practices introduced by Harsh, Brooks, Walker, Browning, and Morrow could not have happened if there had not already been a burgeoning marketplace for Black readers to organize and instruct. Before the middle decades of the twentieth century, though, Black readers who consumed literature were often invisible or deemed altogether nonexistent. As Sterling Brown complained in 1941, "With a small proportion of a small middle class able to afford books, a smaller proportion of readers, and a smaller proportion still of book-buyers, the likelihood of a Negro audience for books by Negro authors is not promising." Indeed, "the job ahead of the Negro author is challenging," he concluded. "It is the job of developing a critical but interested reading public. To have great poets, says Whitman, we must have great audiences, too."[4] But the Renaissance ushered in a new era during which Black readership expanded to a size that allowed it to be taken seriously as a consumer base by the publishing industry. This growth in turn facilitated—even demanded—new reading strategies, methods, and purposes. In this way, the Renaissance provides a missing link between reading practices of nineteenth-century Black literary societies and the blockbuster readership and bestsellers of the late-twentieth-century Black publishing industry.

Third, this growth of Black readership in the Renaissance also bridges a significant gap in the history of Black women's intellectual life and traditions. Bronzeville's literary women inaugurated a democratic reading revolution in Chicago that built on the Black women's club movement of the nineteenth century and looked forward to the Black feminist consciousness-raising groups of the late twentieth. The Black Chicago Renaissance marks a threshold that connects the reading practices that emphasized respectability and refinement (via the white Western canon) with the Black Arts movement of the late twentieth century, an era that linked literary reception to Black radical activism both within and outside the academy. In recovery projects and curricula, radical Black feminists in the 1960s, 1970s, and 1980s formed reading communities that changed pedagogical practices and the literary canon and birthed new academic fields of study. Two decades later, as the millennium approached, this radicalness would become consumerized at an unprecedented rate with a Black readership that numbered in the millions. The women of the Black Chicago Renaissance prefigure much of the "personal is political" language that would become central to the Black literary marketplace and thus the consumption of Terry McMillan and other Black bestsellers at the end of the century. In this way, the Renaissance's women serve as a crucial steppingstone from one experience of literary reception to another for Black readers.

This book demonstrates how Black women readers orchestrated Bronzeville's literary scene, in turn affecting standards of taste regarding African American literature while also recruiting reading and reception practices as political and social acts. It archives how Black women worked within the system and behind the scenes to create new infrastructures and communities of readers. It is not that Black women were at the center of the Renaissance, I contend; they *were* the center. And in being the center, they touched everything—from the production to the promotion of literary life in Chicago at mid-century. *Reading the Renaissance* thus reframes the Renaissance as the story of Black women's literary innovations for a new era.

BRONZEVILLE'S RENAISSANCE

The literary life that Black women orchestrated in Chicago was extensive, a network of readers and reading communities that spanned the city's South Side. Amid the neighborhood's overcrowded conditions—created by redlining, restrictive covenants, and other racist housing policies—a relatively forgotten book culture flourished in the years from roughly 1932 to 1960. In a neighborhood that Cayton and fellow sociologist St. Clair Drake described as "a city within a city—a narrow tongue of land, seven miles in length and one and one-half miles in width, where more than 300,000 Negroes are packed solidly," books and reading were ubiquitous—so much so that by 1947 the neighborhood had become an epicenter of Black-owned bookstores, including one that was managed by Michelle Obama's grandmother.[5] Indeed, books coexisted quite comfortably alongside South Side theaters, ballrooms, and shopping centers—the public hubs of Black life in the city. Books played a fundamental role in the everyday lives of Bronzeville residents; rather than being rare objects tucked away in middle-class homes, they occupied the very streets that inspired them (see Figure 1). As Elizabeth Schroeder Schlabach has written: "Bronzeville was a space rich with outlets and spaces for literary discussion, revision, and review. Bronzeville's pens and typewriters were busy."[6] So, too, were its readers.

The Hall Branch of the Chicago Public Library system anchored this book culture, hosting a Book Review and Lecture Forum created by Vivian G. Harsh, supposedly the city's first African American branch librarian. Considered a "literary salon for the masses," the forum drew an extensive and varied crowd: Bronzeville residents such as Gayden, to be sure, but also writers including Arna Bontemps, Margaret Walker, and Frank Marshall Davis; noted sociologists such as Cayton and Drake; as well as community members.[7] Not far away, Langston Hughes directed the Skyloft Players, a theater troupe based at the Parkway Community House, a settlement house directed by Cayton. Meanwhile, Alice Browning and Gayden created the literary little magazine *Negro Story*, which published Richard Wright and Chester Himes, as well as Brooks and Walker, out of Browning's Vincennes Avenue apartment. Farther south, the *Chicago Defender* ran a poetry column that featured a teenage Gwendolyn Brooks, while the weekly Black newspaper the *Sunday Chicago Bee*—edited by Olive Diggs and staffed entirely by women—had its own book department, which offered mail-order service for

FIGURE 1. Edwin Rosskam, "Books on Display in Shoe Store Window, 47th Street, Chicago, Illinois," July 1941. Farm Security Administration/Office of War Information Photograph Collection, Prints and Photographs Division, Library of Congress, Washington, DC.

readers and also provided financial support for *Negro Story*. Across town, the S. & S. bookstore, independent and Black-owned, sold *Negro Story*, while the Studio bookstore, just across the way, sold out copies of Brooks's poetry collection *A Street in Bronzeville* when it appeared in 1945. And throughout the landscape, at members' homes, the Book Circle, Bronzeville's longest-lasting Black women's book club, met to discuss the day's most talked-about books. Throughout Bronzeville, then, Black women built a dense network of reading communities that shaped the production and circulation of Black literature, art, and culture in the years between the Harlem Renaissance and the Black Arts movement.

Long overlooked as a significant era of Black literary production, Bronzeville's Renaissance has slowly gained recognition as a crucible of Black literary and cultural production after Harlem. Arna Bontemps first made it visible in his 1950 feature, "Famous WPA Writers," which included Wright, Walker, Frank Yerby, and Willard Motley. "Harlem got its renaissance in the middle twenties," Bontemps recounted, "centering around the Opportunity contests and the Fifth Avenue Awards Dinners. Ten years later Chicago reenacted it on WPA without finger bowls but with increased power."[8] Nearly four decades later, Robert Bone was the first to position the Renaissance as a distinct literary movement. Together with Richard A. Courage in 2011, he established the Renaissance as a significant literary period with *The Muse in Bronzeville: African American Creative Expression in Chicago, 1932–1950*, contending that "for a period of fifteen years—roughly 1935 to 1950—Chicago rather than New York was the focal point of African American writing and a major center of visual arts."[9] Other foundational work by Bill V. Mullen, Darlene Clark Hine, and John McCluskey Jr. has further established the literature of the Renaissance as a significant era of Black cultural production, building on social histories of Black Chicago by Adam Green, Robert Weems Jr., and Christopher Robert Reed.[10] Together these important literary and cultural histories have positioned Bronzeville as a place of significant literary, artistic, and other cultural production after Harlem and have enabled the study of this rich period.

But little—if any—attention has been paid to the readers and audiences who received, reviewed, and shaped this production, processes central to the development of African American literature, culture, and consumerism at mid-century. Moreover, while previous scholarship has acknowledged, as Anne Meis Knupfer writes, that "black women were largely involved in promoting the expressive arts, sustaining community institutions, and fostering black solidarity through social protests," no work to date has explicitly examined the role that Black women played in the establishment and circulation of literary values in the Black Chicago Renaissance, the period over which Wright's social realism has long held sway.[11] Indeed, most histories and literary studies of the era center literary *production*—typically, how Wright's social realism influenced a generation of Chicago writers and beyond.

This book thus excavates another kind of cultural work essential to the city's literary influence during this period—that is, the work of cultural *reception*. To illustrate Bronzeville's depth and range of cultural reception, I recover a network of readers, book clubs, public programming, and businesses that directed the development of literary tastes and texts in Chicago. Extensive archival research in various institutions and repositories across the city—from the South Side's Harsh Research Collection and Chicago State University Archives to the North Side's Chicago History Museum and Newberry Library—reveals an overwhelming amount of ephemeral material that narrates the Renaissance from the perspective of the community members who received it. *Reading the Renaissance* places material culture—letters, manuscripts, newspaper clippings, scrapbooks, advertisements, meeting minutes, memos, and other ephemera of local reading practices—in conversation with a series of texts of the Renaissance, both canonical and non-, to demonstrate how reading during the Renaissance was revolutionized as much as writing.

This dynamic ecosystem of reading and reception practices reveals Bronzeville as a community of active readers who not only consumed and celebrated the Renaissance but who also cultivated particular tastes through collective acts of reading and reception. Although the Renaissance has been framed as a community endeavor in that it enabled interdisciplinary activity between various forms of artistic and cultural production—by dancers, musicians, artists, and writers—its literary history tends to revolve almost exclusively around the production of its two brightest stars, Brooks and Wright, with perhaps some attention to Walker and Frank Marshall Davis. This volume reframes Bronzeville's literary production as a grassroots, community-based movement led primarily by Black women. I argue that, while the Renaissance certainly benefited from and was shaped by individual celebrities such as Wright, it was communities of Black women on the ground who engineered and led the movement, thus propelling it forward. Even Brooks,

I show, was not a lone or anomalous genius, as she and Wright have often been characterized, but one of many community members who deliberately used her intellect, social connections, and aesthetic vision to advocate for Black cultural expression in daily practices and in local spaces. In this way I take a collective approach to the Renaissance—as recent scholarship has encouraged—directing "greater attention to cultural institutional history" rather than to "the study of creative individuals in isolation from their social contexts," and therefore building on "the ground on which social history and archivally based literary history meet."[12] I thus shift our focus of the Renaissance from individuals to institutions, from authors to readers.

As it rethinks reading and reception at mid-century, so too does this volume rethink Black literature of the era. I offer an analysis of print and material culture much broader than the traditional Renaissance canon of literary texts, often centered on Wright's bestsellers and Brooks's award-winning verse. Instead, I analyze Brooks's virtually unknown poems which she published as a teenager in the *Chicago Defender* at the same time that I consider the middlebrow reading tastes and texts of the Book Circle, Bronzeville's longest-running Black women's book club—still in existence today. I also devote space to letters, meeting minutes, and essays as well as Bronzeville's popular magazine culture. Surveying texts that circulated throughout this ecosystem—in bookstores, the library, reading groups, and newspapers—allows a different literary history of the Black Chicago Renaissance to emerge, one more attuned to the reading patterns of Bronzeville residents than to the white literary establishment. In this way, *Reading the Renaissance* answers Stephanie Brown's call to consider "what happens when we leave behind the maxims of a largely white critical establishment and turn instead to the everyday practices of a black reading public, gleaned from a consideration of black literary journals as well as book reviews in publications aimed at a black readership."[13] While Bronzeville readers engaged texts of the Black Chicago Renaissance, they also read and were influenced by white middlebrow novels, self-help books, and a wide variety of popular literature. At times they even rejected work by Renaissance writers, most notably Wright. Thus ensued a vigorous debate among Black readers in Bronzeville about the ideal literary aesthetics for racial progress. This book therefore rethinks the relationship at mid-century between Black readers and middlebrow literature, popular reading habits, and citizenship, building on foundational work by Janice A. Radway, Joan Shelley Rubin, Jaime Harker, and Gordon Hutner.[14] In doing so, it investigates how Bronzeville women's reading and reception practices legitimized certain aesthetics and genres over others in the process of building communities of readers.

BRONZEVILLE AND THE GROWTH OF BLACK READERSHIP

Reading the Renaissance joins the work of Elizabeth McHenry, Joycelyn Moody, P. Gabrielle Foreman, Eric Gardner, and others who recover forgotten African American literary communities in order to correct what McHenry calls "the historical invisibility of black readers."[15] While previous scholarship has focused primarily on eighteenth- and nineteenth-century reading practices, this volume restores an important visibility to twentieth-century Black women readers who were central to the formation of a Black middle class and popular middlebrow culture in postwar America.[16] In doing so, it demonstrates how the Black Chicago Renaissance marks a significant shift in the long history of Black readership in two intimately interconnected ways: first, Bronzeville marks a new era of reading habits and practices in the long history of Black readership, and second, it signals the rise of the Black literary marketplace, one that made possible new levels of Black literary consumerism at the end of the twentieth century.

In *Forgotten Readers: Recovering the Lost History of African American Literary Societies*, McHenry offers a history of Black reading societies in the late nineteenth and early twentieth centuries, delineating the strategies and purposes of reading within these groups. "Recogniz[ing] that reading was a potentially transformative activity, not only for individuals but for society as a whole," groups of free African Americans in the North, McHenry writes, "began establishing societies to promote literacy and to ensure that, as a group, they would not be excluded from the benefits associated with reading and literary study."[17] Members of these literary societies read works by white Western canonical authors, "those texts that had traditionally been defined as high culture, thus associating themselves with the prestige identified with genteel society."[18] Literary societies were especially useful for Black women, McHenry notes, because they offered an "invaluable means of educating black women beyond what was considered their 'proper sphere,' preparing them instead to participate in the 'gentleman's course' of study at schools like Oberlin in the 1860s." Moreover, groups such as the Female Literary Association of Philadelphia prompted Black women members to use their education for the improvement of society, "provid[ing] a forum through which black women could challenge the limitations of gender and begin the process of changing the role of women in American society."[19] As Jacqueline Jones Royster has written, such activities granted Black women greater access to the public sphere. Literacy therefore "became a tool for [Black women] inserting themselves directly and indirectly into arenas for action and for doing whatever they could to mediate and manage the critical process of change."[20]

If Black women used literacy to challenge social norms in the public sphere during the nineteenth century, they also did so using more subtle but no less subversive acts of textual reception. Readers of Frances E. W. Harper's *Iola Leroy* (1892), P. Gabrielle Foreman argues, would have been urged to "read aright"—to engage in a kind of reading that recognizes "historical scars and wounds" and rejects "the attitudes and assumptions of the master class." Such reading instruction offers audiences "a way to join a collective project of cultural, historical, and intellectual history that will teach the new nation to read aright."[21] In a similar way, Benjamin Fagan argues that, in *Incidents in the Life of a Slave Girl*, Harriet Jacobs uses the newspaper "as a tool for black liberation." By employing the proslavery *New York Herald* to bewilder the maniacal slaveholder Dr. Flint so she can remain hidden, Jacobs uses the paper against its own intentions, instead recruiting it in the struggle for the emancipation, survival, and dignity of Black womanhood. Fagan thus shows how Jacobs "exemplifies . . . a *rogue reader*, someone who lives outside of the communities imagined by most early American newspapers, has limited if any access to the networks and systems (public roads and post offices, for example) we normally associate with print cultures, but who nevertheless understands print and its pathways as necessarily open and available to revision and manipulation."[22] Through this rogue readership, Jacobs innovates reception practices while teaching her readers new modes of racial resistance independent of highbrow literature. Both "rogue reading" and "reading aright" harness the same power of reading and social intervention that McHenry's literary societies engage, but do so using strategies accessible to a wider base of Black readers in the nineteenth century.

The literary scene on Chicago's South Side gave Black women readers in the next century an especially robust opportunity to engage their community in reading as a political practice. Darlene Clark Hine has illustrated how literary production during the Renaissance offered readers and writers a way to lobby for a better position within the nation's democratic scene. "Chicago's black elites, artists, and workers, men and women and their families, all became cultural consumers, patrons, and agents in the conveyance, if not commoditization, of racial pride," she describes. "They collectively invested themselves in the quest for self-affirmation and imbued each other and their communities with a sense of belonging, the determination to struggle, to stay, and to celebrate achievement in spite of racial discrimination." They did this in one significant way, through the consumption of literature and other print culture. The work of local artists, including Langston Hughes, Gwendolyn Brooks, and others, "was inextricably linked to the basic fabric of everyday life of black citizens. It was but a thin line that separated the black cultural workers from politically engaged steel, meatpacking, industrial, and service workers, and even that line was porous." The result was perhaps a more direct connection between literary and cultural production in Chicago during the Renaissance and the city's South Side. In various forms of writing, for instance, "Hughes took the Black Chicago Renaissance to the everyday working people, and although his humor and insights may not have raised wages, they did raise black self-consciousness."[23] Brooks, meanwhile, demonstrated "a commitment to bring poetry, even at its most difficult, to a wide range of readers," Liesl Olson writes. "Brooks comes out of a tradition of Chicago women devoted to promoting literature for the masses. She taught children; she sponsored poetry contests; she conducted workshops in prisons; she gave countless readings."[24] In this way, much like McHenry's readers of the nineteenth century, the readers of the Black Chicago Renaissance used literary practices to "raise black self-consciousness" of individuals and, in turn, to alter the city's and the nation's racial politics.

Harsh, Brooks, Walker, Browning, and Morrow all aimed to make the lives of Bronzeville residents better through reading. In doing so, these five women entered a long history of using reading to incite personal as well as social transformation, becoming what Gordon Hutner calls "citizen-readers."[25] In the process, they devised new ways of doing so. Rather than advancing one coherent strategy or practice, however, these women promoted a range of habits, values, and purposes. Harsh looked to relevant, accessible texts instead of focusing on highbrow literature, as her predecessors had done, to foster racial pride in her community; similarly, the women of the Book Circle turned to middlebrow fiction as a means to engage the nation's racial politics. Walker and Browning used reading to assemble large-scale audiences of Black readers through, on the one hand, writing best-selling poetry (Walker) and, on the other, building an infrastructure of Black magazine publishing (Browning). Meanwhile, a teenaged Brooks attempted to (re)train readers of the Black press to interpret poetry and their environment more critically. At times, these women imagined reading as a solitary personal endeavor; at others, they framed literary reception as a collective act of racial imagining. Some of the women addressed readers as friends; others used reading practices to introduce new audiences to the legacy of African American literature. Still others, like Brooks, confounded and disoriented readers' expectations.[26] The range of theories and practices these five women promoted, organized, and led allowed them to serve the needs of a nation in flux, one transitioning from the turbulent interwar years to the ambiguous postmodern era.

These new reception habits also created for the women of Bronzeville's reading cultures a more modern and more powerful identity: consumer. The increased literary activity in Bronzeville during the Renaissance signals the rise of the Black reader-consumer, one with the disposable income to purchase literature in a way that Black readers perhaps never had before. Toward this end, this volume complicates previous narratives of Black audiences, readership, and the marketplace which have claimed that Black writers wrote primarily for white audiences—in part because Black audiences did not yet exist in considerable numbers. Jaime Harker writes that "despite poverty and racial oppression, there was a significant black reading audience. Black colleges in the South, founded during Reconstruction, continued their work despite the violent backlash of Jim Crow, producing educated graduates inspired by Du Bois and the activist work of the NAACP. African American literary societies encouraged literary activity and provided appreciative audiences for writers, particularly black writers." Such an "audience wasn't large and prosperous enough, however, to sustain black writers by themselves. A mixed audience was essential."[27] Harker echoes Sterling Brown's concern that in 1941, middle-class Black readers did not exist yet in numbers that could sustain Black writers or the Black publishing industry.

As I demonstrate through archival materials, despite this modest Black reading base, writers such as Gwendolyn Brooks and Margaret Walker nevertheless often wrote for Black readers as their primary and original audience. To be sure, Black bestsellers depended on white readership for their record-breaking sales; nevertheless, this era witnessed an explosion in the numbers of Black readers. This growth in national Black readership—possible in large part because of Bronzeville's rich and robust community of bookselling—thus demonstrates the power of the expanding "Negro market" that the white publishing industry pursued with increasing fervor in the years surrounding World War II. This courtship in turn facilitated the growth of Black reading and reception practices and communities in Chicago, which served as a major hub of literary activity. Bronzeville's various reading habits provide evidence of the growth of Black women readers as a consumer base to be taken seriously and one that, by the end of the century, would become monetized at an unprecedented rate.

Within this history of Black bestsellers, reading practices, and reception strategies, this volume charts the complicated relationship between Black women (and girls), US print culture, and consumerism as documented by Frances Smith Foster, Marcia Chatelain, and Koritha Mitchell, among others.[28] At times a venue of racial uplift and antiracist activism, and at others a means of pressuring Black women into respectability politics, the avenues of print culture that Bronzeville's Black women encountered were varied, even inconsistent. Indeed, this book analyzes the often conflicting and contradictory ways that these women interacted with print culture and literature of the Renaissance. To take up the language of Brigitte Fielder and Jonathan Senchyne, this discussion confronts the tension between "the agency that black writers, editors, publishers, and artists found by participating in print culture" and the "constricting rather than freeing" realities they often faced.[29] Bronzeville's Black readers may have used print culture to navigate the public sphere and to influence (literary) society, but they often did so in ways that were at once triumphant, ambiguous, and even ambivalent.

RECLAIMING A BLACK FEMALE MIDWESTERN INTELLECTUAL TRADITION

Although the women featured in this book often used print culture to facilitate social change, they typically did not explicitly identify as intellectuals or activists during the Renaissance. Yet their reading practices nevertheless engage the rich history of Black women's intellectualism, feminist politics, and praxis, as documented by many Black feminist literary scholars, including Stephanie Y. Evans, Martha S. Jones, and Brittney C. Cooper.[30] The practices and philosophies of Mary McLeod Bethune, Mary Church Terrell, Ida B. Wells, and Fannie Barrier Williams, for instance—all with strong ties to Chicago—echo throughout events organized by Vivian Harsh, poems published by Gwendolyn Brooks and Margaret Walker, literary manifestos penned by Fern Gayden and Alice Browning, and the meetings of Ora Morrow and the Book Circle. The leadership roles in publishing, editing, and other literary endeavors that these women occupied mirror those inhabited by early trailblazers such as Sada J. Anderson, Pauline Hopkins, and Victoria Earle Matthews.[31] Specifically in Chicago, as Olson and Knupfer have shown, there existed powerful, creative women who took artistic and political risks to achieve social progress.[32]

The reading and reception practices advanced by Harsh, Brooks, Walker, Browning, and Morrow contribute in particular to the intellectual history of Black women in the Midwest, as documented by Hine, Wanda A. Hendricks, and Terrion L. Williamson.[33] Even before Emancipation, as Stephanie Y. Evans writes, the Midwest was home to educational opportunities for Black women that were rare in other parts of the country. In Ohio, Oberlin College was one of a handful of institutions that were open to Black or female students in the antebellum era, the majority of which were in the Midwest. "Black women earned their first college degrees in Ohio," Evans notes, explaining, "Oberlin was the only college to graduate a significant number of black women before the Civil War." Moreover, she writes, "in the mid-nineteenth century, many black families moved to the Midwest, especially Ohio, because they were able to gain access to higher education."[34] By the late nineteenth century, Hendricks notes, Illinois in particular served as a vibrant hub for Black women's intellectual and activist work. Just three years after the National Association of Colored Women formed in 1896, the Illinois Federation of Colored Women's Clubs (IFCWC) was created. By 1921, the federation boasted a large following, "claiming nearly eighty groups . . . with at least ten members in each." Committed to uplift and the eradication of inequality, the women of the IFCWC "promoted an African American–based movement built around a racially conscious ideology, successfully blending their private world of club work with the public world of political activism."[35] In their similar community-based efforts to promote reading and reception practices in the service of political advancement, the women of Bronzeville mapped a new geography in the mid-twentieth century of Black women's intellectual traditions in the Midwest.

While these habits and strategies of reading that Bronzeville's Black women readers employed build on previous generations of Black feminist political and public engagement, they also foreshadow the emergence of women who aligned reading with revolutionary political action at the end of the twentieth century, including Audre Lorde and members of the Combahee River Collective, Alice Walker, as well as the scholar-activists of the ground-breaking Black feminist anthology *All the Women Are White, All the Blacks Are Men, but Some of Us Are Brave*.[36] The recovery, reading, and reception of Black women's writing in particular centered the liberation practices of Black feminists and scholars of the 1970s and 1980s. As Courtney Thorsson has written of The Sisterhood, a group of Black women writers who met in the 1970s, including Alice Walker, Toni Morrison, June Jordan, and Ntozake Shange: "They believed in the power of literature as an agent of political and social transformation.... They helped establish Black studies and African American literary studies in the academy."[37] The women of the Black Chicago Renaissance prefigure this revolutionary reading, framing their reception practices in these years as deeply personal as well as politically transformative. This work continues well into the late twentieth and early twenty-first centuries through such venues as Oprah's Book Club, Glory Edim's Well-Read Black Girl project, as well as social media platforms and online groups such as Black BookTok, Book Girl Magic, Mocha Girls Read, the Black Girls Book Club, and the Sistah Girls Book Club. In this way, *Reading the Renaissance* investigates new technologies of readership that similarly aim to bring the personal and political together through acts of reading and reception.

RECOVERY AND RECEPTION METHODOLOGY

In going to the archive to recover lost voices and histories, this volume contributes to the growing field of archive studies, Black memory work, and the complicated history of the politics of access. Specifically, it is informed by what Laura Helton, Justin Leroy, Max A. Mishler, Samantha Seeley, and Shauna Sweeney identify as "a growing tradition of black memory work invested in archive building as a foundation of liberation."[38] This book not only tells the story of Black women such as Vivian Harsh who actively participated in this tradition of recovering, cataloging, and distributing Black texts but also theorizes the methods of recovering this tradition and the limits of contemporary methodology in literary scholarship. I am concerned here with the "tension between recovery as an imperative that is fundamental to historical writing and research—an imperative infused with political urgency by generations of scholar-activists—and the impossibility of recovery when engaged with archives whose very assembly and organization occlude certain historical subjects."[39] As a white scholar, I am especially mindful of how an archive is shaped by white supremacy at the same time that I use it to disrupt literary and cultural histories that erase Blackness. Indeed, as I searched for evidence of reading practices in Black communities, I was confronted by "the state-sanctioned disappearance of black documents, disparaged as worthless," something that scholars of Black print culture in particular know well.[40] This literary and cultural history has therefore been written, in the words of Jill Lepore, "from what can be found."[41]

Informed by these absences and limitations, but also delights, of institutional memory, *Reading the Renaissance* charts a path forward through the archive, assembling a history from unconventional sources inspired by the work of Shanna Greene Benjamin, Carla L. Peterson, Laurel Thatcher Ulrich, and Joanna Brooks.[42] It constructs what Peterson calls a "counter-history"—a narrative that restores "the marginalized, despised, or forgotten" to "the central protagonists." For "unlike official histories, in which one perspective tends to dominate," she explains, "these counter-histories allow a multiplicity of voices to emerge—sometimes in harmony, sometimes in tension with one another."[43] To stitch together such a counternarrative of Black women's reading and reception practices during the Renaissance, I rely on unconventional sources to map out this reception ecosystem: phone directories, newspaper articles, advertisements, business directories, records of purchase orders, marginalia, letters and telegrams, greeting cards, newspaper clippings, scrapbooks, meeting minutes and agendas, journals, notes written on the backs of flyers. In doing so, I aim to engage the process of what Brooks calls an "honoring through care and bringing coherence to the immensely meaningful fragments of experience suspended in the mundanity of time"—"a purpose," as she describes it, "shared by women's work and humanities scholarship alike."[44] This counter-history of the Black Chicago Renaissance thus aims to make visible the "invisible things" that, in Toni Morrison's words, "are not necessarily 'not-there.'"[45]

Each chapter of this book centers on the relationship between a significant Bronzeville figure and a specific culture of reading in mid-century Chicago: Vivian Harsh and the public library system; Gwendolyn Brooks and the Black press; Margaret Walker and Bronzeville's Black-owned bookstores; Alice Browning and little magazines; and, finally, Ora G. Morrow and the neighborhood's literary societies and book clubs. In this way I map a geography of women readers and community leaders who cultivated communal acts of reading and reception.

Chapter 1 documents the relationship between Bronzeville's authors and reading publics formed by the first public library on Chicago's South Side serving primarily African American patrons, the George C. Hall Branch Library, the site of Gayden's dramatic Book Review and Lecture Forum presentation on *Black Boy*. Directed by Vivian G. Harsh, the Hall Branch became a vital community resource when it opened in 1932, incorporating reading practices into everyday Bronzeville life through reading groups, social events, and public programs. Not only were patrons able to attend, free of charge, readings by well-known local writers such as Margaret Walker and Frank Marshall Davis, but they were also prompted to interact with and respond to writers' work in the long-running Book Review and Lecture Forum, created by Harsh herself. This chapter analyzes Hall Branch artifacts such as program flyers, annual reports, and other internal library documents to illustrate how Harsh and her (mostly female) staff positioned patrons to be active consumers of literature. In particular, I examine three listing projects of Harsh's to show how the library normalized the practice of literary reception in Bronzeville and established collective, accessible, and relevant literary tastes and values for readers in the community.

Chapter 2 analyzes how these community norms, tastes, and values came to bear on the early work of Gwendolyn Brooks. While community members were able to access much of Bronzeville's literature in the local Black press—in publications such as *Abbott's Monthly* and *The Bronzeman*—they often turned to the *Chicago Defender*'s "Lights and Shadows" column, which featured well-known local poets like Brooks. Indeed, before she became a national figure, Brooks published dozens of poems in the *Defender*'s literary column as part of a group of poets known as the Lasers. In some of these poems, she models gender and class roles for her aspiring middle-class readers during the Great Migration; in others, she foreshadows the cynicism of her later poems that question the ability of middle-class respectability to solve the social and economic ills of urban life. By recovering Brooks's early newspaper poems, I analyze how her work challenged a politics of respectability—an ideology the *Defender* routinely promoted—rejecting the practices of what I term the *respectable reader* to instead produce a critical, skeptical reader. In this way, chapter 2 also demonstrates how Brooks's early career was shaped by the expectations of Chicago's Black institutions as well as the reception of her work by the city's Black readers rather than the white literary establishment.

Chapter 3 considers the effect of local Black bookstores on the reception, circulation, and consumption of Black Chicago Renaissance texts, particularly Margaret Walker's prizewinning collection of poems *For My People* (1942). Winner of the 1942 Yale Younger Poets prize and selling more than five thousand copies—unprecedented for a poetry collection by an African American woman at this time—*For My People* received little support from its publisher and yielded only a modest response from white readers, and yet it achieved record-breaking sales. This was possible, I show, because of the text's unique blend of aesthetics and accessibility. Mixing sonnets, ballads, and free verse, Walker's collection provides a textual space and reading experience through which Black readers can commune with one another through shared heritage and cultural knowledge. Moreover, Walker's aesthetic arrived in Bronzeville at a moment of exceptional book accessibility on the South Side. At the time, Bronzeville boasted a wealth of independently owned Black bookstores—more than fifteen at its peak in 1947—which gave residents unprecedented access to printed texts and provided an economic base for the Black Chicago Renaissance, funding the movement with Black dollars. Unlike other bestsellers by Black authors in the 1940s—which relied on white readership—*For My People* attracted Bronzeville's Black reading public, demonstrating how the circulation and consumption of literature provided a new kind of purchasing power for African Americans in the 1940s and 1950s. This chapter thus charts how literary consumerism was an integral part of Black Americans' self- and social transformation during the modern era.

Alice Browning and Fern Gayden sought to expand this growing marketplace for Black readers with their little magazine *Negro Story* (1944–1946). Browning took the lead, placing the magazine at the center of the national Black publishing industry and even promoting it to non-Black readers as "A Magazine for All Americans." Her framing was strategic; books and reading had become recruited into the war effort on a national level, symbolizing democracy in a war of ideas. As editor, writer, literary historian, and promoter for and of Black literature, Browning thus explicitly aimed to form attitudes about reading for the magazine's audiences as war raged overseas. In chapter 4 I argue that she did so by launching a Double V victory campaign of her own, publishing stories and poems that recounted Black servicemen's experiences of valor—as well as racial discrimination—at home and abroad. Racial unity was crucial to victory on both fronts, and *Negro Story* charged readers with new responsibilities: to bear witness to threats to democracy at home and overseas. In the process, I show how *Negro Story* also supported Black soldiers by publishing their writing, thus expanding the Black publishing industry that Browning was building in Bronzeville across the Atlantic.

Chapter 5 turns to the middlebrow literary reading practices of Bronzeville's longest-running book club, the Book Circle. Founded in 1943 by a local teacher, Ora G. Morrow, this group of professional Black women met monthly for decades to discuss popular, mostly middlebrow books. The group followed a strict set of reception practices created by Morrow herself and left meticulous records of their activities, including a constitution, agendas, photographs, meeting minutes, and scrapbooks. As these documents illustrate, the group turned to the middlebrow again and again to debate racial injustice in the postwar era. Often branded as escapist or apolitical, the middlebrow instead offered the Book Circle opportunities to engage with social issues and local politics, and members often disagreed about the correct literary taste for advancing racial progress. As the book club routinely turned to the middlebrow, members used mass consumer culture as a way to understand their historical and cultural moment. At the same time, I argue, the Book Circle also looked ahead to the "personal is political" focus of Black women's reading and reception practices of the late twentieth century.

Reading the Renaissance concludes with a discussion of how recovering Bronzeville's reading communities helps tell a larger story of Black women readers in the United States—from nineteenth-century literary societies to Black feminist communities and academic groups of the 1960s through the 1980s—who turned to reading as a strategy for social transformation. Indeed, the deeply "personal is political" reception work carried out by Harsh, Brooks, Walker, Browning, and Morrow in the mid-twentieth century helped pave the way for Black feminist activists at the end of the century who formed consciousness-raising groups and established new academic disciplines that depended on shared reading practices of Black women. In particular, Brooks, Browning, and Walker reemerged in the century's final decades as symbols of reading and reception practices critical to Black feminism. Into the twenty-first century, too, Black women readers have turned to online and digital spaces in which to carry out this important collective work.

As I demonstrate, Black women continue to innovate, creating new practices of communal reading and reception to agitate for racialized and gendered forms of justice.

Today the South Side of Chicago is known more for its supposed violence than its vibrant reading communities—in many ways because, as Adam Green writes, after 1955, Black Chicago would face a "sobering future" of joblessness, poverty, and urban decay. But, Green asks, "what do we miss when we view Black Chicago's history through such a rueful and fatalistic lens?"[46] *Reading the Renaissance* joins current scholarly, popular, and artistic initiatives in documenting the South Side's forgotten histories without ignoring the lived conditions of the community or resigning the neighborhood to fatalism. Since the second decade of the twenty-first century, work by Thomas Dyja, Eve Ewing, Mariame Kaba and Essence McDowell, Nate Marshall, Ethan Michaeli, Natalie Moore, Christopher Robert Reed, and E. James West has begun the process of illuminating the stories of the city's South Side.[47] By recovering Black Chicago's forgotten reading cultures and their impact on American literature and culture, this book constructs a usable history of the South Side, contending that its contribution to national life and letters is far richer than our current literary history has acknowledged. In this way, it participates in a broader cultural movement of asserting that the literary history of Black Chicago—and of Black women—matters.

CHAPTER I

"A Useful and Necessary Part"
Vivian Harsh's Community Reading

Fourteen years before Fern Gayden would stand in front of an audience at the Hall Branch Library and defend Richard Wright's *Black Boy* from local police officers, Vivian Harsh stood accused of trying to incite a race riot in the streets of Chicago. It was the summer of 1931, and Harsh had just been named head of a new, as yet unnamed library to be built at 4801 South Michigan Avenue on a lot donated by the Rosenwald Foundation. The backlash against Harsh was swift, beginning just two weeks after she had been approved by the administration committee of the board of directors of the Chicago Public Library (CPL). First, Oscar De Priest, the noted African American congressman from Chicago (1929–1935), wrote in June 1931 to the CPL chief librarian, Carl Roden, who had selected Harsh for the position, to assert that Blanche V. Shaw should serve as branch librarian instead.[1] Then in August, Roden began fielding complaints from Andrew J. Kolar, the president of the board of the CPL, who demanded that Roden submit a report defending his selection of Harsh. In his lengthy response to Kolar, Roden noted that it was Harsh's extensive experience, qualifications, and training—not "'influence' or 'politics' or pressure of any sort whatsoever"—that had led him to select her. He also made special note of the Rosenwald Foundation's approval of her appointment, writing that both the president and the director of the foundation had "express[ed] their pleasure and satisfaction in the selection."[2] Despite his attempts to quell Kolar's resistance, by October, Roden observed, word had somehow "reached the Mayor to the effect that the books we are installing in the new Hall Branch are likely to cause a 'race riot.'"[3]

The books that concerned Kolar were those housed in Harsh's Special Negro Collection—a collection of books by, for, and about African Americans that Harsh had begun amassing before the Hall Branch was completed. During that summer of 1931, thanks again to the Rosenwald Foundation, Harsh had crisscrossed the country to visit other such collections as inspiration for building her archive. Her collection would eventually number over two thousand items and attract such figures as Langston Hughes, Richard Wright, Gwendolyn Brooks, and John H. Johnson. But the crux of Kolar's concern that summer was one book in particular, Scott Nearing's *Black America* (1929), a provocative treatise on race relations in the United States. Roden assured him in another letter in October 1931 that Nearing's book was not inflammatory, citing reviews from *Book Review Digest* and the *New York Herald Tribune* to make his case. Roden also quoted Alain Locke's response to Harsh's collection. "He went out of his way to praise [it]," Roden reported to Kolar, "saying that it contained all the good items and left out all the 'weeds,' as he put it. If Nearing's book, or any other in our list, was going to cause a 'race riot,' Prof. Locke would certainly have said so to me when he was in my office."[4] In the end, Nearing's book was pulled—not because it was dangerous, Roden clarified, but because "the book was found to be offensive by a number of our Negro patrons"—and Harsh assumed her position as head librarian on January 18, 1932, when the doors to the Hall Branch opened, without scandal or race riot.[5]

Though officials fretted about the potentially incendiary content of Harsh's Special Negro Collection, it was the function of that collection—how she used the list of works within the community and to what end—that proved most radical. As a branch librarian, Harsh focused on building audiences and communities of readers. To this end, she expended a tremendous amount of energy planning programming, organizing events, and otherwise using the Hall Branch as a nexus of public education and community reading. In doing so, she broke from traditional practices of the profession at the time. While "library science literature during the late 1920s and early 1930s echoed ALA president Judson Jennings's insistence that libraries focus on books and on individual patrons," Laura Burt notes, Harsh resisted this top-down, individualistic approach to libraries and instead created an environment that emphasized community reading and reception practices.[6]

At the center of Harsh's democratic reading revolution was listing, a practice she used throughout her career to engage readers, build community, and impart knowledge. Through the lists of works she created, she made reading more accessible and relevant to Bronzeville residents. Harsh has famously been called the "Historian Who Never Wrote," a misnomer that unfortunately haunts her legacy.[7] She gained it primarily because she left few personal records behind, frustrating many who have searched in vain for information about her.[8] Compared with her contemporaries, such as Charlemae Hill Rollins, children's librarian at the Hall Branch, as well as Howard University's Dorothy Porter, both of whom had multiple professional publications, Harsh did not leave a significant paper trail. But she did indeed produce written texts—just perhaps not in the forms or venues that many would have expected of her. For one, much of her writing was created for internal Hall Branch or general CPL purposes. She wrote hundreds of documents, including letters, lists, bibliographies, memos, bulletins, newsletters, annual reports, and even several histories of the Hall Branch—many preserved in the collection that now bears her name. Moreover, what she did publish beyond the walls of the Hall Branch appeared primarily in the local Black press, not in academic journals. That she chose to write for local audiences—colleagues at the Hall Branch as well as readers in her own community—rather than a wider network of colleagues and professionals reveals the community-based, democratic ethos with which she conducted her work throughout her entire career.

In this chapter I examine three listing projects that Harsh directed, as well as the reading practices, reception tools, and knowledges she produced through these lists for Bronzeville readers. In turn, I document how the Hall Branch established a particular culture of reading as well as reception practices throughout the community that emphasized the useful and relevant consumption of books and print culture for its patrons. The Special Negro Collection was one such list that Harsh produced in an effort to create and inform local reading publics, but she made dozens more throughout her career. Yet unlike other lists, bibliographies, and collections in which radical work resides in their *production*—the curating and cataloging process itself—the radical work of Harsh's collection lies in its public *consumption*. In the next section, I detail the production of Harsh's most famous list, her Special Negro Collection, and argue that it emblematizes her dedication to the production as well as to the democratic *consumption* of knowledge in the public sphere.

LIST 1: BUILDING AN ARCHIVE

As Harsh began building the Special Negro Collection well before the Hall Branch opened its doors, she quickly discovered that she would have to rely on her own ingenuity as well as the generosity of others to build the collection book by book. The five-hundred-dollar grant she received in the summer of 1931 from the Rosenwald Fund allowed her to conduct "travel in the field of library science," trips that would continue after this first year so that she could continue to amass books for the collection.[9] She thus spent the summer before the Hall Branch opened visiting different collections of African American history and culture, including the Schomburg Collection at the New York Public Library as well as locations in Washington, DC, Cleveland, Detroit, and Newark. Inspired by her trip, Harsh returned to Chicago and "began acquiring books, pamphlets, clippings, and photographs from friends in the Association for the Study of Negro Life and History."[10] She then "drew up a list of 300 essential books for readers interested in black literature and history. To acquire them, she solicited donations and appealed to booksellers who were friends for discounts."[11] Contributions from friends and colleagues helped. In 1929 Charles Bentley, a prominent African American dentist whom Harsh knew through the Chicago social circuit, seeded the collection with more than one hundred books on African American literature, history, and culture. These included works by Charles W. Chesnutt, Booker T. Washington, and Paul Laurence Dunbar.[12] By the Hall Branch's opening day, Harsh's Special Collection already contained some three hundred volumes.[13]

Over the next two decades, Harsh diligently grew the collection of materials pertaining to "Negro Life and History" with donations from community members and friends. In addition, the Rosenwald Fund contributed another five hundred dollars with which, she notes in her 1934 annual report, she purchased "additional copies and new titles for the Special Collection of books by and relating to the Negro."[14] Harsh also actively solicited books and other materials. "Some very excellent items were donated for the Special Collection through requests by letters sent to authors and publishers," she reported in 1933.[15] Fellow librarians Marian G. Hadley, who assembled an extensive slide collection on Black history, and Charlemae Hill Rollins, who collected children's books, assisted Harsh in growing the collection. Richard Wright contributed various items too, including a draft of "Big Boy Leaves

Home" as well as of "Blueprint for Negro Literature," in addition to drafts of other works, specifically a bibliography he was working on for the Negro in Illinois project and a study of "Ethnographical Aspects of Chicago's Black Belt." Langston Hughes, meanwhile, contributed materials pertaining to his autobiography *The Big Sea*.

Harsh was particularly proud of several rare items in the collection, including "Un Chant Nouveau by Langston Hughes, the first book about his writing in any language; the London edition of the seldom seen Spring in New Hampshire and Other Poems by Claude McKay; the 1878 edition of Henry Flipper's autobiography, The Colored Cadets of West Point; a brochure published in 1829 entitled An Ethiopian Manifesto issued in the defense of the rights of the Black Man in the scale of universal freedom is the earliest work on hand. Interesting also is the narrative, Sojourner Truth, a bonds-woman of olden time published in 1875."[16] Harsh also added various items important to documenting local African American history. These included two WPA (Works Progress Administration) projects: "The Negro in Illinois: The Illinois Writers Project" and one led by Horace Cayton and Elizabeth Wimp that was later published as *The Chicago Afro-American Union Analytic Catalog: An Index to Materials on the Afro-American in the Principal Libraries of Chicago* (1972). And there were still many other materials that Harsh added to the collection, including photographs, periodicals, and pamphlets.

By the branch's fourth anniversary, the collection numbered 793 items.[17] It grew at such a rate that, in 1939, Harsh expressed hope that space would be built on an adjoining lot that would include "a room for the fast-growing special collection of books by and about the Race."[18] In 1940 the collection had expanded to one thousand volumes,[19] and by 1945, it had reached "some 2,000 titles."[20] Having started with only three hundred, Harsh and her extended network of patrons, friends, and colleagues had done impressive work to grow the collection nearly sevenfold in just over a decade. Harsh was pleased with the collection, already noting in her 1937 annual report that "the Special Collection is serving its purpose very well."[21]

While Harsh kept meticulous records of the collection's contents, she left little writing about her philosophy of curation. No rationale or manifesto exists that articulates her principles of inclusion and exclusion or what her overall vision of the collection was. Nor did Harsh ever compile the contents of the collection into a catalog or bibliography; the collection would not be inventoried until 1967, seven years after her death.[22] What little evidence of her purpose or philosophy exists can be gleaned in a few statements she documented about the collection throughout her career. First, it is clear that she considered the collection to be essential work of the Hall Branch; the year before her retirement she reflected, "The most distinct feature about this library which enables it to serve the community so adequately is the special collection of books for and about Negroes." Second, to her mind, the service that the collection provided the Bronzeville community "so adequately" was its ability to build interest in, knowledge of, and pride for Black cultural production. The collection "plays a big part in furnishing information about the Negro in an effort to build pride in [the] race," she declared.[23]

One way that Harsh used the list to shore up racial pride was through her organization of the collection's contents. Though she was certainly hemmed in by the CPL's standardizing methods of cataloging, she nevertheless dignified Black experiences in how she classified volumes of Black literature, history, and culture. Her principles of organizing and cataloging these materials were built on what Laura Helton describes as "a tradition of countercataloging at black institutions" which reoriented classification systems that had long marginalized or altogether erased Black experiences. Like Dorothy Porter, charged with organizing Howard University's Negro Collection (the Moorland Foundation), Harsh rejected the Dewey Decimal number 325.26, the number that came to identify "nearly every object relating to African American life and history," to such a point that "it became a catchall where librarians shelved anything black," Helton notes. Associated with migration, colonization, and emigration, however, 325.26 cemented Black America's epistemological "otherness" in libraries across the nation by classifying Black literature and culture as "foreign to the nation." Finding such racist and exclusionary cataloging practices untenable, "Porter decided to dismantle the tools she learned in library school and remake them to capaciously delineate blackness." To do so, Helton recounts, Porter "did not simply move books within Dewey's taxonomy; instead, she discarded entire sections and rewrote what the decimals signified."[24]

In a similar way, Harsh cataloged items under different numbers, reclassifying them as central to American history, culture, and literature broadly speaking. For example, Booker T. Washington's *Selected Speeches*, often placed at 325.26, appeared in Porter's system under the Dewey Decimal category 815 for American oratory.[25] Harsh, however, used the more targeted Library of Congress call number E 185.6 (United States/Elements in the population/Afro-American/Status and development since Emancipation), thus legitimizing

Washington's work as central to the nation and its history. Harsh made other similar moves: Hallie Quinn Brown's *Homespun Heroines and Other Women of Distinction* (1926) was shelved at 920 (Biography, genealogy, insignia), as was B. G. Brawley's *Negro Builders and Heroes* (1937) and Anna Julia Cooper's *Personal Recollections of the Grimke Family* (1951). Poetry by Brooks (both *A Street in Bronzeville* and *Annie Allen*), Hughes (*The Weary Blues*), James Weldon Johnson, and Frank Marshall Davis appear under the Dewey Decimal category 821 (English Poetry) or the Library of Congress categories of PS 591 (American Literature/Collections of American Literature) and PS 3519 (American Literature/Individual authors). Anthologies such as Alice Dunbar Nelson's volume *The Dunbar Speaker and Entertainer* (1920) appear as 810.8 (American Literature in English), as do histories of Black literature such as B. G. Brawley's *Early Negro American Writers* (1935). Charles Chesnutt's *House Behind the Cedars* (1900), as well as other novels, were predominantly shelved by author and title.[26] By moving such titles out of the 325.26 category, Harsh joined her peers in reimagining a different infrastructure of memory for Black history and culture.

While Harsh expressed a desire through her cataloging practices to dignify Black knowledge, she did not go further in challenging racial bias and white supremacy through cataloging itself. She did not rewrite entire cataloging systems to create her own, nor did she complicate existing ones. For instance, the Dewey Decimal category 326 (Slavery and Emancipation) is used frequently in the collection. While Du Bois sits at history and literature for Porter, he resides at 326 in Harsh's collection.[27] So too does *A Voice from the South* by Anna Julia Cooper (1892) (which Porter placed at 323.2, Civil and Political Rights), and even Richard Wright's *12 Million Black Voices* (1941). Moreover, Harsh did not use subcategories within 326, nor did she subdivide the category; while Porter created one hundred different subdivisions within 326, Harsh used the lone 326.[28] Porter enjoyed a certain freedom, however, that Harsh did not. "Porter's radical revision of standard classification was possible because the Moorland Foundation existed apart from the university's general holdings," Helton explains. Books in the collection "carried the prefix 'M,' and [were] accessible through a separate card catalog." Such separation, however, "was, in part, a legacy of racial segregation: an indirect manifestation of spatial and epistemological rules in which the exclusion of blackness was unmarked and its presence marked."[29] Because she was not employed by a Black institution and was instead bound to the CPL, Harsh could not operate with the same autonomy as Porter. Her collection was thus not a site of revolutionary cataloging; rather, her social intervention lay in her use of the collection as a public good.

Harsh used the Special Collection to build her greatest collection of all—a community of readers. She focused her time and energy on finding ways to distribute the collection and make it accessible to the public to form reading communities. Knowing that an archive was good only to the extent that readers used it, she cared for it and promoted it relentlessly, finding new ways to make it accessible and exhibiting a commitment to the open accessibility of information. In an effort to share and connect information—to map out an infrastructure of knowledge—she assembled a collection meant to be consumed by those outside the library or academic professions. And yet, while compiling a collection that (mostly) did not circulate, Harsh had to find ways, again and again, to make mobile what would otherwise have been a static entity in the archives.

A primary way that Harsh made the collection accessible to the public was its physical location. In the beginning, Harsh kept it in her office. For most of its existence at the Hall Branch during Harsh's tenure, however, much of the collection was available to the public in one way or another, though Harsh experimented with where in the library it would best serve the public. By 1938, it was "becoming so large," she wrote in her annual report, "that better results could be obtained if it was placed together in one room at the branch," recommending that "an ideal arrangement would be to have a trained assistant in charge with a thorough knowledge of what the collection contains. Perhaps we have that to look forward to."[30] Three years later, in 1941, however, only part of her wish had come true and she still struggled to figure out how best to meet public demand for the collection:

> The Special Collection of books on the Negro contains many books that are for room use only, adding in number to the volumes on hand in the 300 and 800's. Since more emphasis is given books on and about the Negro in February, than at any other time during the year, extra copies have been acquired to fill the great demand for books in this field at this period. Requests for material from the Special Collection are increasing throughout the year. Location of the books in this division so that they will be more accessible to those who want them would be a great improvement.[31]

Harsh got her wish. The next year, in her 1942 annual report, she notes that "moving the reference copies from the Office to the cases in the Reference room has added much to the general usability of this material."[32] Just off of the Adult Reading Room, the Reference Room offered the Special Collection a more visible and accessible location, enabling patrons to sit at large tables in the room and browse its contents (see Figure 2). Moving the collection to the Reference Room offered patrons more independence in their use of the materials; readers could browse multiple objects and materials at their leisure—a "great improvement" in accessibility to Harsh's mind indeed. The collection remained there for more than another decade. In 1957, a year before Harsh retired, the Reference Room continued to house the Special Collection.[33]

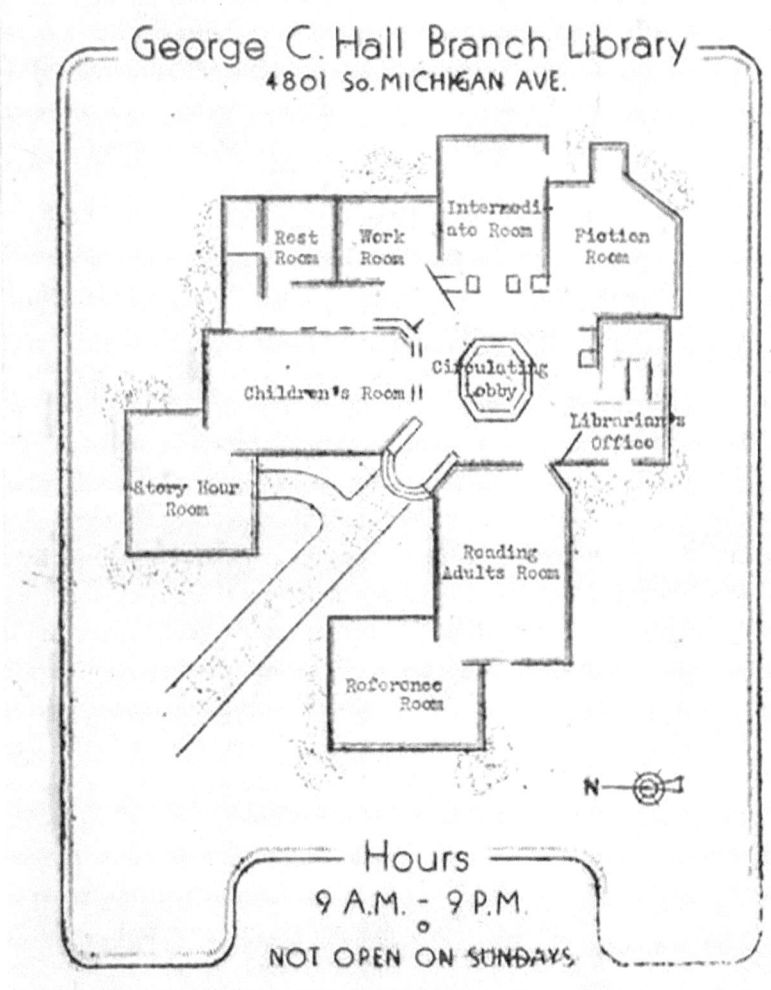

FIGURE 2. Map of the Hall Branch Library, Chicago, undated. Courtesy the Vivian G. Harsh Research Collection of Afro-American History and Literature, Chicago Public Library.

A second way that Harsh made the collection publicly accessible was by allowing some of its selections to circulate. Though extant circulation records for the collection are few, there are repeated references in Harsh's annual reports to this practice. In 1938, for instance, she notes that "circulating copies of books in the Special Collection receive such hard usage that replacements and extra copies are needed at this time."[34] In 1942 she commented: "Books in the Special collection are [illegible] popular. 4283 books were circulated this year."[35] These circulating volumes were novels and nonfiction books rather than rare materials such as manuscripts, pamphlets, photos, and other print culture materials: "Many books from this collection circulate but the rare and autographed copies are kept for reference use only."[36] That Harsh advocated for an accessible location to house the collection in the Reference Room and even then circulated some of its contents attests to her vision of its being an open community resource.

It is no surprise, then, that the collection was popular and used by many, including writers at the center of the blooming Renaissance. Richard Wright, Gwendolyn Brooks, and Margaret Walker all used Harsh's collection. It proved so powerful in "opening up" John H. Johnson to "the world of black history" that the publishing magnate later cited it as an influence in creating his empire.[37] Local teachers also frequently used the collection. Charlemae Hill Rollins referred to it in a 1942 address to the children's section of the Illinois Library Association as well as "a recent project of the Chicago Board of Education" that made use of the collection: "Superintendent William Johnson released two Negro teachers from classroom duty last year to prepare a Course of Study in Negro History to be included in the curriculum of the Chicago Schools," she noted. "These teachers worked at the library with the books and librarians all year. This work has been finished and is now ready to be used in the Chicago schools."[38] What made the collection unique was the fact that a wide variety of constituents used it on a regular basis. In this way, the collection was truly a community resource in that numerous members of the public would visit the Hall Branch to make use of it.

But for those who never set foot in the Hall Branch—to browse the collection in the Reference Room or to check out one of its circulating books— Harsh was mindful of making its volumes mobile in other ways. She did so by lending out materials to various exhibitions and events around the city, especially for Negro History Week, created in Chicago by Carter G. Woodson in 1926. In a special war-themed exhibition celebrating the nineteenth annual Negro History Week, for instance, Harsh lent selections from the collection to the main branch of the CPL which featured "the gallantry and patriotism of Negroes in all of this country's wars ... beginning with Jean Baptiste Point de Saible [sic], a native of Santo Domingo, the first permanent resident on the site of Chicago."[39] Over time, the growth of Negro History Week meant an increase in demand for Harsh's Special Collection. "The heaviest demands on our time and materials occur in February," Harsh wrote in 1950, "since both Negro History and Brotherhood Weeks are observed then. Speakers, book talks, program planning, special exhibits and displays, together with research and reference on many phases of Negro History and Brotherhood are examples of the numerous requests we are required to fulfill."[40]

Moreover, as Harsh notes as early as the 1938 annual report, interest was not limited to Bronzeville, or even to Chicago: "Requests for facts and reference from material in our Special Collection are received from out of town as well as all parts of the city."[41] Indeed, in a feature on the Hall Branch for the *Defender*, Arna Bontemps wrote of the collection that "items in this division are naturally in great demand by patrons of the branch, but residents of other sectons [sic] have also come to look to the Hall branch to supply any particular need which they may have in this field." Moreover, "in the greatest demand among books of the Special Collection are Dunbar's poems and Woodson's 'Negro in Our History.' Books containing information about George W. Carver are requested daily. 'The Chinaberry Tree,' 'Native Son,' and 'Not Without Laughter' are always wanted."[42] To keep up this interest in and use of the collection, Harsh also gave talks on "books for and by Negroes" to various clubs throughout the city as a way to promote the collection. After all, she was mobile, even if certain parts of the collection were not.[43]

Harsh found other inventive ways to circulate her collection—namely, via the radio. In her 1949 annual report she records that "research and reference assistance with our Special Collection material is a source of constant satisfaction to those of us who carry on this work. One outstanding illustration is the use of the books in this special field for the scripts for the popular program 'Destination Freedom' heard Sundays, at 10:00am over WMAQ. The broadcasting station has received several awards for this program."[44] Beyond the borders of Bronzeville, then, the collection served the city as a resource for Black literature, history, and culture. Indeed, Harsh noted in 1948, "use of the Special Collection material, not only by readers from the immediate community but also by other from outside the area, accounts for much of our special reference service."[45]

By making the collection accessible to as many readers as possible—in person, through circulation, via public exhibits, and even over the radio—and in promoting its use by the public, Harsh built a base of readers in Bronzeville and across the city interested in Black literature, history, and printed texts. Less than a decade into the Hall Branch's and the Special Collection's existence, the *Defender* noted an increase in the interest in African American history and literature as evidenced by "the great demand for material on the Race" during Negro History Week programming at the Hall Branch that year.[46] In this way, Harsh not only created interest in Black culture but also democratized access to a variety of source materials.

But it was not enough for Harsh to create accessible archives of Black literature, history, and culture while assembling engaged audiences for them. It was also important that she guide readers' use of the collection by providing reading lists, making books more accessible by grouping them together under various topics. True to the tools of her profession, Harsh made bibliographies and pamphlets that promoted the Collection based on readers' interests, curating lists according to selected themes. She thus guided readers on how to use and experience the collection and its contents. For example, sometime in the late 1930s, the Hall Branch produced "The Negro: A List of Books," a pamphlet that directed readers to selections within the collection according to topic: "History," "Social and Economic Problems," "Literature and Music," "Biography," "Novels," "For Young People," and "For Ready Reference" (see Figure 3).[47]

Selections include Du Bois's *The Souls of Black Folk* (1903), Alain Locke's *The New Negro* (1925), Arna Bontemps's *Black Thunder* (1936), and Frank Marshall Davis's *Black Man's Verse* (1935). The list also features literature by Jessie Fauset, Langston Hughes, Zora Neale Hurston, and Walter White, as well as nonfiction selections by Carter G. Woodson, Benjamin Brawley, E. Franklin Frazier, James Weldon Johnson, and Booker T. Washington. These selections showcase for readers the breadth of accomplishments of the race across a wide range of intellectual pursuits, from poetry to novels, histories, and social theories. The pamphlet even uses asterisks to highlight Black authors (who account for all but eight of the entries). Further, the bibliography produces knowledge about Black identity, preserving a shared

THE NEGRO
A LIST OF BOOKS

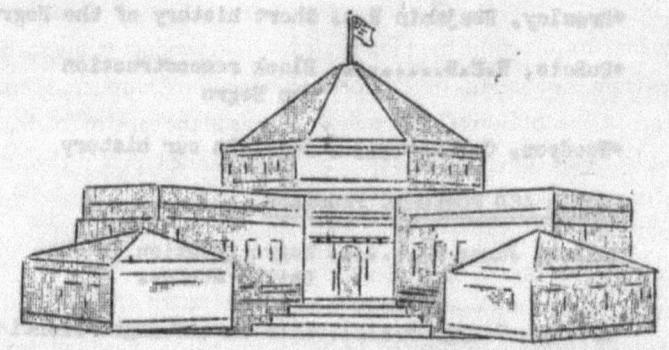

GEORGE C. HALL BRANCH
OF
THE CHICAGO PUBLIC LIBRARY
4801 So. MICHIGAN AVENUE

FIGURE 3. "The Negro: A List of Books," ca. 1930s. Courtesy the Vivian G. Harsh Research Collection of Afro-American History and Literature, Chicago Public Library.

history and teaching it to readers. Through this list, readers learn about great achievements in the past as well as current social and political issues from Black perspectives. The list thus dignifies Black literature, culture, and history for readers and invites them to learn what was otherwise omitted from standard, racist narratives of American history and culture. In this way, the list empowers Black readers by attempting to overcome the racist realities of Jim Crow America. Fittingly, an "Old African proverb" serves as an epigraph to the list: "If you know well the beginning, the end will not trouble you much."[48]

Under Harsh's direction, the Hall Branch would produce many such bibliographies from the contents of the Special Collection. An updated version of "The Negro: A List of Books" appeared sometime in the early 1940s, featuring selections from the collection arranged under the same topics as the previous list. This one includes, for instance, Wright's *Native Son* (1940) and the 1942 edition of Florence Murray's *The Negro Handbook*, noting: "The books on this list, with a few exceptions, are restricted to material on the American Negro published in the past ten years. Other books and pamphlets not included are available in the special collection of 2,000 volumes located at Hall Branch."[49] Other similar lists include "Books by and Relating to the Negro" (ca. 1930s), "We, Too, Are America: A List of Books" (ca. 1944), and "New Books by and about the Negro" (ca. 1950s). While these lists were mimeographed and were of low production quality, the branch also worked with the CPL to create glossy, professionally printed bibliographies that appear to have circulated outside the library and even Bronzeville itself. A fifteen-page pamphlet, *The Negro and His Achievements in America: A List of Books Compiled for the American Negro Exposition*, though produced by the Readers' Bureau of the Chicago Public Library in 1940, bears the mark of Harsh's collection efforts. "With a few exceptions this list is restricted to books on the American Negro published in the past ten years," an explanatory note informs readers. "The * indicates those available only at George Cleveland Hall Branch of the Public Library, where there is a special collection of 1000 volumes by and about the Negro."[50] "On These We Stand: A Selected List of Readings on the Negro" (ca. 1960), prepared by the staff of the Hall Branch, "includes works by Negro and white writers, published over a period of five years, 1946–1950," and supplemented a previous list, "Negro in Our Democracy," from 1946. Like the other lists, this one points readers to Harsh's Special Collection to locate the selected books, though it notes that "many are [also] available at the Central Library and some branches."[51]

Harsh's practice of inviting readers to use the collection and then connecting it to their specific interests and identity ultimately produced new reading communities. Readers responded to these lists with enthusiasm and used them to inform their reading practices. Indeed, Harsh notes in her 1938 annual report that "in connection with Negro History Week a selected book list was prepared and distributed. This list has been so popular that two sets have been run off."[52] In addition to building reading communities, the lists also facilitate use of their contents, directing readers toward relevant and even new topics. In doing so, Harsh's lists legitimize and produce usable knowledge about Black life and history for countless audiences and reading communities in Bronzeville and across the city. And while none of the extant lists bears her name—most pamphlets credit the collective "Hall Branch Library"—they no doubt were overseen by Harsh and needed her final approval. The collective authorship of the lists thus speaks to the democratic ethos of her approach to librarianship—a belief that knowledge is collective, communal, and not owned or authored by any one individual. It belongs instead to the readers who consume it.

In the postwar era, Harsh's Special Collection stalled in numbers and use, eventually disappearing from the public eye.[53] At the time of her death at age seventy in 1960, the collection still numbered about two thousand volumes, roughly the same number as in 1945. At the time, the *Defender* surmised in its obituary of Harsh that the collection "might someday be called 'The Harsh Collection.'"[54] Seven years later, the Special Negro Collection was inventoried, Donald Franklin Joyce reports, and "totaled about 2,000 volumes, most published after 1900," in addition to runs of important African American journals and magazines. The collection was renamed the Vivian G. Harsh Collection of Afro-American History and Literature in 1970, after Joyce had recommended that the CPL do so; he became curator of the collection that same year. In the intervening years, the collection experienced "unprecedented growth," in part because it received over $220,000 from the Illinois State Library and the Field Foundation of Illinois.[55] In 1975 the collection moved to the Carter G. Woodson Regional Library Center and is now the largest collection of African American literature and culture in the Midwest. In April 2023 it was announced that the Chicago Public Library Foundation had received a two-million-dollar grant from the Mellon Foundation to preserve the city's Black history, further securing Harsh's vision: the everyday reading of Black literature, history, and culture.[56]

LIST 2: BUILDING AN AUDIENCE

Beyond her Special Collection, Harsh used the full capacities of the Hall Branch Library to build and sustain a reading base in Bronzeville. She wove her ethos of public access into all of her programming endeavors throughout her tenure there, situating the library as a civic center. Through varied public programming and reading lists, she grounded the branch as the epicenter of community reading in Bronzeville, serving its patrons in myriad ways to meet their reading tastes and practices. Key to Harsh's success was her understanding of Hall Branch readers as well as her belief in serving the needs and desires they expressed. Through countless lists, Harsh and her staff met but also guided readers' tastes and interests to serve the community of Bronzeville and promote lifelong reading practices that were useful and relevant to the branch's patrons.

The year before she retired, Harsh composed a three-page typed manuscript titled "The George Cleveland Hall Branch and Its Social Environment." In addition to offering a profile of the library, she also gave considerable attention in the document to delineating the qualities and characteristics of her patrons. "The George Cleveland Hall Branch Library is situated in one of the world's largest Negro communities," she writes. "This community covers more than one hundred city blocks and it is filled with people who have varied cultural backgrounds, different levels of education and many types of occupations."[57] Though Harsh acknowledges "an oasis of upper middle class families" living in a recent, more upscale housing project built by Julius Rosenwald, she emphasizes that the community primarily "consists of middle and low income families" living in subpar conditions. "Although there has been a tremendous increase in population there has been practically no increase in residential building. The larger population is crowded into existing quarters. The majority of these quarters were built before 1915. The increased population has been accomodated [sic] by tremendous conversion of the existing units into kitchenettes and rooming houses. The people of the area are mostly of the laboring and factory worker class, and there is a high rate of transiency." Given the economic diversity of her patrons, Harsh emphasizes her mission to serve all members of the neighborhood. "Hall Branch Library is an essential and integral part of the community," she continues; thus the variety of programming and reading recommendations must match the variety of the library's patrons. Its books, for instance, "cover a wide range of subject matter varying enough to satisfy the tastes of young and old, the informed and the uninformed."[58] In this way, Harsh ensured that at the Hall Branch, all Bronzeville community members had a place and a purpose—and she did so through the extensive and varied programming that she and her staff provided.

Throughout Harsh's tenure, the Hall Branch functioned as a community center, organizing programming for all ages, interests, and reading levels. Adult programming included such initiatives as the Fifty and More Club (F.A.M.), which "affords social, recreational and educational activities for older adults," Harsh explained, in order to give them "the knowledge that retirement is not a jumping-off point but a challenge and a better way to new interests." Another popular program was the DuSable History Club, "of which the main purpose is research in the field of Negro History." One of the branch's longest-running clubs, the DuSable provided members with educational opportunities as well as the chance to give back to the library by donating "all materials unearthed by this group . . . to the special library collection." The branch also hosted adult education classes, PTA meetings and parent classes, Negro History Week and Public Library Week events and exhibits, film screenings, book festivals, book teas, and many speakers and readings. She also created and helped run, with an advisory board, the popular Book Review and Lecture Forum (discussed in more detail later in this chapter). In this way, as Harsh writes, "adult activities at Hall adequately cover all types of people of the community and its services change as the needs of the community change." And if community members could not get to the library, Harsh and her staff would often come to them—giving talks and providing outreach efforts across the city at schools, women's groups, hospitals, churches, and other community centers. Harsh was also skilled at promoting the library through the local Black press, authoring dozens of articles in the *Sunday Chicago Bee* on books as well as notices advertising the branch's events.[59]

Programming for teens and children was similarly diverse and likewise encouraged interests beyond reading. For these demographic groups, the library hosted summer reading clubs and games, story hours, and a Teenage Forum that organized meetings on topics such as "jazz, teenage dramatics, children's poetry and careers."[60] Over the years there were also plays and puppet shows, a debate club, a Girls Literary Club, a Boys Handicraft Club, study clubs, radio classes, discussion groups, and a camera club. The beloved children's librarian Charlemae Hill Rollins oversaw programming for the library's youngest patrons, helping to produce the next generation of readers.

This rich array of programming enabled the Hall Branch, though underfunded by the CPL, to be wildly successful. "Although the district which Hall branch serves is said to be from Forty-third street to Sixty-first street, in reality it is from northern Wisconsin to southern Mississippi, because from far and near, requests are received for special lists of books, aid in preparing programs, materials for lectures, etc.," the *Defender* reported in 1939. "The increased circulation in the last year shows the interest of those nearby. More than 200,000 books went out into homes during 1938, and strangely, this increase showed itself in books on sociology, science and invention, and fine arts."[61] Fourteen years later, the Hall Branch was still considered a central resource in Bronzeville. "Utilized by children, college students, teen-agers and adults, Hall branch library has become an integral part of the everyday life of Southsiders and is one of the larger branches in the system of the Chicago Public Library," the *Defender* reported in 1953.[62]

Although the library's programming included other activities besides reading, Harsh's intentions were clear: get people into the library and get them reading. For instance, she noted that one of the benefits of the F.A.M. club was that "attendance at the meeting also gives the members an opportunity to visit the library which is an incentive for them to borrow books to read." She envisioned the Hall Branch as a crucial site of community engagement, connecting diverse patron interests with myriad opportunities for reading, and whose goal it ultimately was, as she put it, "to arouse interest in books." Harsh considered this a crucial service to the community and to the nation. "It is readily apparent that the library is a vital social institution in a democracy," she wrote, and "Hall Branch is doing its part to help create thinking, reasoning adults. All of the social group is provided for, readers and non-readers of varying educational background, all are encouraged to make the library a habit, a lifetime habit. This library truely [sic] serves the whole community of which it is a useful and necessary part."[63]

In addition to attracting patrons to the library in the hope that they would start and then continue reading, Harsh also oriented readers' tastes and habits by producing reading lists and recommendations—to guide, in other words, their engagement with the branch and its wide assortment of books, magazines, newspapers, pamphlets, and more. The ever-popular Book Review and Lecture Forum blended both programming and listing, providing patrons with a continuous source of reading recommendations. Launched in 1933 and meeting every other Wednesday evening at eight o'clock over the course of twenty-five years, the forum offered reviews given by the public of books chosen by an advisory committee. The forum attracted literary celebrities like Margaret Walker, Langston Hughes, and Arna Bontemps, who were all regular participants. Community members such as Edward Bland, William Couch, Brunetta Mouzon, and Ollye Coffin also regularly participated, as did other notable names such as Frank Marshall Davis, Henry Blakely (Gwendolyn Brooks's husband), and Horace Cayton. Members of the South Side Writers Group, such as Robert Davis and Russell Marshall, also sat on the forum's advisory committee at various times, as did Era Bell Thompson.[64] In this way, the forum served as an intersection of literary professionals, community members, politicians, and community organizers.

Forum events were free and open to the public and, like all other Hall Branch programming, promoted a range of reading tastes—from novels and poetry to history, politics, and current events. As Harsh explained, the forum "features reviews and discussions of current books with occasional speakers on social and educational topics by those who are specialists in their fields. The bi-monthly meetings aim to enrich the leisure time of those who desire to be enlightened in a cultural and literary way, to draw attention to books and authors, discover and develop local talent and to bring some people to the library for some other purpose than to take out a book."[65] The forum reviewed such literary works as Zora Neale Hurston's *Dust Tracks on a Road* (1942), Margaret Walker's *For My People* (1942), William Attaway's *Blood on the Forge* (1941), Ernest Hemingway's *For Whom the Bell Tolls* (1940), John Steinbeck's *The Grapes of Wrath* (1939), and Wright's *Native Son* (1940), as well as popular novels such as Lloyd Douglas's *The Robe* (1942) and A. J. Cronin's *The Green Years* (1944). Nonfiction selections included Louis Adamic's *My America* (1938), James Ford's *The Negro and the Democratic Front* (1938), Max Lerner's *Ideas Are Weapons* (1939), and John Gunther's *Inside Latin America* (1941). The forum also hosted a wide range of speakers—writers, columnists, academics, political leaders—and moderated roundtable discussions such as "Political Philosophies," "Propaganda in the News," and "Which Way America: Depression or Prosperity?" Often, writers whose work was discussed were invited to meetings. Zora Neale Hurston, "author of one of the popular books of 1933, spoke before the club in November," Harsh recorded in her 1934 annual report. "She was received with enthusiasm by a large audience. The re-action of the public to this activity is most pleasing."[66] The forum soon became the centerpiece of Hall Branch programming, with the *Defender* reporting that "the Book Review and Lecture Forum, with its semi-monthly Wednesday night meetings[,] has become a permanent part of the community life."[67] Harsh herself was particularly proud of the "attractive announcements, mimeographed at N.Y.A. print shop," which, she notes, "have helped to advertise the meetings in advance."[68]

As the forum promoted aspirational reading, it also emphasized pragmatic topics and texts, in keeping with Harsh's philosophy of useful reading. In this way, the forum served Bronzeville, in the words of Jacqueline Goldsby, as "a salon for the masses."[69] It did not subscribe to the erudite reading practices of nineteenth-century Black literary societies, which centered Shakespeare and other white, Western canonical texts; rather, the forum placed books about "the race" alongside popular novels and practical topics of the day. The forum thus grounded Bronzeville readers in relevant reading, speaking to their literary tastes and their daily lives. Though reviews of books given by the public are not extant in the Hall Branch Library archive, the fact that the forum was so popular throughout its existence attests to how deeply the community valued it.

In addition to the Book Review and Lecture Forum, various reading lists and pamphlets that the Hall Branch produced for its patrons promoted this practice of relevant reading. Harsh considered the bibliographies vital enough to the work of the Hall Branch that she tracked their numbers and included them in her annual reports to CPL administrators. Typically, during its first decade, the branch produced between twenty and thirty lists annually.[70] These ranged from, for example, "Vocational Guidance and Training: A List of Books" to "Books for the Modern Reader," "You and Your Health: A List of Books," and "Occupations: Let Us Work to Defend America" (all undated). Mainly these were produced as mimeographed folios and distributed at the branch itself—likely at the front circulation desk. Their purpose of guiding readers toward books that were useful and relevant speaks to Harsh's pragmatic approach to her profession and to her readers. If the lists produced from the Special Negro Collection served readers by instilling race pride, then Harsh's copious other lists demonstrate how reading can serve many other needs in readers' lives—in other words, that reading itself is relevant and useful in a number of ways.

Through authoring these lists, Harsh created audiences, brought communities of readers into existence, and often gathered them together under one roof. Further, she organized and created knowledge about Black history, culture, and identity and democratized access to it within Bronzeville and across the city. By understanding her community of readers, Harsh was able to make the Hall Branch successful in serving, as she put it, "readers and non-readers of varying educational background" and helping them to "make the library a habit, a lifetime habit."

LIST 3: BUILDING A LEGACY

The lists that Harsh assembled at the Hall Branch built Black reading communities in Bronzeville, promoted engagement with Black texts across the city, and democratized access to reading materials and knowledge. Further, she normalized everyday reading practices and programming, encouraging habits that were practical and relevant to her readers. But perhaps Harsh's greatest listing project was not a special collection or a list of recommended readings but rather a directory of people. As demonstrated by the writing she left behind, Harsh wrote as much to connect people as she did to collect and preserve information. Throughout her career, she proved to be a skilled interlocutor, connecting people through the lists she created and distributed. I close this chapter with a discussion of a particularly important listing project of Harsh's that reassembles a lost legacy of Black female librarianship.

Before she was named head librarian of the Hall Branch in 1931, Harsh had already had a substantial career in the Chicago Public Library system. Indeed, her muted presence in the scholarly record misrepresents the central role she played locally and nationally in the library profession. As the first African American branch director within the Chicago Public Library system, or so the history goes, Harsh was part of a significant network of Black librarians, mostly female, dotting the country in the 1930s and 1940s, many of whom also collected and curated Black literature and history. Within Chicago, her network included the noted Black clubwoman Fannie Barrier Williams, who joined the board of the Chicago Public Library in 1924, becoming the first woman, African American or otherwise, to do so. At this point, Harsh had already been working in the CPL system for a decade in assistant positions across various branches and had just recently become head of the Abraham Lincoln Centre Branch in 1922.[71] Harsh no doubt knew Williams, who traveled in the same elite social circles in Chicago as

Harsh did. Williams served on the board until 1926, when George Cleveland Hall filled her position. Harsh already knew Hall through her work with the Association for the Study of Negro Life and History and collaborated with him before his death in 1930 on various projects, including a new branch library that would eventually bear his name and where Harsh would spend the rest of her career.

Beyond Williams, however, Harsh's professional community extended to a larger network of Black female librarians in Chicago. Though to this date little evidence has emerged of this network, as well as Harsh's role in it, a 1925 letter that she sent to W. E. B. Du Bois—likely a connection through Williams—brings this lost history to light, providing valuable information about decades of Black female librarianship in the city. In her letter, Harsh responds to a request from Du Bois to send him information about Black librarians in Chicago for a feature he planned for *The Crisis*. In addition to informing him that she had sent him a photograph of "Mrs. Williams" (likely Fannie Barrier Williams) the day before, Harsh encloses a list of fifteen "colored assistants" working in the Chicago Public Library system (see Figure 4).

Harsh emphasizes that one of the women, a Miss Amelia Platt, had been "in the service for more than twenty-five years."[72] In actuality, Platt's employment in the CPL dated back some thirty-eight years prior to Harsh's letter, to 1887.[73] Further, the CPL employment of several other women on Harsh's list—Rebecca M. Bond, Elizabeth Bell, Emma Shaw, and Blanche Shaw (the librarian whom Oscar De Priest would later recommend to lead the Hall Branch instead of Harsh)—can be traced back to at least the teens. In compiling these names and positions, Harsh's list provides an important record of Black female library employees in the CPL system—but Harsh had more information to share with Du Bois.

In a surprising turn, Harsh identifies two individuals on her list—Miss Elizabeth Bell and Mrs. E. J. Thompson—as "the other two branch librarians." This short phrase raises several important questions: In addition to whom were Bell and Thompson "the other two"? How many African American branch librarians were there by 1925? Were there African American branch librarians before Harsh? Below Bell's and Thompson's names and professional addresses (Hardin Square Branch and Forestville School Branch, respectively), Harsh includes another list of four names: Mrs. Pherell Jewell, Mrs. W. W. Sims, Mrs. Ethel Buster, and Miss Bessie Lowry. Are these the "other" African American branch librarians in addition to Bell

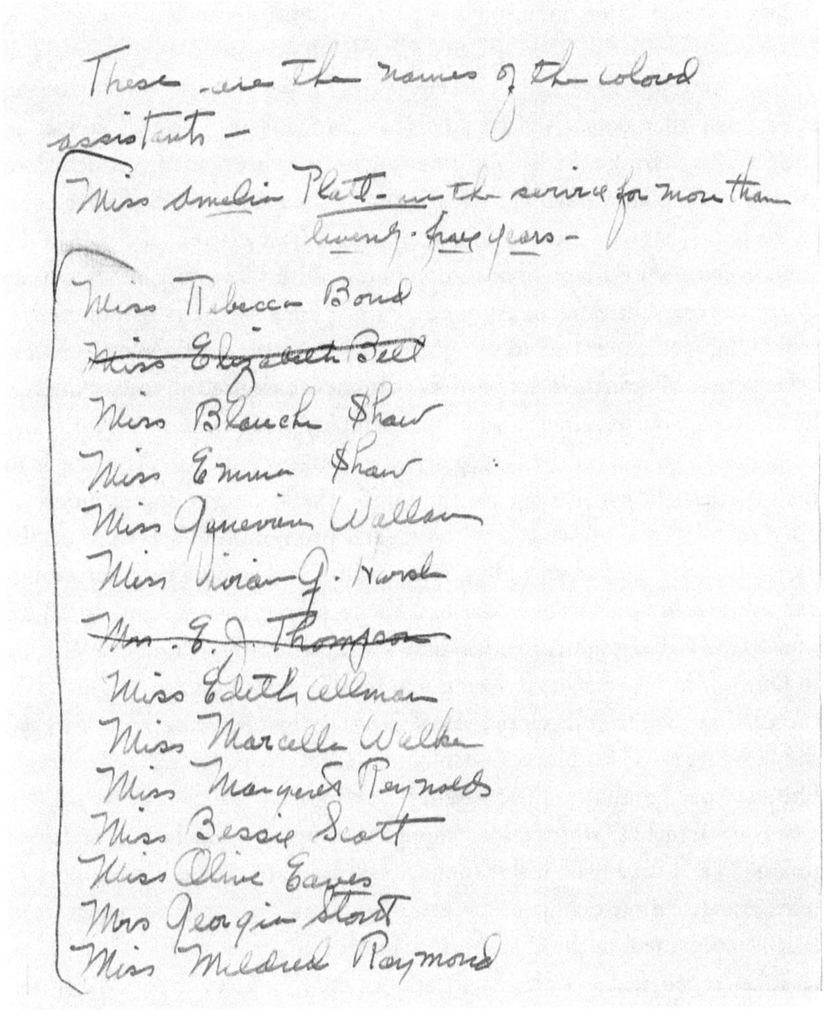
These are the names of the colored assistants –

Miss Amelia Platt – in the service for more than twenty-five years –

Miss Rebecca Bond

~~Miss Elizabeth Bell~~

Miss Blanche Shaw

Miss Emma Shaw

Miss Genevieve Wallace

Miss Vivian G. Harsh

~~Mrs. E. J. Thompson~~

Miss Edith Allman

Miss Marcella Walker

Miss Marguerite Reynolds

Miss Bessie Scott

Miss Olive Eaves

Mrs Georgia Stout

Miss Mildred Raymond

FIGURE 4. Vivian Harsh's list of fifteen "colored assistants" in the Chicago Public Library System. Letter to W. E. B. Du Bois, April 28, 1925, W. E. B. Du Bois Papers, courtesy the Robert S. Cox Special Collections and University Archives Research Center, University of Massachusetts Amherst Libraries.

and Thompson that Harsh alludes to in her letter? Regrettably, she ends her letter without providing any further details.

Regardless of the information it does not contain, Harsh's letter to Du Bois is extraordinary for the valuable information that it does provide. First, it illuminates an interconnected group of African American women working in various roles within the CPL by 1925. Harsh has compiled a directory of African American librarians in the city—from pages and assistants to branch librarians—that dates African American women's professional service in the CPL back to the 1880s. Few other documents provide such insight into African American women in the CPL during the 1920s or at any other point in the library system's history. Five years after Harsh's letter, an article in the *Library Journal* by Louis Shores, librarian at Fisk University, reports these statistics regarding African American employment in the city's library system: "Chicago has refused to recognize Negro readers as different from any other readers. Nevertheless, two of its 45 branches are used almost exclusively by Negroes. Fourteen Negro women are employed in the main building, and a total of 38 women in the Negro branches, but no indication is made as to the capacities in which they are employed. The same training facilities are open to colored as to white applicants, and promotion in service is on the basis of grades applied to all library assistants."[74] The next year, correspondence between Du Bois and Marjorie Kemp, who gathered information for him on the CPL system, provides some additional staffing numbers. Writing to Du Bois in February 1931, Kemp reports that 1,000 to 1,100 employees in the CPL are "white and colored," as of February 1930, seventy-four of whom she designates as "Employees—Colored—(Librarians, Clerks & Janitors)." She also specifies that of these seventy-four, four are assistant librarians ("in charge of Branches," she notes).[75] Though incomplete—she later complained to Du Bois, "I have tried to get some classification of the 70 but the Library refuses to give more definite information"—Kemp's data provide a picture of Black employment in the CPL five years after Harsh's letter.[76]

Taken together, data from Harsh, Shores, and Kemp sketch out a rough history of African American CPL employment over a nearly fifty-year period—from approximately 1887 to 1930. Yet Harsh's lists remain the most illuminating document we have of the numbers and, more importantly, the *names* of African American women working throughout the Chicago Public Library system. Indeed, while Kemp's and Shore's lists note staffing numbers, only Harsh's include the women's identities.

Even more astonishingly, Harsh's 1925 letter to Du Bois seems to suggest that she was not the first African American branch librarian within the CPL, as has always been believed. When Harsh was named head of the soon-to-be Hall Branch, she was already "in charge of our Ogden Park Branch," Roden wrote to De Priest on June 9, 1931.[77] But this was actually Harsh's second branch leadership position. As Melanie Chambliss writes, Harsh quietly became head of the Abraham Lincoln Centre library in 1922 when its head, Frances Rice, was moved to a different location. (Indeed, Harsh signs her 1925 letter to Du Bois from the Lincoln Centre branch). Accordingly, Chambliss writes, Harsh became "the first African American to lead a subbranch."[78] In her 1925 letter to Du Bois, Harsh records that both Bell and Thompson were already branch librarians, three years after she herself had assumed the headship of Lincoln Centre. But this detail raises the question: Did either of these women assume her role *before* 1922? Indeed, Bell appears in 1917 in the CPL records as branch librarian of the Davis Square Branch, making her the first African American librarian to lead a CPL branch.[79]

If Harsh's list provides contemporary information for Du Bois about the status and composition of Black librarianship in Chicago in the 1920s then it also records an important history that is not otherwise legible in the archives.[80] CPL records, after all, do not specify the racial identity of employees.[81] Thus, just as Harsh's lists restore the *names* and *professional titles* missing from histories of African American women's librarianship in Chicago, so too do they restore the *racial identity* of the women librarians and assistants listed in CPL annual reports. Harsh, in other words, provides a crucial intersectional nexus that makes Chicago's African American women librarians visible in the archives.

Beyond Chicago, Harsh's network of African American librarianship extended to an even larger network throughout the country, including Dorothy Porter at Howard, Sadie Peterson Delaney at Tuskegee, and Catherine Latimer at the 135th Street Branch of the New York Public Library. Once again, correspondence with Du Bois fleshes this network out considerably to librarians and branches in other parts of the country. Though Du Bois's profile on African American libraries never materialized, as he later lamented, his friendship with Harsh grew, and he wrote in 1931 to congratulate her on being named head of the Hall Branch.[82] Five years later, he visited the Hall Branch to view her Special Negro Collection himself in search of source materials for a new project, *Encyclopedia of the Negro*, that would ultimately take him to Africa, where he would die in 1963. Just months before his visit—on February 17 or 18, 1936—Du Bois had sent Pauline A. Young, a librarian and niece of Alice Dunbar-Nelson, to visit Harsh's Special Negro Collection over the 1935–36 holiday season in search of information for his *Encyclopedia*.[83] But Du Bois wished to see Harsh's collection for himself. What exactly Harsh showed him and what they discussed that February of 1936 remains unrecorded, yet his letter of gratitude to her upon his return to Atlanta documents another list of African American librarians that Harsh had provided him in person, this time to aid in his new project: he reports writing to Sadie Peterson Delaney at Tuskegee, as well as Dorothy Porter, Mollie Dunlop of the *Journal of Negro Education* at Howard University, and others whom Harsh had recommended.[84] In her response three days later, Harsh lists two more contacts for Du Bois: Mrs. Florida Ridley of Toledo, Ohio, who "has some very valuable records and books on the Negro," and Edward H. Morris of Benton Harbor, Michigan, who "also has documents and information of value about the Negro in Chicago."[85] Du Bois took Harsh's advice, writing to more than a dozen librarians, the majority of whom Harsh herself had recommended.

It is worth noting that Du Bois already knew Delaney and Porter; he had corresponded with both women since at least the 1920s.[86] Yet he does not appear to have contacted them about his *Encyclopedia* project until Harsh recommended that he do so. As their correspondence reveals, Harsh was a trusted resource for Du Bois concerning information not only about African American collections and primary sources but also about African American librarians and their expertise. In her various lists, in person and in letters, Harsh maps out for him a network across the country, from Chicago to New York City to Indianapolis to Los Angeles to Kansas City to Illyria, Ohio. Harsh's lists thus encapsulate the work at the center of her profession: to collect, organize, preserve, curate, and then share vital information that might otherwise be lost. But her lists also make visible the epistemological nature of her work: the production of knowledge made possible by constructing a historical narrative of African American women librarians.

Harsh's lists of African American women librarians and their professional histories contribute to the long tradition of African American women's intellectual work in significant ways. Indeed, Harsh's directories of African American librarianship in the 1920s and 1930s echo lists published by African American women around the turn of the century, such as *The Work of the Afro-American Woman* (1894) by Gertrude Mossell (published under the name "Mrs. N. F. Mossell") and Pauline Hopkins's serialized list "Famous Women of the Negro Race," which appeared in the *Colored American Magazine* from November 1901 to October 1902. In both cases, Mossell and Hopkins showcase Black women such as Phillis Wheatley, Ida B. Wells,

Frances E. W. Harper, and other figures who contributed to racial uplift in a variety of ways. For race women like Mossell and Hopkins, documenting and showcasing the accomplishments of African American womanhood was a crucial part of uplift ideology that provided, in the words of Fannie Barrier Williams, "the badges of race respectability."[87]

A century later, this work was just as critical to the Black feminist activists and scholars who compiled, collected, and circulated reading lists of "forgotten" Black women writers and artists. At the center of these projects was the landmark anthology *All the Women Are White, All the Blacks Are Men, but Some of Us Are Brave: Black Women's Studies* (1982), edited by Gloria T. Hull, Patricia Bell Scott, and Barbara Smith, a collection that compiled dozens of bibliographies, syllabi, and lists of influential Black women in the United States in an effort to make visible their body of cultural production which had been categorically neglected. Listing these women and their various forms of literary and artistic production anchored recovery work as Black feminist praxis. Jean Fagan Yellin's "Afro-American Women, 1800–1910: Excerpts from a Working Bibliography," for instance, defines this important intellectual work of recovering and compiling Black women's writing. "Their presence is what is most important," Yellin writes in the preface to her bibliography. "If we are unaware of Black women in nineteenth-century America, it is not because they were not here; if we know nothing of their literature and culture, it is not because they left no records. It is because their lives and their work have been profoundly ignored. Both as the producers of culture and as the subjects of the cultural production of others, however, their traces are everywhere." The remedy for this systemic omission, Yellin concludes, is to restore the work of Black women and their influence on American culture, encounter by encounter. "Rather than express surprise when we encounter Black women in the study of nineteenth-century America, we need to ask why they are missing when we do not. Then we need to search and find them."[88]

The syllabi included in *But Some of Us Are Brave* do exactly that. They feature courses in women's studies, Black studies, Afro-American studies, history, and English departments and programs, and range from large state schools (San Jose State University) to small liberal arts institutions (Hampshire College). These syllabi, such as Gloria Hull's "Black Women Writers," for the fall 1976 semester at the University of Delaware, and Frances Foster's spring 1976 "Black Women Writers," recover many writers that Mossell and Hopkins documented but add Ellen Craft, Elizabeth Keckley, Anne Spencer,

Jessie Fauset, and others. Many of the syllabi put nineteenth-century Black women writers in conversation with contemporary writers such as Alice Walker, Audre Lorde, Mari Evans, and Ntozake Shange. In doing so, the syllabi produce accessible genealogies of Black women's intellectual and creative traditions that circulated both within and outside of academia. What is more, many of the syllabi offer frameworks through which to read and understand the work presented. Fahamisha Shariat's 1979 syllabus "Blakwomen Writers of the U.S.A. Who Are They? What Do They Write?" not only provides "An Outline of Literature by Blakwomen in the U.S.A." but also offers readers lists based on "Thematic Groupings," such as "Black Girlhood," "Black Woman to Black Woman," and "Black Love." As an appendix, Shariat also supplies "Assigned Topics for Research and Discussion," as well as "Other Suggested Topics" that range from "The cookbook as a literary genre" to "Blaklesbian writers."[89] Like Harsh's lists, the bibliographies and syllabi that make up *But Some of Us Are Brave* construct a legacy of Black intellectual and creative labor and, in the process, produce new reading communities and strategies.

Harsh connects these traditions that bookend the twentieth century by showing how, in the middle decades of the century, Black women continued the intellectual work of building what Helton has called "infrastructures of black inquiry" through lists of their own.[90] Certainly Harsh's contemporaries such as Porter and Latimer were also invested in list-making—and produced capacious numbers of them—but their work focused primarily on cataloging authors, primary texts, and other archival materials of Black print culture. Harsh's intellectual work is thus unique in that it documents the information infrastructure itself. She lists the librarians and catalogs the collectors.

The intellectual work that binds these generations—from Mossell and Hopkins to Harsh, Latimer, and Porter to Yellin and Hull—constitutes an important practice at the heart of Black feminist praxis, what Brittney Cooper appropriately terms *listing*. This process, "in which African American women created lists of prominent, qualified Black women for public consumption," Cooper explains, "situate[s] Black women within a long lineage of prior women who have done similar kinds of work." As a result, "naming those women grants intellectual, political, and/or cultural legitimacy to the Black woman speaking their names."[91] Harsh's lists in her 1925 letter to Du Bois are particularly valuable in that they construct such a genealogy of race, gender, and librarianship in Chicago, similarly granting those women their own historical and cultural legitimacy. By placing the current generation of African American women working in Chicago's libraries in 1925—including herself—alongside such library veterans as Amelia Platt, Harsh establishes "a long lineage" of African American librarianship in the city, revealing its status as long-standing tradition rather than modern phenomenon.[92]

In a similar way, her 1936 lists of librarians across the country build an infrastructure of African American women professionals for Du Bois to consult for his project. As an intellectual project, then, one that invests itself in knowledge production, Harsh's lists constitute what Cooper describes as a "critical edge, without which the broader history of African American knowledge production would unravel and come apart at the seams." To be sure, Harsh's list-making "create[s] an intellectual genealogy," as previous Black women's work has done, one that constitutes "a practice of resistance against intellectual erasure."[93] To this end, it is interesting to note that Harsh includes herself in her 1925 list of African American CPL library assistants, attesting to her desire to be visible in this profession and tradition of African American librarianship. Since Du Bois of course already knew her position in the CPL system—which is why he queried her in the first place—one must wonder who else Harsh had in mind as readers of her list.

But Harsh was not finished giving Du Bois lists. In addition to catalogs of librarians and libraries, collectors and collections, Du Bois wanted bibliographies, specifically a bibliography of the Negro in Chicago.[94] Harsh obliged, sending him one later that spring.[95] In this way, Harsh's lists are also evidence not only of the long tradition of Black women's intellectual work but also of her personal philosophy of knowledge production as communal and openly accessible. Like Porter and Latimer, Harsh produced bibliographies, but rather than publishing them in academic or trade journals, she instead provided open access for public consumption, circulating them—as flyers, pamphlets, handouts, and letters—throughout Bronzeville and beyond. Indeed, she considered list-making serious reference work, central to her responsibilities at the Hall Branch Library. "I think making lists and reading courses should be listed as reference service also," she wrote in 1934.[96] But as the other women who created lists knew, lists were useful only if audiences consumed them—in other words, if the list circulated even if the physical texts did not. The lists she made for Du Bois follow this logic: though they never made it into print, they were ultimately created with the intention of being shared with a wide, nonprofessional audience.

Harsh's story contains one final grace note that illustrates the significance of her listing projects and their impact on Bronzeville's reading practices and cultural productions. An inconspicuous internal document from the Hall Branch papers—likely authored by Harsh—provides a directory of Hall Branch employees. The list is mostly perfunctory and unremarkable, except for the last name on the list, which reads: junior assistant, Miss Annie Allen.[97] As a resident of Bronzeville nearly her entire life, Gwendolyn Brooks, whose tour de force book of poems *Annie Allen* (1949) was awarded the Pulitzer Prize in 1950, was a frequent patron of and speaker at the Hall Branch Library. Little information about the Hall Branch Annie Allen exists, though she did co-author at least one article in the *Sunday Chicago Bee* with Harsh. In this article, Harsh and Allen offer a feature on "war books with a purpose." That purpose, they write, "is the advocation of a permanent peace based upon the equal co-operation of men and nations. Such a peace would involve the recognition of the essential dignity of every human being regardless of race, creed, or color and bring to full realization the true meaning of a democratic world."[98] In recommending books dedicated to this cause, Laura Burt writes, the women showed "that books could help readers, especially Bronzeville readers, envision a democratic and just postwar society."[99] Accordingly, Harsh and Allen conclude their feature by insisting, "Thus, it behooves us as members of a minority group to whom democracy has at times been denied, to read and understand them."[100]

By 1948, Annie Allen was working at the Oakland Branch of the Chicago Public Library system.[101] Located at 700 Oakwood Boulevard, the library sat less than two miles from the Hall Branch on Bronzeville's northern edge. I cannot locate any other significant information in the archives to document Allen's role in the CPL system or in Bronzeville writ large. Yet Harsh's list of colleagues suggests that Brooks may very well have had in mind a librarian she knew at the Hall Branch when she was thinking up a title for her next book of poems.[102] Though the chapters that follow focus on four other influential Bronzeville women and their various reading communities and reception practices, they nevertheless also show how the Hall Branch wove itself into the everyday fabric of Bronzeville life, influencing all of its readers—Pulitzer Prize winners or not—in unexpected and delightful ways.

CHAPTER 2

Bad Girl Brooks

Refusing the Respectable Reader in Popular Poetry

Although she was not accused of attempting to start a race riot, as Vivian Harsh had been, Gwendolyn Brooks nevertheless found herself in trouble in the spring of 1937. The writer, then twenty, was still more than a decade away from becoming a celebrated author and Pulitzer Prize winner, yet her success publishing dozens of poems in the *Chicago Defender*'s weekly literary column "Lights and Shadows: A Little Bit of Everything" had already fixed her as an emerging figure in Bronzeville's literary scene. As early as 1934, while she was still in high school, Brooks began submitting short, lyrical, and often sentimental poems to Dewey R. Jones, the longtime editor of "Lights and Shadows," who enthusiastically published them. Soon Brooks became a regular contributor, publishing around seventy-five poems in the column from 1934 to 1938 and becoming affiliated with the Lasers, a disparate group of poets who regularly contributed to the column.[1] By 1937, however, Brooks had provoked the ire of one popular Laser, William Henry Huff. A lawyer by trade, Huff began writing poems for the column in the 1920s, frequently heralding the virtues of traditional womanhood and thus feeding the respectability politics that the *Defender* espoused to its readers. Dubbed the "Defender's Poet Laureate," Huff found a wide readership and garnered the praise of fellow Lasers, including Brooks herself, who, in 1935 commended his "strength of soul / To cry the wholesome thing you're crying."[2]

But in 1937, the young poet's lyrics worried him. After Brooks published one particularly sour poem in March of that year, which was ironically titled "Happiness" and cynically advised readers to "put thought / Of happiness away,"³ "But Gwendolyn, O Gwendolyn," he scolded her in the column the following month:

> Happiness is everywhere
> 'Tis in the valleys, on the hills
> And in every breath of air
> That you and I and all inhale
> God is your happiness and mine.

Huff's irritated mansplaining in this first stanza turns to outright exasperation in the second:

> Ah Gwendolyn, dear Gwendolyn
> Just why did you say such a thing
> When happiness is all about.
> Can't you hear the angels sing?
> There's happiness for you and all
> O Gwendolyn—Gwendolyn divine.⁴

As a fellow poet, Huff does not object to Brooks's style or subject matter; both conform to the type of verse that populated "Lights and Shadows" for a decade. It is her affect, her refusal to make readers feel good—in a poem titled "Happiness," no less—that provokes his response as a reader. Instead of writing poetry that reassures and comforts her readers—that reaffirms happiness for them—she mocks and frustrates them. "Happiness is your desire?" Brooks derides her readers:

> Happiness was mine!
> Like a true though distant gem
> It ever appeared to shine.
>
> But every time I reached the spot
> Where it had seemed to be,
> No sign of sofe [sic] resplendence could
> I see.
>
> Ha! Ha! Ha!
> Happiness, you say!
> Better put thought
> Of happiness away.⁵

Rather than affirming the "wholesome thing" that Huff celebrates in his verse, Brooks denies its very existence, advising readers to put happiness out of their minds entirely. Just as happiness was a trap that frustrated the expectations of Brooks's speaker, so too is "Happiness" the poem for her readers.

Brooks's poem thus constructs a radically different relationship to readers than Huff's does. Hers berates, withholding pleasantries and comfort. It agitates, discomforts; it embraces futility. It trades one affect—happiness—for another: anxiety. Brooks even laughs at her readers, admonishing them for desiring happiness as she once did. Huff's response to Brooks, however, puts readers' minds at ease by putting the young poet firmly in her place. He does so by correcting her about where to find happiness ("happiness is all about"), questioning her ("Can't you hear the angels sing?"), and condescending to her throughout the poem ("O Gwendolyn—Gwendolyn"). Huff thus quells the anxiety that her poem provokes, reaffirming the positive affect that her poem denies its readers.

By refusing to do this emotional work, Brooks in turn refuses to subscribe to a politics of respectability that she was expected to adhere to as a Black female poet writing in the *Defender*. At its core, this is the source of Huff's outrage: Brooks does not conform to the prescribed literary and gender norms that, at the time, were intertwined with the Black press, print culture, and the project of racial uplift. Indeed, a politics of respectability was central to the newspaper's mission; transmitting this respectability to readers was even more important. Such "respectable reading," as I term it, was considered a primary way to advance the race, and Black women writers in particular were supposed to offer themselves and their work to this cause. As a Black female poet publishing in the Black press in the early decades of the twentieth century, Brooks has a role that is very much prescribed for her: she is there to nurture, comfort, and guide her readers. And yet, as her "Lights and Shadows" poems demonstrate, she repeatedly refuses this role, teaching *Defender* readers a new way of engaging popular Black poetry.

In this chapter I argue that Brooks troubles popular conventions of reading by writing poetry that foregrounds anxiety, frustration, failure, and even disillusionment. Her poems deny readers the comfort and security that poetry in the *Defender* routinely offered. By deflecting back to readers the sentimentality that they expected from her, Brooks's poems construct experiences of feeling alone, lost, disappointed, and unfulfilled. The dozens of poems Brooks published in "Lights and Shadows" question the aesthetics, affects, and politics of respectable reading. Instead of facilitating this relationship by evoking a readership that reaffirms class and gender norms, Brooks encourages a kind of reading that is skeptical of, even cynical toward, middle-class respectability. In doing so, she rejects an entire infrastructure of early-twentieth-century racial uplift that links race pride, reading, and Black print culture. As she did so, Brooks wrestled with the role that poetry and print culture should play in serving Bronzeville's community and remained unconvinced that it should "civilize" Black readers, especially migrants coming from the South.

Brooks's early *Defender* poems in turn challenge our own reading and reception practices by urging us to read her work anew. Her "Lights and Shadows" lyrics not only innovate new ways of reading and writing popular poetry in the early years of the Black Chicago Renaissance—providing an alternative to ways the Black press advocated—but also prompt us to rethink the trajectory of her long career and its relationship to Black readers. In other words, they instruct us on how to read her, facilitating for us a new reception of her career. Though Brooks would go on to reject her early work as being "assimilationist" and written for a white audience, these poems instead illustrate that she was writing for a vibrant and engaged Black reading community in Bronzeville as early as the 1930s.

PRODUCING THE RESPECTABLE READER IN PRINT AND POETRY

From its beginning, the *Defender* committed itself to respectable reading—the idea that one could acquire respectability through reading and that reading itself was a marker of racial progress, success, and refinement. The newspaper's founder, Robert S. Abbott, frequently promoted the trappings of the middle class, framing "culture" as the ticket to upward mobility for the race. "Once upon a time man's ignorance of the fine things of life was excused on the grounds of insufficient opportunity, inadequate provisions and lack of leisure," he wrote in 1934. "But today, with library facilities, with the establishment of free schools conveniently located and scheduled, with free public lectures on all conceivable subjects, there can hardly be a justification for not tasting the savorous fruit yielded so abundantly by the tree of knowledge."[6] Abbott's mission with the *Defender* carried on the legacy of previous generations of the Black press. As Kim Gallon writes, "The early Black Press centered around its perceived ability to guide and shape behavior" and "stressed a class-inflected social responsibility in conformity with white conceptions of humanity that prefigured the 'politics of respectability' used by middle-class blacks at the turn of the twentieth century to regulate the behavior of working-class blacks." By the early twentieth century, she continues, Black newspapers such as the *Defender* "remained invested in a collective ideology that racial progress would be attained by broadcasting the merit of black humanity," and thus acted as "arbiters and conveyors of temperance, sexual restraint, and thrift."[7] These newspapers could "challenge dominant stereotypes of Blacks and recreate the group's wider public image to challenge the historical degradation of African American identities by the dominant White public," writes Catherine Squires.[8] To be sure, the *Defender* invested itself in building a community of readers for financial gain, to boost sales, but also in the more admirable goal of "broadcasting the merit of black humanity." Through the pages of his weekly newspaper, Abbott created a particular experience for readers—one that transmitted community values and norms through reading, encouraged reading as a means of racial uplift and respectability, and illustrated a "new" refined image of the race for outsiders.

For the *Defender* in particular, race progress in the form of greater economic stability and social advancement via the Great Migration were facilitated through acts of reading. In one way, reading provided African Americans in the South with pragmatic information as well as inspiration for moving north. As an "acknowledged catalys[t] of the Great Migration," the newspaper circulated throughout the South, aggressively advertising the better lives and jobs available in the North, thus helping to build Chicago's Black Metropolis as the city's Black population ballooned from 44,103 in 1910 to 109,458 in 1920.[9] In another way, reading the newspaper offered readers the chance to imagine better conditions—both for themselves and for the collective race—by escaping the poverty and racial violence of the South. Readers of the *Defender* regularly acknowledged the newspaper's ability to do so. "Being a regular reader of your most valuable paper (The Defender) I am impressed with the seeming unlimited interest that paper is taking in the welfare of the army of emigrants comeing [sic] from the south," one reader wrote to the newspaper in 1917. "My greatest desire is to leave for a better place but am unable to raise the money," another wrote. "I can write short stories all of which potray [sic] negro characters but no burlesque can also write poems.... [T]hese things will never profit me anything here in Natchez. Would like to know if you could use one or two of my short stories in serial form in your great paper they are very interesting and would furnish good reading matter."[10] So effective was the *Defender* at mobilizing people that it became an illegal artifact of Black reading practices, banned in some southern cities for inciting the migration north.[11]

At the same time that it worked to build a vibrant Black population (of readers) in Chicago, the *Defender* also conspicuously attempted to mold and manage that population on multiple fronts—to groom readers in the image of middle-class respectability. In Chicago, this impulse to cultivate readers intensified during the height of the Great Migration when the *Defender* frequently published articles and editorials that advised or lectured migrants—whose "habits and customs," one article complained, are "far different than those found in the north"—on proper norms of decorum.[12] As the sociologist E. Franklin Frazier reported in his 1932 study *The Negro Family in Chicago*: "Many members of this class of Negroes in northern cities viewed with alarm ... the influx of the ignorant masses from the plantations into their communities. They saw their neighborhoods deteriorating and met racial barriers where none had existed before. Moreover, to them the migrants constituted a threat to the standards of behavior which they had safeguarded as a heritage," believing "that all their achievements were being threatened by these 'hordes of barbarians.'"[13] The *Defender* thus positioned itself as "the migrant's book of dreams and etiquette" for Chicago, one that would, as Bill Mullen writes, "'civilize' the southern migrant."[14] Alongside popular etiquette columns in the 1920s and 1930s, articles explicitly directed toward new migrants to the city enforced a strict code of conduct.[15] "It is the duty," a February 10, 1917, editorial stated, "of every Northern organization, every pastor and every good citizen to guide and direct these newcomers so that their coming will prove an asset rather than a liability to the community they select for their future home."[16] The newspaper also instructed migrants directly, publishing such advice as "Don't let your property run down," "Don't sit around in the yard and on the porch barefoot and unkempt," and "Don't talk so loud, we're not all deaf." Moreover, the *Defender* directed migrants to cultivate aesthetic practices that aligned with respectability politics. "Do plant flowers in your yard," it directed, "Do dress nice and clean, but not gaudy," and, of note, "Do have good newspapers and books."[17]

To create an audience of respectable readers—race men and women who placed "good newspapers and books" at the center of their daily lives—the *Defender* needed to educate readers and guide them to the "right" kinds of books and other print culture to read. In other words, it needed to create a community not just of readers but of *respectable readers*—those who read the "right" things. Indeed, the kinds of print culture, media, and other forms of leisure and entertainment that new migrants consumed took center stage in this anxiety about respectability. The *Defender* saw its guidance as especially important as new migrants flooded the city and apprehension mounted among the Old Settlers about the kinds of print culture, media, and other forms of leisure and entertainment these new residents consumed. For instance, an early book review warns readers of "the thousands of books annually thrust upon an unsuspecting public"—"as though," Zoe Trodd explains, "the new community might need defense from literary as well as civil and physical assaults." Subtitled "Two Good New Books," the review highlights two recent publications that "deal with subjects in which we are especially interested, and of which the public at large know little": *The Progress of a Race* and *The Dunbar Speaker and Entertainer*. The review concludes by linking reading to social mobility: "We are getting out of the rut, we are becoming self conscious, we are taking pride in things that are ours. And the enormous sale of these two books is evidence of our growing desire to learn more of the things that vitally concern us."[18] Editors at the *Defender* may have thought that the paper's "unsuspecting" readers needed protection from the sheer number of books "thrust upon" them, but they worried more about their readers picking up the *wrong* books.

The *Defender* thus guided its "unsuspecting public" through columns and features that promoted cultural norms of middle-class propriety to become respectable readers. This advice even included educating readers on the proper way to handle a book. A 1912 column titled "Book Don'ts" reads much like the paper's columns for new migrants:

> Good books are treasures, and they should be handled with the greatest of care by everyone. Here are a few rules that should be observed:
> Never drop a book upon the floor.
> Never turn leaves with the thumb.
> Never lean or rest upon an open book.
> Never turn down the corners of leaves.
> Never touch a book with soiled or damp hands.
> Always place a large book upon a table before opening it.
> Never pull a book from the shelf by the binding at the top, but by the back.
> Never close a book with a pencil, tablet or anything else that is bulky between the leaves.[19]

Everything" in 1926.²⁷ Though Jones would leave in 1931 when he entered journalism school at Columbia and then later return, he permanently left the *Defender* staff in 1935. Dan Burley and David Orro served as editors of the column after Jones until "Lights and Shadows" eventually folded altogether in 1942 at the onset of World War II.

Under Jones's editorship, "Lights and Shadows" flourished, evolving from a lighthearted column of miscellany and verse into a centerpiece for Abbott's mission to showcase racial progress and enculturate readers. Authors such as Georgia Douglas Johnson, Frank Marshall Davis, Langston Hughes, Countee Cullen, Era Bell Thompson, and of course Brooks herself contributed to the column throughout the 1920s, 1930s, and early 1940s, yet the majority of "Lights and Shadows" contributors were amateur poets—educated Black professionals with both the knowledge and the time to write. Many were lawyers, teachers, or other professionals. Over its more than twenty-year existence, "Lights and Shadows" published hundreds of Black amateur writers from all corners of the country, including New York, Colorado, North Carolina, Texas, Pennsylvania, California, and Washington state. In the spirit of the column's at times playful tone, many contributors adopted lighthearted pseudonyms such as Bubbles, The Pirate, Ann Accident, Wyoming Bozo, Apple Blossom, Ima Twin, I. N. Cahoots, and The Nutty Nebraskan. Era Bell Thompson published letters, poetry, and other commentary in the column under the name Dakota Dick, yet most writers who used pseudonyms remain unknown. Additionally, many contributors were strangers to Chicago's literary world who simply wrote in, pitched a poem or two, and hoped Jones would publish them. Some made note, in a somewhat embarrassed way, of their amateur status. One, signed "TREE TOP TALL," from Des Moines, Iowa, confessed:

> I ain't no Contee [sic] Cullen
> Nor a budding Claude McKay,
> But just a long tall corn'er
> From out in IOWAY.
> (Where the tall corn grows.)²⁸

Notably, Jones encouraged and accepted many of these "cold call" poems, establishing a kind of open door policy akin to that of Harriet Monroe's *Poetry* magazine, which held court on the north side of town.

In large part because of this democratic approach to poetry, a friendly, convivial atmosphere developed among contributors. In addition to entering poems, jokes, and amusing anecdotes, they often wrote poems to and/or about one another, flung witty banter back and forth, engaged in friendly competitions, critiqued one another's work, and even romantically pursued one another. Indeed, as Delaney Hall writes, contributors wrote "as much to flirt, joke, and participate in a community of peers as to fulfill any serious literary aspirations."[29] For instance, "Will you please ask 'Langston Hughes,'" a Miss Independence wrote from Los Angeles in 1926, "to please, please, send me his picture? When I saw it in the Defender my heart turned five flops backwards."[30] By this time the group of regular contributors whom Jones named the Lasers had emerged. This group—including Cullen, Hughes, and Brooks—admired and fought one another fiercely; celebrated one another's accomplishments (such as Era Bell Thompson breaking track records); engaged in friendly rivalries; mourned the deaths of several of its members; and often wrote letters to and poems about one another. They even adopted a fraternity name, Lambda Alpha Sigma, and distributed membership pins.

Despite their playfulness, however, many Lasers and other contributors to "Lights and Shadows" were connected to the literary world. There were tributes to James Weldon Johnson; queries about Edna St. Vincent Millay's newest work; reviews of Hughes's *Weary Blues* and Claude McKay's *Home to Harlem* ("an assortment of glorified, highly perfumed fertilizer");[31] a stinging rebuke of Wallace Thurman; slightly gentler critiques of Jessie Fauset and Zora Neale Hurston; and even a gentle teasing of Gertrude Stein. Such engagement was most often prompted by Jones himself, who nudged both his contributors and his readers toward a more sophisticated literary palate by publishing the "good reading matter" that Abbott wished for his readers. A 1927 full-page feature on "Lights and Shadows" by Jones lauds the many literary accomplishments of the Lasers and notes that the column holds "a premier position among columns" and "ranks among the best columns in any newspaper printed in the United States" (see Figure 5).[32]

Readers noticed, often citing the column's role in advancing the race. In 1925 a Chicago reader, Robert M. Crawford, wrote to the *Defender*:

> I think the Lights and Shadows in your paper are just fine. That is the first thing I look for every week. I think it's very nice of you to give your readers space for their poetry and jokes. We learn so much by reading the other fellow's thoughts.
>
> I have been reading the Defender weekly for ten years and I really think it has the right name. It defends us from the lies the Chicago Tribune writes about our race. And it puts forth every effort to get us a fair deal at law, and it is a great help to the Negro race in every way. I know it is the world's greatest weekly, so therefore I am sure it has the right name. I am with you![33]

FIGURE 5. Dewey R. [Jones,] "Defender Column Contributors Win High Honors," *Chicago Defender*, July 30, 1927.

A decade later another reader similarly wrote: "We are constant readers and boosters of The Chicago Defender, the Worlds [sic] Greatest Weekly, and our eyes always find the column 'Lights and Shadows' and we like the poems, just keep them coming."[34] Even as late as the 1960s, "Lights and Shadows" was remembered as the column that added culture and refinement to the *Defender*. Concerned by "bizarre headlines" about "horrible sex and crime cases," a Chicago reader, Mrs. Lonnie Richard Garner, suggested to the *Defender* in 1962 that "the old 'Lights and Shadows' column could be revived and it would help inspire young poets and at the same time add culture to the paper."[35]

For nearly a decade, then—roughly half the column's existence—Jones constructed a virtual national Black poetic community that produced "good reading matter" for the *Defender* and, in turn, promoted respectable reading. Jones took the task seriously. "This isn't a matrimonial bureau to encourage love-sick maidens and sighing sheiks," he wrote in 1926 in an attempt to raise the profile of the column. "Nor is it a medium of communication between estranged personages. It is just a column conducted to give meager expression to our readers who are interested in the sort of thing it tries to offer."[36] And while initially Jones seems to have espoused an apolitical aesthetic—demanding in his inaugural column, "Don't send us any poems about lynchings, 'Going North,' or the 'Rising Race,' etc."—the column regularly offered a mix of politics and poetry throughout his tenure as editor, including lynching statistics published right alongside poems.[37] Jones thus built the column out of poetry that protested racial injustice, showcased literary accomplishments of the race, and, above all, reinforced social norms within Bronzeville and Black communities across the nation. In the process, he used poetry to affirm the new image of the race that Abbott wished to project, establishing "Lights and Shadows" as one of only a few venues in the country that published Black poets in the 1920s, 1930s, and 1940s. Meanwhile, across town, when asked "how many Negro poets the magazine has published," *Poetry* magazine editor Peter De Vries answered, "What the hell has that got to do with poetry?"[38] As Jones and contributors knew well, "Lights and Shadows" was a significant space in which Black readers and writers could enjoy poetry that spoke to the experiences of being Black in America.

"Lights and Shadows" was a source of refinement and culture, perhaps the most visible way that the *Defender* encouraged habits of respectful reading during the early to middle decades of the twentieth century. But it was also a complicated nexus of reading, respectability politics, traditional gender norms, and popular poetry. Much of the literary labor of creating respectable reading practices relied heavily, though not exclusively, on Black female poets. Moreover, the women who contributed to the column were held to exceptionally high standards. The column adhered to strict ideas about gender, championing "traditional" Black womanhood, as William Henry Huff did in his response to Brooks in 1937. Though respectable reading offered Black women writers like Brooks the opportunity to participate in the larger public sphere of the Black press, it also held them to sometimes unachievable expectations, ones that Brooks would eventually abandon.

RESPECTABLE READING AND THE BLACK WOMEN POETS OF "LIGHTS AND SHADOWS"

The textual environment that Brooks entered in 1934 with "Lights and Shadows" offered a very narrow role for the Black female poet. The pressure on Black girls and women to conform to a politics of respectability and serve as public figures for the race was especially acute in Chicago. At the time, the city was an epicenter of Black women's club activity, promoting respectable Black womanhood in service of bettering the race. Wanda Hendricks writes in her capacious history of Black women's clubs, *Gender, Race, and Politics in the Midwest: Black Club Women in Illinois* (1998), that the state saw "an unprecedented proliferation of black female clubs" in the late nineteenth and early twentieth centuries.[39] During this time, Chicago was home to "more than seventy social and political clubs," reports Anne Meis Knupfer.[40] "The mobilization of these middle- and upper-class African American women was based on a shared belief that they had to collectively tackle the issues contributing to the destruction of the African American community," Hendricks continues. "They saw their social welfare crusade as improving both their own lives and the lives of those around them" as well as "elevating the image of middle-class black womanhood."[41] At the head of this progressive activism in Chicago were such leaders as Fannie Barrier Williams and Ida B. Wells. Indeed, the Black clubwoman was "the real new woman in American life," Williams argued in 1900:

> She is needed to change the old idea of things implanted in the minds of the white race and there sustained and hardened into a national habit by the debasing influence of slavery estimates. This woman is needed as an educator of public opinion. . . . She has come to enrich American life with finer sympathies, and to enlarge the boundary of fraternity and the democracy of love among American women. She has come to join her talents, her virtues, her intelligence, her sacrifices and her love in the work of redeeming the unredeemed from stagnation, from cheapness, and from narrowness.[42]

The influence of race women in the city would echo throughout the following decades of the twentieth century. In Chicago, as the sociologists St. Clair Drake and Horace Cayton would note in 1945, "Bronzeville is somewhat suspicious, generally, of its Race Men, but tends to be more trustful of the Race Woman.... The Race Woman is idealized as a 'fighter,' but her associated role of 'uplifter' seems to be accepted with less antagonism than in the case of the Race Man."[43]

This discourse intensified during the Great Migration, Marcia Chatelain writes, when Black women, and especially girls, were charged with the task of healing what was often depicted as a fragmented Black community. "Black clubwomen's advocacy for girls revealed their belief that black girlhood was indeed multifaceted and critically important to black survival and progress," Chatelain argues. "Black organizations steeped in racial uplift ideologies—a communal investment in overcoming stereotype through a commitment to piety, industriousness, and chaste living—believed that black girls needed to represent their race by limiting their expressions of sexuality and desire and displaying the values of the black middle class." Panic about "destabilized black families" spiked again after the Depression, she notes, spurring more rhetoric about Black women's and girls' morality, sexuality, and behavior.[44] Throughout this era in Chicago, the Black press played an important role in defining and propagating the image of a respectable race woman. As Aria S. Halliday shows, Katherine E. Williams-Irvin, editor in chief of *Half-Century Magazine* (1916–1925), and Olive Diggs, editor of the *Sunday Chicago Bee* (1925–1942), used their "periodicals to publicize and perform a New Negro womanhood for the twentieth century. These women castigated, challenged, and condemned improper behavior for black women migrating to the black metropolis," thus reinforcing the importance of respectability for Chicago's Black population.[45]

The Black women who contributed to "Lights and Shadows" were similarly looked to as models of propriety and race pride through the use of popular poetry.[46] Poets such as Georgia Douglas Johnson and Beatrice Abbott—both of whom overlapped with Brooks in "Lights and Shadows"—established this persona of the respectable Black female poet in Jones's column in the years just before and during Brooks's participation. Though she is more often associated with the Harlem Renaissance, Georgia Douglas Johnson contributed to the *Defender* throughout her life—in "Lights and Shadows" during the 1920s and 1930s, and in another column, "Verse a Day," from 1960 to 1962—as well as to *The Crisis* and other Black publications, including the short-lived little magazine, *Music and Poetry*, published and edited in Chicago by Nora Douglas Holt, classical music critic for the *Defender*.[47] An admitted fan of Huff's poetry, Johnson herself was praised by the *Defender* as having "a fine and never failing good taste."[48] Elsewhere, Dewey Jones included Johnson in his 1927 feature on the Lasers as well as his 1931 short list of "young poets who have established themselves as people to be considered when the American world of letters is being discussed, thus "prov[ing] that the Race would be articulate poetically if it chose to be."[49] Johnson upheld the image of the refined Black woman for readers of "Lights and Shadows" through such poems as "A Song of Courage" and "Hope."[50] These early contributions to the *Defender* prefigure her nationally syndicated advice column "Homely Philosophy," which appeared in Black newspapers across the country, including the *Defender* from 1926 to 1932.[51] Appearing on the same page as "Lights and Shadows," just two columns over, "Homely Philosophy" aimed to comfort and nurture readers by giving advice on topics such as "Mastering Your Tongue," "Count Your Blessings," "Keeping Friendships in Repair," "Shaping Your Own Destiny," "Making the Best of Things," "Master Your Moods," "Find Pleasure in Common Things," "Don't Hurry Through Life," and "Chin Up." These columns guided readers, helping them to navigate difficult and uncertain social situations while imparting good manners and good culture, including advice about good books. In her February 9, 1929, installment, "Good Books," Johnson lauded the importance of good reading:

> Good books inspire great thoughts and great thoughts make men great! That which we feed upon mentally day by day soon becomes a part of us; we grow into the likeness of our own thoughts.
> If upon reading certain books we feel lifted, stronger, more hopeful, more able and determined, those books are good and by reading them our path lies upward!"[52]

Linking racial uplift with "good books," Johnson reinforced the larger message of the *Defender* in both prose and poetry.

Writing from Newark, New Jersey, Beatrice Abbott published regularly in "Lights and Shadows" as a member of the Lasers, and as a friend of Brooks's, from 1933 until just weeks before the column ended in 1942.[53] Like Johnson, in her writing she instructed readers on morality and social norms while embodying a respectable Black woman persona. In 1936 alone, Abbott published such pieces as "Hymn of Humility," "Belles Lettres," and "Good Neighbor," all of which modeled the kinds of values *Defender* readers, especially women, were supposed to emulate.[54] Her poetry embraced the figure of the nurturing and supportive Black woman poet who guided readers and served as a moral compass. Sounding much like an installment of Johnson's "Homely Philosophy," the speaker of "Contrast," for instance, embodies the kind of respectability expected of "Lights and Shadows" readers and contributors:

> Someone said an unkind word today—
> Someone hurt me in a wicked way.
> For a time, I thought I'd like to do—
> Something just as mean, to Someone, too.
> But I cannot find within my heart,
> Urge to ape the mean one's nasty art.
> I decided I don't want to be—
> Like that one who was so mean to me.
> So, I shall begin this very day . . .
> To be kind in all I do or say.[55]

Much like the *Defender*'s various "Do and Don'ts" advice columns, and echoing the kind of role Black women (poets) were supposed to have as a moralizing force within the community, Abbott's poetry modeled good and respectable reading for "Lights and Shadows" readers.

In some ways, the teenage Brooks seems to have been eager to fulfill her role as a model for respectability in the same ways that Johnson and Abbott did. After all, she came from a class in Chicago, as her biographer George Kent writes, that "Horace Cayton and St. Clair Drake called the 'respectables,' people not of self-conscious class, color, educational, or aristocratic distinctions but somewhere in the middle, the good-doing people determined to live within a firm moral ordering."[56] Born in 1917 in Topeka, Kansas, Brooks grew up in Chicago in the 1920s and 1930s immersed in this social world. She was surrounded by such "respectables" and learned respectability politics firsthand: her parents emphasized education and exposed Brooks and her younger brother to reading and writing at a young age. "As soon as we were old enough, my mother got us library cards; and there were many books in the house, including the Harvard Classics," she later recalled. "Our parents were intelligent and courageous; they subscribed to duty, decency, dignity, industry—*kindness*."[57] Indeed, good writing and good manners were central to Brooks's sense of self in the years when she wrote for the *Defender*, and she prided herself on both. In a list of new year's resolutions for 1934—the year she began publishing in "Lights and Shadows"—Brooks set both literary and personal goals for herself:

1. Have at least ten stories accepted and paid for by January 1st, 1935.
2. Have at least twenty-five poems (new poems) published by January 1st, 1935.
3. Become softer mannered.
4. Become pleasanter.
5. Found, "The Pioneer Star," monthly. To include 4, original, typewritten stories, 4, original, typed poems, 4 original drawings. Nine issues by January 1st, 1935.
6. Earn, during the year of 1938, from forty dollars to _____, by literary work. At any rate, not less than forty dollars.
7. Write and publish *good* book. 20 chapters, about 40,000 words. From $400 to $800, net results.[58]

Though ambitious, Brooks's resolutions to write "*good*" material while becoming "softer mannered" and "pleasanter" illustrate the seriousness with which she dedicated herself to fulfilling the good girlhood that was expected of her and that she clearly aspired to at this young age.

Brooks was well positioned to enter "Lights and Shadows" as a respectable (and respected) poet. It is no surprise, then, that many of her poems for the column invest in these gendered norms and the mission of "refining" a migrant population in Chicago as well as a larger, national population more broadly. Following Johnson and Abbott, many of the earliest of these poems present the teenage Brooks as a sage writer advising her readers with conventional wisdom; some are even didactic. Many moralize. In the anti-materialist poem "Wealth," Brooks reminds her readers that "courage is the truest wealth of all."[59] "Selfish" values compassion, altruism, and generosity, while "Life Is Too Short" advises readers not to worry about "What comes or goes, what goes or comes."[60] Indeed, "Life is too brief to waste it / Grasping for the moon," she lectures. "Too precious, precious, and too brief; / The death flute shrills too soon."[61] In a similar way, "Count No Day Lost" insists, "And when the day comes that yourself / You lift, oh, wondering soul, / Count that day as your day of days— / Mark it, now, as your goal."[62] "Genius," meanwhile, exhorts humility, framing "the tie / Of simple friendship" as more precious than intellect, which, ultimately, "Geniuses wake to find . . . gone, one day."[63] "Shadows" emphasizes perseverance: "As long as I am firm and whole / And bright and clear and warm of soul," the speaker vows, "I think that I can reach my goal / In shadows."[64] Embracing piety, "A Song of Thanksgiving" declares, "All things I thank Thee for, / Divine and worthy King! / Gifts great and small, thank Thee for all—/ True thanks for everything."[65] Likewise, "A Christmas Story" restores the speaker's wavering faith by affirming the redemptive power of Christ's love to heal the "weightiness" and "Heavy resentment" she experiences by being poor.[66]

Other poems offer more practical advice for readers on maintaining the social fabric of their community. For example, "One Little Quarrel" exhorts readers to avoid petty arguments such as one that *ruined two lives* and can lead to *"blinding tears"* and *"Regret."*[67] Much like the *Defender*'s various "Do and Don'ts" columns that direct readers not to "act discourteously to other people in public places" or "allow yourself to be drawn into street brawls," Brooks's poems remind readers of the importance of social bonds.[68] They especially revere the bond of friendship. Brooks wrote several poems expounding on her loving friendships both within and outside of the Lasers: "Corner in a Portrait Gallery," "Sonnets for Beatrice," "For Semuel H. Randolph (Ima Twin)," "Two Songs for

Friends," and "Friend," which defines friendship as "The purest lesson / Flesh can learn."[69] Brooks herself was the subject of other Lasers' verse celebrating friendship as well. In 1936, Ima Twin praised Brooks by writing, "I searched my treasures, carefully, / And you were the brightest gem."[70] Brooks was also the subject of two poems by Abbott. In the 1935 "For Gwendolyn Brooks (Appreciation)," Abbott praised the comfort that Brooks's poems offered readers: "Into our lonely hearts you come—/ To ease our stress and strife"; "You have a sense of humor, too—" she continues, "Which is a precious thing."[71]

Brooks's poems similarly celebrate the bonds of the nuclear family—the social unit that reformers in Chicago looked to for stability in the Black community, especially during the flux of the migration. In "To My Parents," the poet lovingly paints a blissful domestic scene of her mother and father "In a relaxed and tranquil cheer." Admiring the "sparkle in her eyes" and the "patience in his smile," the speaker muses:

> I like to watch them at this hour
> When calm falls on them lke [sic] a shower
> Serene and gentle, for the day
> Has such an over-brilliant ray
> That it outshines those qualities
> Which glisten in nocturnal peace.

The poem ends with the speaker confessing, "But this I say most honestly: / More than all gold are both to me."[72] In this way, the poem prizes emotional wealth over material wealth, asserting that the bonds of family are the most valuable possession of all.

Revering the Black family was particularly important, given anxieties surrounding Black life during this era of migration. By 1932, E. Franklin Frazier had already condemned the effects of the Great Migration on the Black family. "The movement of the Negro to the city [Chicago] creates a crisis in his life," Frazier wrote. "It means the loss of the intimate association of friends and relatives and the status that he has in the small town or rural community of the South." This in turn causes "the migrant [to be] liberated from the control that the church and other forms of association exercised in the rural South"; as a result, "freedom from these controls makes the migrant subject to all the forms of suggestion that the city offers." This "crisis" led to a moral panic about sex, illegitimacy, vagrancy, juvenile delinquency, and unmarried women—a fear of what Frazier called "the disintegration of Negro family life in the city."[73] As Adam Green notes, "The growing impermanence of black families [was] covered with particular intensity in *Ebony*" and other Black periodicals of the day. "The emerging ritual of the black family reunion, widespread by this time, offered evidence of the dedication to maintaining family ties in spite of dislocation," while "at the same time, it registered widespread anxieties over African Americans' capacity to do so."[74] Much of the responsibility for this social anxiety fell on Black women, writes Chatelain, resulting in a "call for better black mothers" as "a direct response to mounting fears about the fate of African American families in Chicago as they struggled to adapt to their new surroundings and exercise their newly found freedoms."[75] The result was an acute social anxiety displaced onto judgments of the moral fitness as well as the bodies of Black women.

By painting a scene of a respectable Black family in "To My Parents," then, Brooks does much more than honor her parents; she demonstrates that she is a good daughter and community member—one who fulfills gendered expectations that help instruct and stabilize Bronzeville's Black population by employing a politics of respectability. She does exactly what the *Defender* and social reformers in Bronzeville would have her do: in Chatelain's words, "carry the weighty responsibilities of race progress."[76] Together, many of Brooks's *Defender* lyrics serve as a kind of primer for Bronzeville readers, using verse to help readers navigate their complex social terrain in the same ways that Abbott's poems and Johnson's advice columns do.

The young Brooks, alongside Johnson and Abbott, thus carries out the literary labor of "Lights and Shadows" to refine the *Defender*'s "unsuspecting public." Their writing constituted important cultural work. First, it united readers around a common vision, establishing standards and guidelines for respectable Black living (and reading) in the modern era. And second, Abbott, Johnson, and Brooks provided readers a degree of comfort and safety. In other words, the affect their writing produced in readers was more important than the aesthetics they deployed in their verse. The repetition of themes, speakers, perspective, personas, characters, and emotions created a predictable reading experience in a bewildering and often violent urban North. Not only did these three poets repeat themes and morals in their own poetry—reiterating messages within their own bodies of work—but also they repeated one another, accruing a catalog of poetry that revisited similar if not identical topics and messages. It would be easy for readers to conflate poems by Abbott, Brooks, and Johnson because such repetition was the point. This "repetitive consumption," to use a term from Janice Radway, of respectable reading creates emotional responses to make readers feel a certain way.[77] That, more than the poems' form or even content, is important in this context.

The affects produced by such repetitive consumption of respectability may in turn prove transformative for the readers of "Lights and Shadows." In the context of nineteenth-century serial novelists, Dale Bauer suggests that repetition can create alternative futures. "Nineteenth-century serial writing is about transforming a few plots into a series of other possibilities, particularly for women," she explains. "These plots and characters may be combined in different ways, but their accretion yields a surpassing vision: the need to establish a code of conduct that will help to reorder personal and family relations in a new vision of Americanized pain and recovery—what ails American women and how they might recover."[78] Similarly, the repetition of images of respectable Black life and identity allowed readers of "Lights and Shadows" to envision a common purpose—a way to overcome and "recover" from pain and trauma. Brooks's poems help readers envision the future, much as the *Defender* did in the early days of the Great Migration, when it nurtured a collective imagination of what life *could be*. Brooks thus offered recuperation, transformation, and stability in a vision of Black life in the North around which readers in Bronzeville could cohere.

To be sure, the poems of "Lights and Shadows" and the advice in "Homely Philosophy" did not effect a resolution to racial violence or white supremacy. But the repeated imagery that readers encountered week after week provided a level of comfort and predictability, safety and security in familiar shared values enabling racial cohesion. Such national cohesion was, writes Green, still developing in the 1930s and 1940s. "African Americans broadly speaking were not yet a national people," he explains, "because they still lacked capacity to think of themselves in nationalized terms." Though this would change in the next decade as "African Americans throughout the country would be moved to see themselves in such simultaneous terms by purveyors of music, radio, and journalism: individuals already disproportionately concentrated in Chicago," the lackluster attendance at the 1940s Negro Convention in particular "indicated that they could not be called on, because they were not yet adequately developed."[79] In multiple ways, reading the *Defender* helped Black readers in Bronzeville and across the nation cohere by inducing in them shared experiences, shared feelings, and thus, ideally, a shared community. This, ultimately, is the work of respectable reading: making visible a collective future and allowing readers to feel comfortable and safe in that repeated vision. "Lights and Shadows" was at the center of this cultural work, calling on Black women to do the labor of racial cohesion through predictable and comforting poetry.

The repetition in these poems was also important cultural work for Johnson, Abbott, and Brooks because it elevated Black women in "Lights and Shadows" into the role of "educators of public opinion" that Williams promoted at the turn of the century and that other race women have embodied before and since her. Personifying this important position in Black society helped them combat negative stereotypes of Black women, even in their own column. Indeed, as problematic as respectability politics were, the strategy served a crucial purpose for Black women. Brittney Cooper explains that such gender norms "made Black women's and men's lives legible as humans rather than as chattel and has subsequently created deep affective investments in Black communities over the last 150 years. Thus, we cannot only see respectability politics as a problematic mode of articulating class identity, though it certainly is that. It is also a complicated, contingent, and (rightfully) contested mode of articulating Black gender identity vis-à-vis the social resuscitation of Black women's sexual morality." Engaging this tradition of respectability politics gave the women of "Lights and Shadows" the armor they needed to protect themselves in the public sphere. "In a world predicated in the surveillance of Black bodies," especially Black women's bodies, Cooper continues, a politics of respectability and its close counterpart, a culture of dissemblance, emerged as "two key strategies that Black women used to navigate a hostile public sphere and to minimize the threat of sexual assault and other forms of bodily harm routinely inflicted upon Black women."[80] While this strategy has been theorized in large part in relation to white audiences, it nonetheless proved important for the women writers of "Lights and Shadows," who, as women, faced insults from other contributors to the column.

At times, "Lights and Shadows" harbored abusive and demeaning depictions of women; at others, it criticized and condescended to them. At the center of much acerbic discussion of the New Negro Woman was William Henry Huff. As the most popular poet in "Lights and Shadows" in the 1920s and 1930s, Huff was one of the key factors in the success of the column as well as one of the greatest supporters of Black poetry and literary life in Chicago. But his repeated championing of traditional Black womanhood—steeped in purity, submissiveness, and self-sacrifice—is troublesome because of the desire his poems express to control and police Black women. Many of them explicitly focus on praising women who conform to traditional notions of womanhood and ridicule those who adopt different standards, much as he did with Brooks. Disgusted by the New Negro Woman in "The Ultra-Modern Wife," for instance, Huff's speaker laments:

> She thinks a man is made to dance
>   To her discordant notes;
> She seems to want to wear the pants,
>   To search his eyes for motes.
> She does not seem to understand
>   That men are human, too,
> But longs to drive with whip in hand
>   Like masters used to do.[81]

Huff's astonishing simile likening modern Black women to enslavers reveals the degree to which he excoriated New Negro womanhood. Huff would further expound on the types of traits that desirable respectable women share in other poems such as "Womanhood Then and Now," which longs for a time "when women stood / Beside the spinning wheel / With apron on and snow white hood" and "did not rock and reel / From whiskey, wine or gin or beer."[82] Further, others such as "A Stitch in Time," "O Mother Dear," "Girls Should Neither Smoke Nor Drink!," and "The Girl Who Answered No" similarly fantasize about controlling women, manufacturing nostalgia for a time when women were supposedly passive and compliant.[83] In this way, Huff's poems use male complaint and injury to instruct readers in traditional notions of Black womanhood that frequently descend into misogynoir.[84]

Much of the humor of the column, too, came at the expense of women, who often found themselves serving as the punch line of ugly "jokes." In 1924, "Handling a Woman Electrically" advised, "When a woman is sulky and will not speak—Exciter. / If she gets too excited—Controller. / If she talks too long—Interrupter."[85] In 1937, Dan Burley, who took over the column after Jones, commented, "Right now the trend seems to be for men to keep their seats in the presence of women because the ladyfolk have an idea of eventually running a female for President of this great Republic—which would never do!"[86] More extreme examples of the column's sexism include a 1935 interlude between poems, most likely also by Burley, which reads: "WIFE BEATING is an art. Few people realize the various difficult steps one has to take before he can be accepted into the ranks of the 'Free and Accepted Ancient Order of

Wife Pummeler.' Your fists have to be of a certain hardness at certain times of the year. Your eye has to be able to take on a flinty glare while your weight must border at 190 pounds stripped."[87] Though Black women's poetry was regularly promoted and prized in the column, such "humor" nonetheless reveals great anxiety about changing gender norms—as well as competing with Black women in the literary marketplace—in the first half of the century.

The respectable images that Johnson, Abbott, and Brooks repeatedly offered in "Lights and Shadows," then, push back against negative images of Black women so casually and routinely circulated in American culture, even in their own column. Moreover, investing in the politics of respectability facilitated entrance into a public sphere that could have been closed to them had they crafted different personas. The persona of nurturing, pious, and chaste womanhood afforded Black women (limited) freedom and agency they might not otherwise have been able to attain. Within the context of the *Defender* and "Lights and Shadows," writing this poetry and using this persona allowed them to contribute in a central way to the Black public sphere through literature, becoming a dominant force in the future of the race. Brooks's ability to conform to the "Lights and Shadows" aesthetic and mission allowed her entry into a group that had prestige, thus marking her as a serious writer. Her experiences with "Lights and Shadows" greatly leveraged her future career, including nearly landing her a first job. She later recalled how Jones attempted to secure employment for her as a reporter at the *Defender*. "When Gwendolyn wrote to him, [Robert] Abbott's reply setting up an appointment was cordial and obliging," Kent relates. But the hopes of the writer and her mother, who accompanied Brooks to the meeting, "were dashed at the start of the interview, when Abbott's face changed expression upon sight of Gwendolyn.... Gwendolyn remembers that the interview was cold, perfunctory, almost hostile.... and after the interview Gwendolyn did not hear from him again." Brooks later surmised that "his change arose from her old source of rejection: skin color" because Abbott was known to have "an obsession about white-skinned black women," while Brooks was dark-skinned.[88]

That tension as insider/outsider—as one who gained praise but also reprimands from fellow columnists—would come to define this early stage of Brooks's writing. At the same time that she aligned herself with the *Defender*'s and the "Lights and Shadows" column's respectability project, she also expressed anxiety about this role and the values it espoused. She may have later characterized these poems as mere "pleasantries," but the verses are deceptive, working more to dismantle than to shore up the role she was supposed to model for readers.[89] Underneath even her most saccharine verse lurks an ambivalence, at times a pessimism, about the ability of middle-class respectability to solve the economic and social ills of the urban North. Again and again, Brooks's *Defender* poems *worry*.

RESISTING THE RESPECTABLE READER

For all of their confidence, Brooks's "Lights and Shadows" poems express doubt, frustration, cynicism, even anxiety about the "good manners" and "good reading" promoted by the column and the *Defender* writ large. While the poems set sentimental scenes and scenarios, they ultimately refuse readers the pleasure of fulfilling those visions. In doing so, they frustrate readers, denying the safe and secure role of popular poetry in the Black press at the time. Moreover, they demonstrate a lack of agency, reminding readers that they cannot control their own destiny—that instead, their lives are determined by such social forces as those documented in Drake and Cayton's *Black Metropolis* and Wright's social realism. In this way, her poems train readers to read their world (and literature) skeptically, uneasily.

Take the final stanza of the sentimental "To My Parents," an ending that disrupts the domestic scene established earlier in the poem. In the final lines, the speaker tells us that "Neither [parent] is perfect—who can be! / There is so much infirmity, / Nothing escapes debility / That treads earths [sic] doubtful radiancy."[90] Here, Brooks no doubt hits a nerve with her readers. By aligning the Black family with "infirmity" and "debility," she expresses uncertainty about the ability of this social unit to survive in the North, an anxiety at the center of the Great Migration experience.[91]

Brooks similarly represents heterosexual romance—positioned as the very foundation of the Black family—as a failure. Her early poems are littered with lyrics devoted to unrequited love, failed romances, and parted lovers. It is tempting to interpret them as the melodramatic musings of an imaginative teenager. Some of these poems certainly rely on romantic clichés and tropes. One, for instance, mourns: "Music is not music, / Since you have gone from me! / Since you have gone, there is no song, / No stinging melody."[92] Another confesses, "Knowledge that you're desired / By someone you desire, / Warms much more completely / Than fire."[93] To some degree, Kent writes, such melodrama is to be expected: "It is typical for the youthful writer to tend toward pathos and the tragic, to the imaginative exploration of the emotional universe, and even to the enjoyment of pain." Brooks's poems "are thus part of the usual development of adolescence and young poethood. In addition to the spillover tensions from real life, they partake of the romantic love of the movies and the romantic postures of other poets, with Byron and Sara Teasdale at the foreground."[94]

But for the few that fulfill this familiar teenage persona, many more poems reject love altogether as a category of fulfillment and stability for Black women, ultimately departing from traditional lovesick verse that—despite its melodrama—ultimately values love as a category of personal fulfillment. Repeatedly, Brooks's love poems associate romance with loss, disappointment, injury, even death. In "Plaint," the speaker "bitter[ly]" complains that "One love was all I asked" but "I have all now but that / One thing."[95] "Gift" grieves, "That which I love, yet cannot know, is dear, / But oh, so far, so far away from here."[96] "I Loved You Best" complains, "I loved you most, I loved you most, / You loved me not at all."[97] The speaker of "After Christmas" gripes, "But you, whom I have treasured most, / Proved to be most untrue. / You failed to give the sweetest gift of all, / The gift of you."[98] "How Can I Keep My Mind Away" recounts "love that is dead. / Love that is no more love, but ash instead; / Love that succumbed on being overfed."[99] The speaker of "I Thank You for Your Kindness" offers a more somber message about love: "I thank you for your kindness. / But dear, an I-don't-want-you / Is just an I-don't-want-you, / No matter how soft the covers / That enfold."[100] Alternatively, another speaker matter-of-factly denies feeling grief at the end of a relationship: "I give myself no time to nurse my ache— / I have my floors to sweep, my pies to bake."[101] The speaker of "You Say I Am in Love" rejects identification as a person in love: "I am in love, you say? / You know there is no love."[102] The speaker of "Star Love" complains that "loving you is / Like loving a star, / And I am tired of / Reaching so far."[103] Finally, another speaker compares love to bubbles that—in their fragility—are "Not to be trusted."[104]

Even when one of Brooks's *Defender* poems does seem to want to invest in a romantic relationship, doing so is ultimately framed as an uncertainty. "Prayer" offers a sobering request: "Now timidly I pray / I may a lover find / Who knows / How to be kind."[105] The speaker of "You Need Not Bring Me Roses" echoes the cynical verse of Dorothy Parker by rejecting roses from a beloved, instead instructing: "Bring this—your mute affection, / Warm and strong and pure. / This is—I pray!—a gift / That will endure."[106] At times love even causes injury and harm: the distraught speaker of "The Bright Star" laments, "such a star was never meant for me," and thus wonders "Why blind me with this brilliance all too bright?"[107] "Solace" recounts the escapades of a cruel lover: "You took my heart home with you, / And laughed, 'A souvenir.'"[108] In a similar way, the speaker of "Possession" addresses a lover who has left her "A tortuous life": "Oh, you have taken and devoured my soul, / And you have taken my heart's substance, too."[109] In a similar way, "Sonnet" ironically uses the traditional poetic form to reflect how love has reduced the speaker to an object: "I am a thing that you have thrust away, / To save until a darker, colder day."[110] Meanwhile, the speaker of "Kismet" watches her beloved suffer from afar: "She will abuse him and she will deceive / Him whom I love and always shall love so."[111] Alternatively, the speaker of the experimental piece "Jingling Judy's Journal" "screamed, 'Say, better guys than you, Dan Doe, have run from me!' . . . So back to home, and into bed, without my customary meal; I cried until my eyes were red, so rotten, rotten, did I feel."[112] "Never Enough," depicts love as fundamentally unsatisfying: "There's never enough of what I want" and "Never enough of what I desire! / Satisfactions are few! / Never enough of your love, / Enough of you."[113]

For Brooks, heterosexual love fails to be a salve for economic and social problems, or to be personally fulfilling, ultimately offering little respite from the instability of life for many in Bronzeville. Further, many of Brooks's poems express anxiety about one's lack of agency in life altogether, musing on day-to-day uncertainties. "Postscript to Suffering" wonders, "What, must the Cup of Sorrow / Be drained by me alone? / Or will a smile tomorrow / Gleam where the tears have shone?," while "Destiny" questions if it would be better to "know / Of cumbrances that I must meet." Instead, the speaker confesses, "Ah, but I shrink, and am afraid, / Perchance mans [sic] destiny should remain / A thing unpondered and unsaid, / A thing untold by wind or rain."[114] Rather than finding comfort in this collective vision of race progress, Brooks's poems leave readers unsure and uncomfortable.

In denying readers comforting, reassuring verse, Brooks disrupts a pattern of respectability, fostering reader anxiety, to be sure, but also allowing for a greater range of experiences and identities for Black women. After all, Chatelain reminds us, "for most, migration produced ambivalence, disappointment, and confusion about rights, responsibilities, and roles in this new era of black life."[115] This is precisely what Brooks's poems do: give voice to the range of emotions and experiences, frustrations and failures, that Black women experienced but the respectability poet persona could not provide. As much as that role offered Black women a place in the Black public sphere, it could also flatten the nuances of Black womanhood, eschewing the subjectivity of Black women in order to dictate community norms—piety, chastity, modesty, and heterosexual longing. In their attempt to convey those standards, Johnson's and Abbott's poems often created one-dimensional types from which they rarely broke.[116] Abbott even admitted as much in 1934 when she acknowledged that her poems used just that—a persona—because readers expected it. "My sonnets sigh for love that's lost," she writes, "My stricken soul seems desolate—...."

> And yet—were you to spy on me,
> Dear reader of my ranting rhymes—
> You'd make the strange discovery,
> That I am having glorious times.
>
> Now, don't berate me—gentle friends.
> It's all *your* fault, as you must know,
> My tearful tales bring dividends—
> Because my public likes 'em so.[117]

Here, in an unusually frank moment, Abbott reminds her readers of their influence on her work—the public imperative that Black women perform a particular role in print.

But Brooks is not invested in the project of using poetry for moral leadership or moral readership; she instead uses poetry to explore the emotions and experiences of Black womanhood on her own terms. "Myself," one of Brooks's last "Lights and Shadows" poems, showcases a more confident, self-possessed speaker, indicating that her verse was evolving in new ways:

> Myself is all I have.
> Myself is all I need;
> Should grain and blossoms be?—
> Myself can plant the seed!
>
> Myself requires no other
> To help her better know
> Dawn splendor, gold of noon,
> Or ruddy sunset glow.
>
> Myself requires no teacher—
> Herself knows how to sing!
> She is full strong enough to be
> A lone and quiet thing.[118]

Brooks would develop the wisdom and self-assurance of this "lone and quiet thing" in her final "Lights and Shadows" poem published five months later. "An Old Apartment Building" breaks from Brooks's other poetry in that it is not written in the voice of a young woman. Instead the speaker is the old apartment building itself. "So I'm condemned," the speaker begins. "I, who was the finest of my time." But, after years of living, the building confesses:

> My stairs creak,
> And if you trod too firmly,
> They sag in.
> Ho!
> Look at those windows,
> Once so clear and strong!
> Glass all wasted now.
> (The stones of little boys z z z z
> Have visited them.)

And yet, it is precisely because of this wear and tear, the building tells us, "I know everything."[119] In the same poem where Brooks abandons the respectable Black female poet persona, she also abandons rhyme and meter, using free verse to symbolize the liberation she has finally achieved from a persona that had confined her for years. In this way, the young poet previews a new persona that would mature in her later work, such as "A Song in the Front Yard," whose young female speaker declares: "I've stayed in the front yard all my life. / I want a peek at the back / Where it's rough and untended and hungry weed grows. / A girl gets sick of a rose."[120]

Brooks's new poet/speaker in turn demands a new reader. She complicates and expands the representation of the respectable reader that Black writers were expected to appease in the Black press and that the *Defender* worked to promote. Her poems instead imagine a different reader, one who is not fulfilled by compliant poetry or truisms, but is challenged to think anew about one's environment as well as the norms that define movement through that social landscape. Brooks's critical rather than respectable reader, then, inhabits a new way of reading the textual environment of Black Chicago as well as the streets of Bronzeville itself.

Decades later, Brooks would reflect with some embarrassment on this phase of her writing as her "integration stage"—a period when she wrote poetry to appease a white audience.[121] "During my sixteenth and seventeenth years I had seventy-five poems printed in the *Chicago Defender*, in the 'Lights and Shadows' column which they no longer have," she recalled in 1967. "Aside from these pleasantries I didn't publish a poem in a well-known magazine until I was twenty-eight, even though I had sent poems to poetry magazines for fourteen years.... I thank the editors, now, for not publishing the first things I sent in. I would have been thoroughly ashamed of them."[122] For Brooks, these "pleasantries" and her other early verse served as evidence of inauthentic, even assimilationist expression. Authenticity would come only after 1967, she later claimed, when she attended the Second Black Writers' Conference at Fisk University. There she met young Black writers of a new generation who catalyzed her epiphany that "Black poetry is written by Blacks, about Blacks, to Blacks." This change came not just from meeting "those young people who could really see what was happening all around them and were kind enough to let me know too" but also through reading: "They recommended books to me, that I read. Such books as *Report from Iron Mountain*, of the possibility and the desirability of peace, and *The Rich and the Super Rich* and *The Choice*, which are books that I am always recommending to people now. Also the *Autobiography of Malcolm X* really influenced my changes."[123] As a result of her experiences in 1967, Brooks parted ways with her longtime publisher, Harper and Row, and signed with a Black publisher, Broadside Press. She also embraced a new aesthetic in her poetry to reach Black readers. As a result, Brooks's later poems are fueled by an intense fidelity to Black aesthetics and Black audiences not found in her early work.

But Brooks's "Lights and Shadows" poems show us that her work was deeply engaged with Bronzeville's Black community from its start—that her poems literally were, as she described them, "conditioned to the times and the people."[124] Despite their traditional form and white, Western aesthetic, these poems respond to the lived realities of Black readers—not white—more than forty years before she explicitly articulated a desire to do so. This fact in turn prompts us to read Brooks herself anew and to reconsider the narrative of her career, especially the pre/post-1967 divide. There is a tendency to ascribe authenticity to Brooks's later work, a characterization that the poet herself promoted. But there is a danger in focusing on post-1967 Brooks as the "true" Black poet—the only Brooks who wrote poetry "about Blacks, to Blacks"—because this obscures the fact that she was writing for Black readers in Bronzeville as early as the 1930s. Brooks later claimed that in these early years, "Blacks didn't seem to be buying our people's work in great quantity, not even Langston Hughes's books. It was whites who were reading and listening to us, salving their consciences."[125]

While it is true that a majority of the purchases of *A Street in Bronzeville* and even *Annie Allen* were likely made by white readers, her "Lights and Shadows" poems show us that Black readers in Bronzeville were Brooks's first and main readers when she began publishing poetry. It was for these readers that she wrote, without a white audience in mind, from the beginning. And even if the demographics of her readership changed in the 1940s from Black to white, it was the work she accomplished in "Lights and Shadows," as well as the Black reading base her poems created, that paved the way for her later success. After all, it was during this period that she "realized that writing about the ordinary aspects of black life was important."[126] Such writing resonated deeply with Black readers long after Brooks's "Lights and Shadows" poems, as evidenced by the popularity of her work in the 1940s and 1950s with Bronzeville readers. Take *A Street in Bronzeville*. Just weeks after Brooks's first book of poetry was published on August 18, 1945, the *Sunday Chicago Bee* reported that three local bookstores had already sold out of all of their copies (see Figure 6).[127] The Marshall Field bookstore, situated farther north in the Loop, served primarily white patrons. But the two other bookstores listed—the Studio and the S. & S.—were independent Black-owned bookshops in the heart of Bronzeville that served a predominantly Black clientele.

As this unassuming notice demonstrates, Bronzeville's Black reading base

FIGURE 6. "Honored," *Sunday Chicago Bee*, [September?] 23, 1945.

HONORED. Gwendolyn Brooks was honored at an autographing party Sunday night at the Southside Community Art Center by an overflow crowd of book lovers. Saturday, Marshall Field's book store, the S and S book store and the Studio book shop had depleted their stock and were turning away disappointed customers who wished to own this unique volume of verse.

did indeed buy Brooks's work—so much so that local bookshops on the South Side could not keep up with demand just weeks after the publication of the poet's first book. In the next chapter I detail changes in Bronzeville's reading base after Brooks's "Lights and Shadows" period to illustrate how the neighborhood would emerge in the next decade as a national hub of Black bookselling, providing an infrastructure that made possible the first bestseller "written by Blacks, about Blacks, to Blacks": Margaret Walker's *For My People*.

CHAPTER 3

For My People

Bronzeville's Bookstores and the Making of Modern Black Readership

Margaret Walker could not have had better timing. In October 1932, the seventeen-year-old boarded a bus in New Orleans and made her way to Chicago, where she entered the rich textual environment that Vivian Harsh, Gwendolyn Brooks, and others were building. Walker quickly settled in. She enrolled at Northwestern University in suburban Evanston, earning her BA in 1935. She joined the South Side Writers Group and befriended Richard Wright, with whom she would have a complicated relationship for decades. She frequented the Hall Branch Library, where she reviewed books for the Book Review and Lecture Forum, and read books recommended by Harsh, including *Their Eyes Were Watching God*.[1] She went to work for the WPA in 1936. And she wrote poetry. Energized by the literary environment flourishing in Bronzeville when she arrived, Walker composed poems that enabled a newfound freedom of expression. In Bronzeville she also found an audience for this work, reading her poems at the Hall Branch one evening in April 1937 and publishing several of them in *Poetry*.

One such poem was "For My People"—a striking free verse composition whose speaker sings of "my playmates in the clay and dust" who attempt "to fashion a better way from confusion, from hypocrisy and misunderstanding, trying to fashion a world that will hold all the people, all the faces, all the adams and eves and their countless generations."[2] Years later the poem would serve as the opening piece in Walker's first collection of poetry and provide the book's title. Then, in October 1942, exactly a decade after Walker first set foot in Chicago, *For My People* won the Yale Younger Poets prize, garnering the poet national attention. This compilation of free verse, folk ballads, and sonnets celebrating Black identity bore the imprint of her experiences in the Black Metropolis with other Black writers and readers, marking a culmination of those exciting years. "My whole education and training have been with one purpose and view in mind," she would later write in her journal as an MFA student at the University of Iowa in 1940: "for the service of my people—for the creation of one masterpiece poetic and lyrical yet solid and real and sincere and honest as the earth itself."[3] With the publication of her award-winning collection two years later, Walker accomplished this purpose—the creation of a masterpiece in the service of her people. To be sure, her title says it all. The poems were written "for my people," a dedication that presumes there were readers for them to begin with. As sales soon showed, there were.

When it appeared in October 1942, *For My People* was hailed by Stephen Vincent Benét, the editor of the Yale Younger Poets series and the judge who selected her work, as demonstrating "a controlled intensity of emotion and a language that, at times, even when it is most modern, has something of the surge of biblical poetry."[4] A month later the collection was already in its second printing, and by May 1943, some seven months later, it warranted a third.[5] From there it continued to find "a surprisingly large number of readers, requiring publishers to authorize [even more] printings to satisfy popular demand."[6] Indeed, a fourth printing soon followed, with sales topping more than four thousand copies by March 1944, less than a year and a half after it first appeared. In total, the collection went through six cloth editions for Yale University Press, totaling over five thousand copies.[7] These sales figures were enough to secure Walker—the award's first African American recipient—the title of "Yale Press' best-selling poet" and *For My People* as the series's best-selling collection for nearly three decades.[8] Unlike the vast majority of the award's recipients, Walker's collection has never gone out of print. By the time *For My People* appeared, nearly a quarter of the previous volumes in the series were already out of print.

Although other bestsellers of the 1940s by Black writers would sell into the hundreds of thousands (like *Native Son*) or even into the millions (like the novels of Frank Yerby), Walker's five thousand copies is a stunning accomplishment.[9] "Simply getting a book of poems published would have been unlikely enough [during this period]," one of Walker's obituaries would later note; when the volume "went into a second printing within two months, [it was] a sign of successful verse in any era."[10] To put Walker's five thousand in perspective, Brooks's collection *A Street in Bronzeville* (1945) would sell 4,762 copies and *Annie Allen* (1949) would reach 2,841, though both would be out of print by the early 1960s.[11] At the time, then, *For My People* was the best-selling volume of poetry by a Black woman. And while it received one of the country's most prestigious poetry prizes, the collection exceeded even Yale's expectations, surpassing the series' previous bestseller, Muriel Rukeyser's 1935 *Theory of Flight*. As "one of the books that put the Yale Series of Younger Poets on the map," Ruykeyser's volume sold only five hundred copies in six months—"which was modest but nonetheless a distinct improvement over earlier sales in the series," George Bradley notes—and would go on to reach three printings, ultimately selling "more than fourteen hundred copies."[12] When *For My People* appeared seven years later, it dwarfed the figures for Rukeyser's bestseller, more than tripling its sales.

For My People's commercial success is more than just an impressive accomplishment by a young poet, though, or an anomalous blip in literary history. It is evidence of a robust culture of book buying and selling in Bronzeville that bolstered Black writing of the era. The reading culture that flourished in Chicago after the Depression was layered and complex, catalyzed by a growing base of Black reader-consumers as well as various local businesses centered on the consumption of books. This extensive culture of book buying in Bronzeville provided an economic base for the Black Chicago Renaissance, helping to support the movement with funding from local Black businesses and consumers. By relying on the Black dollar, Bronzeville's reading culture in turn provided African Americans with a new kind of purchasing power. Davarian Baldwin, Adam Green, Robert Weems, and others have interpreted how film, sports, radio, and other popular media proved central to the rise of Black consumer power after the Depression—and rightfully so. "Mass consumer cultures of beauty, film, gospel music, and athletics," Baldwin writes, did indeed constitute a "consumer marketplace of [Chicago's] Stroll," which "was one of the only sites where New Negroes could buy and sell culture, dreams, and products of self-transformation and create both personal and communal desires for a different black metropolis and a different world."[13]

But what the surprising sales of *For My People* demonstrates is that the purchasing of books was an integral part of this process of self- and social transformation too, particularly in Chicago. Beginning in the early 1940s, the growth of "the Negro market" fueled an increase in the commercial consumption of books by Black readers which then incited new reading and reception practices that promoted book buying. These changes in turn, I argue, gave rise to a new type of Black reader—a "reader-consumer"—one for whom the purchasing of books constituted an important way to participate in popular American consumer culture. As this chapter demonstrates, Black bookstores and Black readers helped cultivate the conditions to boost Walker's sales to bestseller status in the Yale Younger Poets series. *For My People* was likely read and bought primarily by Black reader-consumers and would not have achieved its bestseller status without them. In this way, Walker's bestseller serves as an important missing link in the history of Black readership—situated between the relatively small number of Black Americans in the nineteenth century who purchased books and those in the late twentieth who found themselves at the center of a booming Black book industry fueled by bestsellers like Terry McMillan's *How Stella Got Her Groove Back* (1996). Before that could happen, though, Bronzeville's web of book writers, buyers, and readers facilitated the growth of Black readership through the collective acts of writing, reading, and buying poetry.

ASSEMBLING *FOR MY PEOPLE*

For My People was well received by Black readers because it spoke directly to them, assembling a community of Black readers through the consumption of Black poetry. In a transcendent, even Whitmanesque way, Walker provides a textual space and reading experience in which Black readers can commune with one another across time and geography. William Scott writes that Walker's poems "can be read as a series of imaginative rememberings, or representations, of what it might mean, historically, to *be* and to *belong to* a people."[14] While *For My People* certainly meditates on what it means to "be" Black, the poems seem to assume that Walker's readers already belong to a people; they just need a conduit to one another. Her poems provide precisely that. Specifically, Walker's poems connect readers through shared identity and heritage. In these poems, reading allows Walker's audience to convene with individual but also collective ancestors as well as with one another. Indeed, Benét prefaced the poems by noting that the language of Walker's "biblical poetry" "comes naturally to her and is part of her inheritance." Consequently, "when she speaks of and for her people older voices are mixed with hers—the voices of Methodist forebears and preachers who preached the Word, the anonymous voices of many who lived and were forgotten and yet out of bondage and hope made a lasting music."[15] By tapping into this fount of "forebears," Walker's poems connect readers to one another and frame reading as a way to access their shared heritage.

Walker convenes her community of readers, in one way, with her repeated use of "we," which calls into being an existing collective identity. "We have been believers believing in our burdens and our demigods too long," the third poem in Walker's volume declares. "Now the needy no longer weep and pray; the long-suffering arise, and our fists bleed against the bars with a strange insistency."[16] "Delta," the longest poem in the collection, documents the collective labor and suffering of a "hunted desperate people / stricken and silently submissive." The speaker recounts how "We tend the crop and gather the harvest / but not for ourselves do we labor." Nevertheless, the land offers inspiration: "Into our troubled living flows the valley / flooding our lives with a passion for freedom."[17] In both poems, "we" and "our" connect contemporary readers to a shared history of oppression in another place and time. Meanwhile, the volume's final poem, "The Struggle Staggers Us," speaks of more contemporary woes. "Ours is a struggle from a too-warm bed," the speaker observes,

> too cluttered with a patience full of sleep.
> Out of this blackness we must struggle forth;
> from want of bread, of pride, of dignity.
> Struggle between the morning and the night.
> This marks our years; this settles, too, our plight.[18]

In this poem, "our" allows current readers to commiserate over shared experiences such as the "want . . . of dignity," binding disparate lives together through reading.

Walker's recurring collective "we" also engenders strength, fortitude. For instance, "Our Need" ends with these words:

> We need a wholeness born of inner strength:
> sharp thinking running through our stream of days,
> having certain courage flame with honest rays
> like slaps of life along the body's length.
> We need the friendly feel of human forms
> and earth beneath our feet against the storms.[19]

Here, such use of "we" and "our" grounds readers in a shared purpose and vision of the future, much like "People of Unrest," which directs readers to "Stare from your pillow into the sun" and "Be glad to be washed in the sun. / Be glad to see."[20] The collection's eponymous poem, "For My People," similarly honors the struggles of the past. "For my people everywhere singing their slave songs repeatedly," the speaker begins, "praying their prayers nightly to an unknown god, bending their knees humbly to an unseen power." Born out of the protest tradition of the 1930s which Walker came to know so well during her time in Bronzeville, the poem builds to its powerful final lines that command her reader:

> Let a new earth rise. Let another world be born. Let a bloody peace be written in the sky. Let a second generation full of courage issue forth; let a people loving freedom come to growth. Let a beauty full of healing and a strength of final clenching be the pulsing in our spirits and our blood. Let the martial songs be written, let the dirges disappear. Let a race of men now rise and take control.[21]

Here, the collective—encapsulated in "a people" and "a race of men"—becomes active rather than merely descriptive, inspiring united movement.

Other poems in Walker's collection situate readers within a shared heritage through references to personal and collective histories. "Since 1619" asks a series of semi-rhetorical questions, ending with "When will I burst from my kennel an angry mongrel, / Lean and hungry and tired of my dry bones and years?"[22] Through the repetition of "I" in nearly every line, the poem accumulates a legacy of "I"s who have raised the same questions about freedom and oppression since that historic year. "Lineage" likewise looks to the past, assembling a genealogy of "My grandmothers" who "were strong" and "are full of memories."[23] "Today" directly addresses readers: "I sing these fragments of living that you may know by these presents that which we feared most has come upon us."[24] This poem directly precedes part two, a section composed of folk ballads. In these poems, heroes, bootleggers, misfits, and other outlaws engage Walker's audience through shared cultural knowledge. Indeed, Walker knew that such "fragments of living" in the form of Molly Means, Bad-Man Stagolee, Kissie Lee, Big John Henry, and others would be recognizable to Black readers. In this way, part two of the collection links Walker's work to a shared Black cultural history through the reading of poetry. Further, some readers might even connect Walker's use of the folk to other Black writers' use of it. Walker's poems thus situate the poet within a Black literary tradition that includes such writers as Sterling Brown and Langston Hughes.

In other poems in the collection, Walker uses the body as a geography that joins individuals to a collective past. The second poem of part one, "Dark Blood," declares, "There were bizarre beginnings in old lands for the making of me," before imagining a homecoming: "Someday I shall go to the tropical islands of my birth, to the coasts of continents and the tiny wharves of island shores. I shall roam the Balkans and the hot lanes of Africa and Asia. I shall stand on mountain tops and gaze on fertile homes below."[25] The speaker of "Delta" mourns, "I go up and down and through this valley / and my heart bleeds with my blood here in the valley. / My heart bleeds for our fate."[26] "Sorrow Home" declares, "Warm skies and gulf blue streams are in my blood," while crying out, "O Southland, sorrow home, melody beating in my bone and blood!"[27] In "Southern Song" the speaker yearns, "I want my body bathed again by southern suns, my soul reclaimed again from southern land," and "no fiend to stand between my body's southern song—the fusion of the South, my body's song and me."[28] Through these repeated references to embodiment, Walker establishes a link between the body of her work and the bodies of her people who share not only the blood but also the heritage symbolized by that blood. In this way, her poems allow Black readers to commune with one another through a particular reading experience that comes to symbolize the blood that she and her readers share.

That these poems resonated with Black readers is clear given the dramatic difference in reception from white and Black reviewers. Though an award winner and bestseller in the prestigious Yale Younger Poets series, the collection "drew lukewarm reviews, especially from traditional critics," Walker's biographer Maryemma Graham writes.[29] Reviewers within the white literary establishment offered mixed praise at best for the volume. Many recognized Walker's talent but bristled at her choice of form as well as her incorporation of folk material. Mary E. Burton, writing for Louisville's *Courier-Journal*, contended:

> There is promise here of much that she may do when she is more sure of what she wants to say. In this volume of twenty-six poems, some four or five are all we need to see that she has ability and ideas. The rest are either too subjective to be of interest or are too obviously derivative, both faults that time and hard work will overcome. Ten of the poems are not poems at all, but humorous sketches of the "bad" men and women she has known.

They are worthy neither of her art nor of her race. We must know more of the lives of the able Negroes like Miss Walker, less of people like her Bad-Man Stagolee, who "killed a cop and turned out bad," of Kissie Lee, the "toughest gal God ever made," who "drew a dirty, wicked blade."[30]

The *Christian Science Monitor* judged somewhat more generously that "while the ballads in dialect are not above the average, the serious poems in the book are of superior quality."[31] The *Hartford Courant* conceded that while she "handles the Whitmanesque free verse, steeped with Whitmanesque love of freedom and democracy[,] with natural ease," Walker "works hard at the sonnet."[32] Another review in the *Louisville Courier-Journal* derided the ballads of part two, asserting that "Miss Walker falls into the trap laid by the theatrically picturesque that has overbalanced our Negro-motivated literature."[33] Even Nelson Algren, whom Walker had adopted as one of her "closer friends and trusted advisors" in Chicago, wrote a mixed review of the collection for *Poetry*.[34] Describing Walker as "intense and forthright without being oratorical," as well as "terse and demanding without loss of rhythm," he praised "Delta" for its ability to "posses[s] the restless music that oppression makes in the human heart, and recreates the mood of the human mind under the lash." But he also criticized her "fondness for alliteration," which "sometimes compromises her depth and originality," as well as the "conventional romanticism" of some pieces. In her final section, he attests, "she is just another poet writing sonnets. Although none are bad—since she does not write bad poetry—several do smell of the midnight oil."[35] Perhaps the kindest treatment Walker would receive from the white press was her inclusion in the *New York Herald Tribune*'s "Guide to the Outstanding Fall Books" for 1942, which complimented the collection, albeit blandly, as "poems that speak eloquently of the Negro race."[36]

Black reviewers, by contrast, enthusiastically praised Walker's collection, emphasizing her ability to connect deeply to Black experiences and cultural past. Arna Bontemps, writing for the *New York Herald Tribune*, highlighted Walker's treatment of social problems: "She sees her people rebelling against hypocrisy—meaning, presumably, against the dissimulation by which the bitter, offended black man is often forced to live in some sections. She marks a struggle between pride and pain, the near-hopeless task of trying to maintain dignity under indignities.... Simply put, her complaint is that her people are deceived and cheated." Regarding Walker's form, Bontemps praised the ballads and sonnets, writing: "They show that preoccupation with the greater problems of her 'playmates in the clay and dust' have in no wise detracted from Margaret Walker's understanding of their folk ways. She has a genuine sympathy for low-down folks like 'Molly Means,' 'Poppa Chicken' and 'Kissie Lee.'"[37] In a similarly laudatory tone, Frank Marshall Davis asserted that Walker's book "is far and away the best book of poetry written by a Negro to be published in the last five years." Writing for the Associated Negro Press, he praised the "modern . . . style and approach" of Walker's free verse in part one as well as "her own kind of sonnet, on display in Section III." The "section of ballads," meanwhile, "has a spiritual kinship with work in similar vein of Langston Hughes." Though he references a "minor fault"—that Walker "occasionally repeats a word or phrase in such a way that it dulls the emotions of the reader"—Davis ultimately finds her work "smooth, easy flowing, dynamic and rhythmic, always majestic and occasionally rhapsodic."[38] Countee Cullen concurred: "The poet speaks in vibrantly beautiful accents of values that count most in a social-minded and war-activated world. Her book is at once a denunciation, a hope, and a prophecy."[39]

The stark difference between the white literary establishment's lukewarm reception of *For My People* and Black reviewers' applause is telling; it reflects the fact that Walker had hit a nerve with Black readers. The poems, dense with collective emotions and memories, provided Black readers a familiar textual environment and reading experience. White readers could access no such experience while reading the poems, thus leveling accusations, as Mary Burton did, that they were too "subjective." Indeed, Walker knew her audience. And yet, even she could not have known the number of Black readers who would turn out to purchase her book.

AN UNLIKELY BESTSELLER

Despite the positive reception from Black readers, *For My People*'s sales are nonetheless surprising considering the modest bookselling climate of the early 1940s. Indeed, up until the later years of the twentieth century, actual bookstores—shops devoted to the selling of books—were rare, with most book sales coming from drugstores, department stores, and other general merchandise establishments. Laura Miller writes that in 1930 there existed only 4,053 book outlets in the United States, many of which were not bookstores but actually "drugstores, gift shops, and rental libraries (places that rented books to patrons for a few cents a day)." By the late 1940s, though, this number had increased to "3,041 book outlets . . . plus another 5,000 drugstores and variety chain stores," bringing the total to just over eight thousand. The number of establishments that sold books, then, doubled in this period, yet still remained low overall, primarily because the bookselling industry was slow to rationalize. "Most booksellers were still small and independent," Miller notes, and "with the exception of department stores, mass retailers played a relatively minor role in bookselling during the first half of the twentieth century." This meant that "for a large portion of the country's population, access to books for purchase remained extremely limited."[40] Bookselling in Black communities mirrored this national trend. The *Negro Year Book*, for instance, reports that there were only fifteen bookstores with "Negro proprietorships" in the entire nation in 1939, just three years before the publication of *For My People*.[41] Such a limited bookselling climate did not bode well for books in general and especially not for a "niche" collection like Walker's which explored Black identity and experience.

Sales of *For My People* were also surprising considering that Yale University Press did little to advertise the book. Rather than promote its first Younger Poets collection by an African American writer, the press chose instead to throw its advertising efforts behind another book it released in the fall of 1942, *How to Be Fit*, an exercise manual claiming that "the maintenance of our physical fitness is a matter of national concern."[42] In November 1942, Yale announced that it was "planning a big campaign" for *How to Be Fit*, starting with "a full-page coupon ad in the *New York Times Book Review*" and promising that such efforts were "only the opening gun."[43] Yale even took out a full-page ad in *Publishers' Weekly* to advertise the upcoming *New York Times Book Review* ad—of which an image was included in the *Publishers' Weekly* ad itself—as a way to hype the book. Yale also neglected to include Walker in its fall promotional campaign "Books from Yale for Fall," featuring instead five other books, including *How to Be Fit*.[44] Whatever ads included *For My People* did so in a minor way, especially compared to other books published by Yale, such as *How to Be Fit*, which received multiple full-page treatments. Instead, Yale chose to promote Walker's book quietly—as an unremarkable volume in which "a young Negro speaks of and for her people."[45] Yale's lackluster promotion of *For My People* also pales in comparison to the advertising for other best-selling books by African American writers in the early 1940s. Take Wright's *Native Son*, appearing two years before *For My People* on March 1, 1940. Though it was selected for the Book-of-the-Month Club, it had not won any awards at the time of publication, as Walker's book had. Nevertheless, it enjoyed a robust ad campaign from Harper & Brothers that featured multiple full-page promotions.

Considering its modest national profile—despite its award and series best-seller status—it is no surprise, then, that *For My People* never appeared on the *New York Times* bestseller list or the *Publishers' Weekly* list, two indexes of white readership. Nor did it ever make the country's most popular reading poll, "What America Is Reading," published in the *New York Herald Tribune*. Charting the most commonly purchased fiction and nonfiction books in the nation, this weekly poll surveyed bookstores across the country, from Albany to Houston, from Fort Wayne to New Orleans to San Francisco.[46] *For My People* never appears in the survey, though *Native Son* did when it was published in 1940.[47] Nor did *For My People* break into regional bookselling polls either, such as the *Chicago Tribune*'s "Best Sellers in Midwest."[48] It is worth noting, however, that the Chicago bookstores regularly surveyed by these national and regional polls—Brentano's, Kroch's, and Marshall Field's—served a predominantly white clientele.[49]

But *For My People* did not require the support of white America because it appeared right in the middle of Bronzeville's book explosion after the Depression. Indeed, small, independent Black-owned bookstores had a vibrant and visible presence on Chicago's South Side throughout the late 1930s and 1940s, contributing in large part to *For My People*'s strong reception and sales. We know well that theaters, taverns, jazz clubs, and other venues of commerce constituted the financial and social heart of Bronzeville. But, it turns out, bookstores were right there alongside them, serving a central need in that community: the consumption of books.

BRONZEVILLE'S BOOKSTORES

Black-owned bookstores were not new to Chicago when *For My People* appeared. Though locating these bookselling establishments and their histories is now difficult—few materials documenting their existence have been saved—Black business guides and city directories date Black bookstores in the city back to at least 1905. One of the first such establishments, Faulkner's News and Book Store—"A Reliable Place for Leading Race Papers and Books"—located at 3104 State Street, operated from at least 1905 until 1912.[50] Such early bookshops typically lined business-packed State Street, known as the Stroll, and served the Old Settlers of Black Chicago, the middle-class respectables who consumed literary culture as a marker of distinction. Indeed, a 1915 syndicated column in the *Chicago Defender* promoted a new strategy of racial uplift called Buy-a-Book. The movement encouraged readers "to have every family and single man and woman buy at least one book written by a colored author during the year 1915." Owning "a bibliography of the worth-while books," the article noted, promised "to both instruct and stimulate the colored people to greater effort."⁵¹

By 1918, according to *Black's Blue Book: Business and Professional Directory; A Compilation of Names, Addresses and Telephones of All Chicago's Colored Business and Professional People and Guide to Others Active in Church, State, Club and Social Life*, there were two Black bookstores in the city; three years later, *Black's* reported seven.⁵² One of them, Hayes' Book Store, had existed since at least 1912 and sold "Negro Literature" as well as "Books, Magazines and Newspapers of Chicago and Everywhere."⁵³ Two years later, the 1923 *Simms' Blue Book and National Negro Business and Professional Directory* listed only two Black bookstores in the city, one of which was Hayes'. By comparison, Simms lists none in New York City, one in Atlanta, and one in Charleston, South Carolina, though in his preface acknowledges: "We do not claim that this is a complete directory of the businesses and professional people of our race. . . . But we do claim that it is a good beginning."⁵⁴

Black book businesses steadily increased over the next several decades in Chicago—so much so that by the 1940s, Bronzeville had become a center of book buying and selling. The 1947 edition of *Scott's Blue Book*, a directory of Black businesses in "Greater Chicago," reports *eleven* independent bookstores on the city's South Side—bookstores on South Michigan Avenue, State Street, Cottage Grove, East 47th Street, and other central locations in Bronzeville.⁵⁵ The 1947 list includes one bookstore specializing in religious texts, as well as two used book shops; there were also four renting libraries, bringing the total number of Black establishments on the South Side devoted to bookselling to an impressive fifteen—the very same number of "Negro bookstores" in the entire country less than a decade earlier. Note that this tally does not factor in drugstores (of which *Scott's* reports thirty-five), gift shops (ten), variety stores (eleven), and other novelty and department stores that very likely also sold books and other reading materials. In other words, fifteen is a low estimate. Even so, in 1947 there were more booksellers in Bronzeville than carpenters, roofers, plumbers, movers, locksmiths, optometrists, upholsterers, or painters. There were more bookstores than jewelry stores, hardware stores, dairy stores, or vegetable and fruit markets.

Scott's Blue Book highlighted this rapid increase of Black-owned bookstores in Bronzeville. A feature in the 1947 edition reports that eight existed in 1939 and 1940, seven in 1941 (just before *For My People* appeared), and eleven in 1944.⁵⁶ From 1923 to 1939, then, there was a fourfold increase from two to eight, and nearly a doubling from 1939 to 1947. These numbers indicate that Bronzeville was a bookselling hub throughout the 1940s, and in turn, that bookstores were at the center of Bronzeville commercial life during the Black Chicago Renaissance, indeed, quite literally. They lined the corridors of 47th Street and the Stroll, rubbing shoulders with the Regal Theater, the Savoy Ballroom, and the South Side Community Arts Center. For a neighborhood only one and a half miles wide and seven miles long at the time (roughly half the size of Manhattan), Bronzeville boasted an impressive number of bookselling establishments, attesting to the centrality of books and reading in Black Chicago at mid-century.

In this way, again, Walker had good timing. It is this infrastructure of bookselling and consuming in Bronzeville that helped *For My People* achieve the unlikely sales figures it did. While Yale University Press may not have advertised or promoted Walker's book in any meaningful way—nor did any East Coast newspaper or publication, for that matter—Bronzeville's reading culture did. Both bookstores and major periodicals based on the South Side actively promoted Walker's collection, suggesting that the book was well received in Chicago's Black community. Though bookstores did not typically advertise in local newspapers or magazines—instead, publishers did—one such extant ad illustrates how Walker in particular benefited from Bronzeville's bookstores and their connection to the larger literary world in Chicago (see Figure 7). Published in 1947 and featuring *For My People*, this ad was placed by a Bronzeville bookstore, illustrating the role played by local Black businesses—not Yale University Press—in the sales and promotion of the book. Moreover, the ad appears five years after the book's publication, securing its place in the canon of African American literature alongside such classics as Wright's *Native Son* and *Black Boy*, Era Bell Thompson's *American Daughter*, and Langston Hughes's *Shakespeare in Harlem*. Indeed, the ad promises "a careful selection of the latest best-sellers as well as the best books of the past," which are sure to provide readers with "reading you'll remember."[57] It is a testament to the importance of *For My People* in Bronzeville that a local bookstore would continue to advertise the book five years after its initial publication. Finally, the local bookshop that placed this ad was not just any bookstore but rather one associated with a major Black magazine based in Chicago, *Negro Digest*, published by John H. Johnson, who also founded *Ebony* (and, later, *Jet*). Furthermore, this ad for *For My People*, being sold at the Negro Digest Book Shop, appears in *Ebony* magazine.

FIGURE 7. "Best Buys in Books," advertisement for Negro Digest Book Shop, appearing in *Ebony*, March 1947. Special thanks to Ebony Media Group, LLC.

This last point exposes an important link between bookstores, print culture, and literature of the Black Chicago Renaissance. Local bookstores often helped promote and finance Bronzeville's literary scene, supporting the Renaissance in vital ways. For instance, the Studio Bookshop, managed by Doris Evans Smith and Eloise M. Boone, advertised itself in the 1947 *Scott's Blue Book* as selling "books—art objects—stationery—greeting cards."[58] But it was also a local business that supported Black writers, helping to create a community of reading and writing in the heart of Bronzeville. Located at 4657 South Michigan Avenue, Studio was well positioned in Bronzeville's commercial district. Just north of 47th Street, it was mere steps from another prominent bookstore (the S. & S.), one block north of the Hall Branch Library (located at 48th and South Michigan Avenue), and only a half-dozen blocks west of the Regal Theater, Roseland Ballroom, and the South Center Department Store. This location situated it at a major intersection of commercial and book-buying activity in Bronzeville, a service it readily provided for Bronzeville residents. Recall that the Studio, alongside the S. & S. bookstore (and Marshall Field's), sold out its copies of *A Street in Bronzeville*, "turning away disappointed customers" less than a month after the volume appeared in 1945.[59] The Studio is also one of the few Bronzeville bookstores that semi-regularly advertised Black book selections in newspapers. A dozen or so of its ads can be found in issues of the *Defender* from the 1940s.[60]

Nearly kitty-corner from the Studio, the S. & S. bookstore (located at 107 East 47th Street) likewise held a prominent place in Bronzeville and supported Black writing. "Featuring a Complete Line of Books By and About Negroes plus All Current Best Sellers," the S. & S. also offered magazines as well as "Engraved Invitations and Announcements." It even served as a recording studio.[61] Its proprietor, Lewis Simpkins, supported *Negro Story*, a major though short-lived literary magazine of the Black Chicago Renaissance discussed in the next chapter. Created by Alice Browning and Fern Gayden, and running from 1944 to 1946, this Bronzeville little magazine published literature by Black writers of the era, including Brooks, Richard Wright, Langston Hughes, Chester Himes, and Walker herself. The S. & S. bookstore served as a newsagent for *Negro Story*, selling the magazine in its shop and likely otherwise financially supporting the publication. In this way, S. & S. offered its business and its status in Bronzeville to support the little magazine and the writers, including Walker, whom the magazine published. A complex network of relationships thus emerges: one of Bronzeville's

Black-owned bookstores (S. & S.) funded one of the leading publications of the Renaissance (*Negro Story*), which published Walker, who in turn was promoted by two other major Black publications in Chicago (*Negro Digest* and *Ebony*), both of which also had bookstores, at least one of which sold *For My People*.

This connection between Black bookstores, literature of the Renaissance, and local print culture illustrates another important point: many of the periodicals published in Bronzeville at this time operated their own book departments or actual bookstores, providing residents convenient access to a wide variety of books and other print material; many of them even offered mail order. Indeed, while local Black bookstores and magazines built a reading infrastructure in Bronzeville that bolstered the Black Chicago Renaissance, so too did the local Black press. In addition to *Negro Digest* and *Ebony*, for instance, the *Sunday Chicago Bee* also offered bookselling services, which it advertised in every issue as a full-page notice, "Books About Negroes" (see Figure 8).

Also like the S. & S., the *Bee* made financial contributions to *Negro Story* as a "friend." With the inclusion of Black periodicals based in the city that also staffed book departments and/or offered bookselling services, the number of Bronzeville bookstores increases to at least seventeen by 1947, which is still a conservative estimate.

In addition to selling books, the Black press supported Black writing during the Renaissance through other promotional efforts. The *Defender* proved central in supporting Walker in particular; this was not true of white newspapers—in or outside of Chicago. A comparison of the *Chicago Tribune* and the *Defender*, for instance, proves illustrative. From the summer of 1942 (when Walker's award was announced) to the end of 1944 (when the book was already in its fourth printing), fifteen articles featuring Walker and/or *For My People* appeared in the *Defender*, while only five appeared in the *Tribune*. In the *New York Times*, for comparison's sake, the book fared a bit better, with ten articles or ads about *For My People*, thanks to its book review section (where Yale University Press tended to advertise). *The Crisis*, meanwhile, announced the award in December 1942 and regularly included *For My People* as one of its "Books about Negroes" available through its mail order service as well as at the Crisis Book Shop. Otherwise, though, it did not feature or promote *For My People* in a significant way.

The *Defender*, conversely, published special features on Walker that promoted her collection and her career. Langston Hughes, for instance, devoted one of his weekly *Defender* columns in April 1943 to Walker's rise to fame.

The Chicago Sunday Bee

WILL FILL ORDERS PROMPTLY FOR ANY

BOOKS ABOUT NEGROES

(IN PRINT), AT THE PUBLISHERS RETAIL PRICE-POSTAGE PAID

THIS MONTH'S OFFERING

Native Son — -$ 2.50	12 Million Black Voices — - 3.00	
by RICHARD WRIGHT	by RICHARD WRIGHT	
The Negro In Our History — - 4.25	God's Trombone — - 2.50	
by CARTER WOODSON	by J. W. JOHNSON	
The Negro Handbook — - 3.50	American Unity and Asia — - 1.25	
by FLORENCE MURRAY	by PEARL BUCK	
Sharecroppers All — - 3.00	A Time For Greatness — - 2.50	
by DeA. REID and ARTHUR ROPER	by HERBERT AGAR	
The Lost Zoo — - 2.50	Slave Insurrection In	
by COUNTEE CULLEN	U. S., 1800-1865 — - 2.00	
	by JOSEPH C. CARROLL	
The Biology of the Negro — - 5.00	The Child's Story of the Negro - 1.25	
by JULIAN HERMAN LEWIS, Ph. D., M. D.	by JANE D. SHACKLEFORD	
Books of Negro Spirituals — - 3.00	Blood On The Forge — - 2.00	
by JAMES WELDON JOHNSON	by WILLIAM ATTAWAY	
Complete Poems — - 3.00	Negroes In Brazil — - 4.50	
by PAUL LAURENCE DUNBAR	by DONALD PEARSON	
Marian Anderson — - 2.50	Railroad to Freedom —	
by KOSTI VEHAMEN	by HILDEGARDE HOYT SMITH	

SUNDAY CHICAGO BEE

BOOK DEPT.

3655 South State St.   Chicago, Illinois

FIGURE 8. Advertisement for *Sunday Chicago Bee* book department, *Sunday Chicago Bee*, December 5, 1943.

He recounts a reading of hers in New York, highlighting the renown *For My People* has already achieved and mentioning its favorable reviews "all over the country." As he describes Walker "surrounded by an admiring crowd, autographing copies of her first book in New York's intellectual forum,"

Hughes assures the *Defender*'s readers that "in Margaret Walker's eyes there is strength and determination and dignity and intelligence and lots of things of which the Negro people can be proud."[62] As the only Black publication to follow Walker's success—tracking her reading tour and radio appearances and otherwise actively promoting her—the *Defender* helped mobilize her reception, arousing interest in and likely sales of *For My People*.

If Margaret Walker arrived in Bronzeville at the right moment to write the poems that would fill *For My People*, influenced as they were by the city's vibrant literary environment of the late 1930s, then she had even better timing in publishing them just as Bronzeville's bookstores were on the rise in the 1940s. Bronzeville's network of Black bookstores, magazines, and newspapers had a direct impact on the surprising sales of Walker's prizewinning collection of poetry and likely on many other texts of the Black Chicago Renaissance. This network not only served Black readers in the city but also supported Black writing, promoting and even funding the Black Chicago Renaissance with Black dollars. Literary magazines like *Negro Story* and writers, particularly Walker, directly benefited from Bronzeville's bookselling culture, gaining promotion and even financial support from some of the neighborhood's most successful establishments. This was made possible in part because of larger national trends that shifted both consumption and reading patterns for Black Americans.

THE NEGRO MARKET AND THE RISE OF THE READER-CONSUMER

Walker's bestseller signals the rise of the Black reader-consumer, one with the disposable income to consume literature in a way that Black readers had largely been unable to do before. In the nineteenth and early twentieth centuries, Black readers with the time and money to purchase books had not been numerous enough to support the literary marketplace—particularly writing by Black authors—in a significant way. By the middle of the twentieth century, little had changed on the national scene. Richard Wright, for instance, depended on white readers to become the first best-selling Black author. Recall, too, that in addition to the Studio and S. & S. bookstores, Brooks sold out Marshall Field's, which primarily served white customers—a testament to the importance of white readers to the reception and sales of *A Street in Bronzeville*. For decades, Jaime Harker contends, African American writing thus necessarily relied on "a mixed audience." It was not until the late twentieth century, she continues, "that African American reading communities, supplemented by (mainly) white women readers, supported writers like Alice Walker, Gloria Naylor, and Toni Morrison, and more recently Terry McMillan."[63] "To put it plainly," Liesl Olson adds, "black writers at this time had to write for white readers if they wanted to sell books."[64]

To be sure, Black audiences could not sustain national bestseller lists—but they could sustain Black reading communities like Bronzeville. As *For My People* demonstrates, it was possible for Black writers like Margaret Walker to sell books without white readers—to sell books, in other words, "for" but also "to" "My People." Given her reception from Black reviewers and the support of Bronzeville's bookselling infrastructure, Walker's five thousand sales likely came from mostly Black readers, not white. But her audience constituted a new kind of Black reader who emerged as part of a powerful economic base in the postwar era. This reader-consumer not only valued reading as a means of cultural and political uplift but also specifically valued buying books as a way of participating in postwar consumerism. The reader-consumer—who reads to consume and consumes to read—thus illustrates a shift between consumer practices of the late nineteenth and the late twentieth centuries whereby Black readership becomes increasingly associated with book *buying*. A decade after Harsh's Hall Branch library sowed community investment in reading practices through lending and borrowing books—collective acts of sharing community resources—*For My People* reveals new reading habits that focus on individual commercial consumption.

This practice of Black book consumption reverberated throughout Bronzeville, but if residents needed an extra push to spend their money on books, there were two prominent voices that advocated spending the Black dollar at Black bookstores: Langston Hughes and Alice Browning. Hughes used his *Defender* column, "Here to Yonder," to champion books and specifically book buying for the Black community throughout the 1940s. Just months after his feature on Walker in the fall–winter of 1943, Hughes pitched books as the ideal holiday gift for black consumers. "Books make very good Christmas presents," he writes. "Especially for people doing their last minute Christmas shopping, books are easy to select, the bookshops will mail them for you, and books are presents that always have tone, class, taste—providing you choose good books." He then speaks to the growing interest in owning books within the Black community: "Many people nowadays are forming Negro libraries, or adding to their Negro collection of books. A volume by a contemporary Negro author," Hughes suggests, "would be, in most homes, a welcome Christmas gift."⁶⁵ Hughes's column advocates and reinforces a culture of reading—and specifically legitimizes book consumption—encouraging readers to start their own personal libraries of Black reading material. And he does so after having just featured Black literature's newest and best-selling collection of poetry a few columns earlier.

Alice Browning likewise promoted the reading of books and encouraged readers to purchase (not only read) those books. For example, an ad placed unassumingly on the back cover of *Negro Story*'s anniversary issue in 1945 (and conspicuously next to an ad for Wright's *Black Boy*) provocatively inquires, "Have You Been Missing Something?" It continues:

> Are you making the most of the tremendous untapped gold mine that books offer you? Books can probably do more for you than you have ever really dreamed possible. They can give you relaxation and forgetfulness of your everyday troubles; they can broaden your whole outlook on life and improve your social presence by giving you a solid background of culture; often they can help you to succeed in business; above all they can give you continuous and unfailing enjoyment.
>
> ... We have all noticed that most successful men and women are usually well-informed, interesting people with keen minds and compelling personalities. As a rule these people are successful not because of a college training, but because all through their lives they have been reading, studying, sharpening their wits and accumulating information, some of which they keep in their memories—some of which they keep on their library shelves. These people have all learned the importance of balanced reading. They know that to get the most of what books have to offer, they must cultivate the habit of reading books of all classifications.⁶⁶

In its emphasis on forming good habits and achieving personal success, the ad reads like a promotion for a self-help program. Instead, however, it is an ad promoting *Negro Story* book clubs—Browning's attempt to mobilize audiences to form reading groups and, specifically, to purchase books (and the literary magazine) so they might improve themselves.

Browning here emphasizes that reading by itself is not enough to procure these desirable results. Book readers must also be book *owners*. "The easiest way to acquire this habit [of balanced reading]," she continues, "is to buy books and own them in your own library at home."⁶⁷ For Browning, like Hughes, the benefits of reading are grounded not just in reading books but specifically in purchasing and owning them—amassing a particular cultural capital and occupying a distinctive class position. Accordingly, Browning advocates a certain *way* to read—as a consumer, a participant in the literary marketplace. To this end, Browning positioned *Negro Story* as an outlet not only for Black reading but also for Black purchasing: "We want to be an organ for advertising good books to our many readers—all of a highly selective book-buying group," she declared in 1945. "Mention *Negro Story* when you write these publishers for books."[68] Whatever reading lists she includes, then, as well as book reviews and other recommendations, become a way to provide book shopping lists for readers; moreover, she is able to curate lists of "good books," directing readers to appropriate literary taste. Browning thus also buttresses the growing book-buying market through her little magazine, recruiting readers into financially supporting the broader literary marketplace in Bronzeville and beyond. "Buy books from our advertisers as they are helping the Negro," she directs her readers in the book club ad: "Mention *Negro Story* when you order, so they can see that *Negro Story* is in turn helping to enlarge the book-buying market."[69]

The rise of the Black reader-consumer—as well as the South Side's somewhat dizzying and entangled reading infrastructure—was made possible by a postwar phenomenon: the growth of the "Negro market." It was the general increase in Black Americans' ability to inhabit the national marketplace as consumers that allowed for this shift in consumption habits and the rise in the number of bookstores in Bronzeville. By the late 1940s, white businesses had begun courting the increased populations of African Americans in northern US cities who, Robert Weems Jr. reports, had an "estimated $10 billion aggregate income in 1946."[70] In the spring of 1947, *Tide* magazine, the advertising industry's trade publication, devoted its cover story to the "question" of the growing Black market. On its cover, a huge (white) question mark is superimposed on a photograph of African Americans; inside, its feature story declares: "The Negro Market . . . is plagued by too few statistics and it needs a more businesslike press, but the postwar Negro market seems to deserve serious consideration by advertisers." Furthermore, "the largest and most important of these markets—and the greatest unrealized opportunity, perhaps—is among Negroes," it continues. "In population and in buying power, they are growing rapidly and give every sign of continuing to do so." This growth of the Black market, the article contends, was facilitated by the Great Migration, which "improved the Negro market and made the Negro a more accessible and prospective customer," in addition to gains in education and particularly literacy. Before the advent of other widespread and accessible popular media, print advertising in the Black press and the growing Black magazine industry was crucial for businesses courting the African American market; reading was thus the primary way of engaging consumers. "Generally, Negroes are probably better educated than the average white person is apt to think," the article concludes.

> They have made astounding progress. In 1870, more than 81% of all Negroes 10 years and over were illiterate. By 1930, the last year the Census Bureau obtained figures, the ratio had reversed itself: about 80% of all Negroes 10 years old and older were literate. By now the literacy figure would be even higher—and perhaps that is the most revealing point of all about the Negro market of the future. For a rising literacy rate not only helps to produce bigger and healthier magazines and newspapers; it also creates higher tastes and better demand and, coupled with an increase in purchasing power, a higher standard of living and a better market.[71]

Black Americans looked to this new consumer power to achieve "a higher living standard" and even "higher tastes," to be sure, but more important were the greater freedoms that consumerism promised. As Cynthia Lee Henthorn writes, African Americans "saw an empowering potential in the techno-corporate order's narrow view of commercialized democracy that mainstream business had promoted so ruthlessly to white consumers during the war." In the postwar era, Black consumers now wanted a bigger share of the market as a way to lobby for the race. "By aligning democratic freedoms with consumerism," Henthorn explains, "blacks conceptualized their race as an economic aggregate that agitated for equality and full citizenship through purchasing power. Excluded from the image of progress, blacks leveraged capitalism's contradictory and self-serving assumption that consumerism and free enterprise represented the ultimate expression of American liberty."[72]

Bronzeville was well positioned to serve this growing Black marketplace. As early as 1938, the neighborhood was already nationally recognized by *Time* magazine as "the centre of U.S. Negro business."[73] As Elizabeth Schlabach writes, "A small but vibrant black leisure class was emerging, and 47th Street offered black Chicagoans a sense of freedom and purchasing power they couldn't find anywhere else in America at that time."[74] Indeed, the 1921 *Black's Blue Book* reprinted an article on the back of their guide that announced, "More Negroes in Business: Increase in Local Commercial Enterprises of Colored People." Tracking the growth of Black business in Chicago, the article reported that:

Negro business enterprises, large and small of all varieties, have increased from 1,200 in 1919 to 1,50 [sic] in 1920, according to a canvas completed for 'Black's Blue Book of Chicago.' The compilation lists. [sic] 651 industrial and commercial houses conducted by persons of the colored race on South State Street, 549 on principal cross streets, and an estimate of 300 as the number of new establishments on other streets.

The increase in 31st street is from nine negro business places in 1918 to 45 in 1919 and 71 in 1920. In 35th street two years ago were 47; last year, 64; this year 77. The congestion of housing about 35th street is given as the cause of the movement to 31st street.

Cottage Grove Avenue is listed as having 57 colored business establishments from 28th to 45th street. These include nine grocery stores, three drug stores and two undertakers. From 31st street to 47th, Indiana avenue has 68 business places chiefly at intersections of 31st, 35th and 39th streets."[75]

This growth of Black businesses in Bronzeville during the early decades of the century would soon help fund the Black Chicago Renaissance with Black dollars.

Perhaps the first to anticipate the effect of the growing Negro market on book consumption was the Black publishing industry. As *Ebony* would report in its very first issue in November 1945, "a book boom is here." The article declared: "After a long century of frugal, fruitless writing, Negro authors are finally hitting pay dirt.... Along Book Row in New York's mid-forties, publishers are frantically grabbing at any and all manuscripts which touch on the Negro." Publishers began targeting Black writers, in other words, because they wanted to attract the growing base of Black readers. Indeed, the article notes, "the book clubs are finding novels about Negroes sell well and they vie with each other for first distribution rights." The article concludes that the winners in the industry's race to gain the Black dollar include "book stores around the nation," "book clubs," and even individual authors, who "stand at the threshold of financial as well as artistic success for the first time."[76] On-the-ground reports from the publishing industry supported *Ebony*'s assessment. A *Washington Post* survey found in 1946 that "of particular interest is the observation of booksellers and librarians alike that the Negro reading interests are somewhat more serious than those of white residents. Brentano's stated that Negroes comprise 40 per cent of the membership of the store's Home Reading Club, a recently established mail rental library."[77] *Publishers' Weekly* also picked up on this development in national reading demographics. In 1947 Isidor Schneider reflected that "another major trend" driving readership in the years since World War I was "the development of a large Negro reading public, Negro self-expression and growing interest, in general, in Negro–White relations."[78]

This race to gain the Black dollar was not lost on Yale University Press. When the 1942 Younger Poets Prize was announced, the press anticipated the benefits of having an African American winner of their prestigious prize in a growing "Negro market." In June 1942, a senior editor at the press wrote to congratulate Stephen Vincent Benét on awarding the year's prize to Walker. "We are all greatly pleased with your selection," he writes, adding: "We feel that a volume by a negro has unusual possibilities. In fact, we are so enthusiastic that we would like to get some material into the hands of sales representatives who are already on the road. Therefore," he continues, "send us a few sample poems and if possible your introduction . . . [and] we could make up something that the salesmen could sell from." He concludes by adding, "Any advance selling we can do will be all to the good." Even in 1942, the shrewd staff at Yale recognized the "unusual possibilities" of backing a Black writer in a growing market of Black readers.[79]

As *For My People* demonstrates, then, independently owned Black bookstores on Chicago's South Side, in conjunction with Black magazines and newspapers, wove together an extensive culture of reading that, when catalyzed by a national push for the Black dollar, made it possible for a small book of poems to break records. In the process, this culture of reading allowed Bronzeville residents to participate in mid-century American consumerism in new ways. As a consequence, *For My People* achieved record-breaking sales without the help of white readership, at least to any significant degree, making it a bestseller among a growing contingent of Black reader-consumers—something national bestsellers like *Native Son* and *The Foxes of Harrow* cannot boast. In this way, then, we might consider *For My People* the first Black bestseller: not only written by, about, and for Black Americans but also, more importantly, *bought* by Black Americans as an expression of a collective impetus to "rise and take control" of their communities and destinies.

Margaret Walker had good timing in one final way. As it turned out, 1942 was an important year for books and reading. In February, two months after the nation's entry into World War II, the *Pittsburgh Courier* launched its Double V campaign. Recognizing the hypocrisy of sending Black soldiers to fight for democracy overseas, the campaign promoted victory at home and abroad through the end of racial injustice. In response, Black writers were called upon to join the cause, producing literature that waged war against racial discrimination, domestic and foreign. Also in early 1942, the Victory Book Campaign declared its own victory, having achieved its goal of collecting ten million books for the armed services overseas. At the same time, the Council on Books in Wartime launched a series of initiatives to promote reading in the service of the war effort. That May, about the time he was judging the Yale Younger Poets series submissions, none other than Stephen Vincent Benét took part in one such initiative, writing and producing a radio play deploring Nazi book burning. *They Burned the Books* (1942) offers a dramatization of the May 10, 1933, Nazi book burning in Berlin. Incorporating the voices of Mark Twain, Walt Whitman, Milton, and other canonical writers, it produced a dramatic, effective rallying cry to save books and thus democracy. "Books are not men, and yet they are alive," the narrator declares. "They are man's memory and his aspiration, / The link between his present and his past, / The tools he builds with." Urging listeners and readers to support the war by defending books, the narrator asks listeners to "Suppose it happened here. / Suppose the books were burned here."[80]

By the fall of 1942, books and bullets were in the air, and reading Black literature had taken on a new relevance on the national scene. When *For My People* appeared in October, then, it offered a rallying cry of its own at just the right moment, signifying even greater pride as Black servicemen fought with distinction overseas. As Countee Cullen emphasized in his review of Walker's collection, "The poet speaks in vibrantly beautiful accents of values that count most in a social-minded and war-activated world." Over the following few years, this confluence of reading, race, and books would only intensify as casualties of the war mounted. The next chapter details how one institution within Bronzeville's reading culture responded to this crisis. When Alice Browning and Fern Gayden launched *Negro Story* in the spring of 1944, they in turn offered audiences new reading strategies and habits to intervene in the war of ideas.

CHAPTER 4

"A Magazine for All Americans"

Negro Story's *Wartime Reading*

In *Negro Story*'s spring 1945 anniversary issue, celebrating the magazine's first year in print, Alice Browning declared: "Now is the time to read. This is a period of enormous social change."[1] This was not the first nor would it be the last time that this little magazine of the Black Chicago Renaissance explicitly linked reading with social change. Throughout the magazine's run, from 1944 to 1946, editors Browning and (for a time) Fern Gayden positioned reading as a civic duty that was central not only to the nation's racial politics but also to its democracy. After all, both women knew firsthand how powerfully reading and literary reception could threaten the racist status quo. Gayden, of course, found out that same spring when she reviewed *Black Boy* in front of a room of threatening Chicago police officers at the Hall Branch Library. Browning understood as well. In the same anniversary issue, she reported that "Chicago police officials" had recently "made a raid on a Loop book store and seized copies of *Lillian Smith's, Strange Fruit*," a best-selling novel about interracial love. "Charges of obscenity against the book and several others were dismissed, thank God," she reassures readers.[2] As a writer, editor, and publisher, Browning clearly understood the power—as well as the risks—of reading while Black, and used *Negro Story* to direct reading and reception practices that would incite political and social change.

Browning considered Chicago the up-and-coming base of the growing Black literary marketplace and situated *Negro Story* at its center. As sole editor for six of the magazine's nine issues, she envisioned the magazine as a new space in which Black writers could renovate the image of Black Americans through the short story.[3] When it first appeared in the spring of 1944, *Negro Story* positioned itself as a crucible of new and boundary-pushing fiction—a periodical devoted to realistic representations of race (and racism) in America that in turn created a new space for Black writers. "We feel that, with few exceptions," Browning and Gayden wrote in their inaugural issue, "the Negro creative writer has not yet achieved the same degree of maturity as say the Negro artist in the field of music or in the fine arts or the Negro in other phases of life."[4] *Negro Story* offered African American writers that space—a place in which they could experiment with an array of writing styles, subjects, and experiences of Black America. In doing so, the magazine sought to bring nuance to a flat literary marketplace regarding representations of Black identity and experiences within the national scene. To this end, the magazine emphasized a fidelity to reality that would break racist stereotypes and connect readers through texts that promoted Black pride, much as Margaret Walker had with *For My People*.

But if Walker (and even Gwendolyn Brooks before her in the 1930s) imagined a specifically Black readership, then *Negro Story* sought a considerably wider (and whiter) one. Rather than "for my people," Browning and Gayden pitched *Negro Story* as "A Magazine for All Americans," as its masthead read. This shift was due in part to the changing literary landscape that emerged as World War II raged. The magazine appeared at a time when reading was being aggressively recruited across the country for the war effort. Though Walker's 1942 volume had also been published in wartime, ten months after Pearl Harbor, it appeared just as reading was being framed as a way to help win the war. By the spring of 1944, when *Negro Story* first hit newsstands and bookstores such as the S. & S., the national discourse had intensified, and the magazine entered into a completely different cultural landscape and national mindset. The war offered Browning—and the larger world of Black publishing—both a problem and an opportunity. On a fundamental level, the war raised critical questions about the role of Black readers. What does it mean to be a reader during wartime, especially a Black reader in Jim Crow America? Moreover, what are the responsibilities of readers during wartime? Does wartime demand new reading strategies? Can one engage texts and print culture in ways that better ensure the survival of democracy? What relationship does reading have to social change—and racial progress specifically—during wartime? What does reading "A Magazine for All Americans" mean in the midst of a global crisis?

Browning seized this crisis as an opportunity, using her editorial acumen to assemble a multiracial community of readers that consumed Black literature as a way to support the war effort. Further, through the stories it published, the magazine highlighted issues of racial injustice, drawing attention to the plight of Black servicemen at home and overseas during the war. *Negro Story* thus presented a different image of the country's war effort and positioned readers with new responsibilities—namely, to bear witness to threats to democracy at home and abroad. In this way, as I argue in this chapter, Browning launched a literary Double V campaign of her own, using the reading and reception of *Negro Story* to support the battle for democracy on two fronts. She did so by publishing material that produced a particular culture of reading in wartime, facilitated certain tastes in reading and democracy, and promoted specific modes of reception through which to understand the war from Black perspectives. Through analysis of short stories, poems, advertisements, letters to the editor, lists of recommended books, literary news, notes and notices, as well as other miscellany in the magazine, I demonstrate how *Negro Story* instructed readers about what to read, why to read, and how to read—all against the backdrop of the nation's entrance into World War II. As Browning and Gayden declared in their first issue, "We emphasize the belief that the future of the world is at stake during this World War II."[5] The story of *Negro Story* is one that narrates how reading Black literature took on not just local and national but also international importance.

READING IN WARTIME

As it had been during World War I, reading was recruited into the Second World War effort, symbolizing freedom, civilization, and democracy. "As Hitler waged total war, America fought back not just with men and bullets, but with books," Molly Guptill Manning writes. "Despite the many advances in modern warfare—from airplanes to the atomic bomb—books proved to be one of the most formidable weapons of them all."[6] In some sense, the emphasis on books and reading came naturally in this crisis. From the rise of *Mein Kampf* (1925) to the book burning demonstrations in Germany in the 1930s, books and reading seemed to be at the center of the war. In response to this destruction of intellectual material, the conflict was framed as a war of ideas that reading was uniquely positioned to fight. As one librarian wrote in 1942: "There is a book that is now near to blowing the world to bits. It is called *Mein Kampf*. Maybe there are other books, as charged with power, but of a different kind, the power of many men, struggling to survive, to live in a world without hunger, tyranny, or want. If one book could stir millions to fight for intolerance and oppression and hate, cannot other books be found to stir other millions to fight against them?" After all, she notes, "the soldier at the front needs to have a cause in his heart as well as a gun in his hand."[7]

Franklin Roosevelt himself framed the crisis in similar terms and repeatedly emphasized "the growing power of books as weapons," insisting that "a war of ideas can no more be won without books than a naval war can be won without ships." He elaborated: "Books, like ships, have the toughest armor, the longest cruising range, and mount the most powerful guns. I hope that all who write and publish and sell and administer books will . . . rededicate themselves to the single task of arming the mind and spirit of the American people with the strongest and most enduring weapons."[8] The publishing industry responded in kind. Echoing Roosevelt, Frederic Melcher, president and co-editor of *Publishers' Weekly* wrote: "We need books which will help us to be a united people, books which tell what we are fighting to preserve and what we and our allies are to do with the peace. Here is a high challenge to publishers and booksellers."[9] Meanwhile, W. W. Norton, president of the famed publishing house, argued:

> I believe it is . . . the responsibility of bookmen in a democratic society to take the initiative and the leadership in presenting the ideas which will be most influential in advancing the thought and answering the human needs of our time. And I believe that the book offers the best medium of expression for presenting these ideas. Newspapers and magazines have limitations of space as the radio has limitations of time which the book by the very nature of its form transcends. Let those of us, then, who live and work by books, redouble our efforts in the face of inevitable difficulties to fulfill our responsibility, which is that of offering to our fellow citizens the finest books that have ever been created and produced during any wartime in our country's history. In so doing we will be making our contribution to the winning of this war.[10]

In response to such calls, both the government and the private sector sprang into action to arm the nation with books. The American Library Association announced its Victory Book Campaign in January 1941, an initiative that ultimately collected more than ten million books for the armed services.[11]

Working in tandem, the Council on Books in Wartime—a nonprofit organization of publishing industry leaders as well as educators—organized a series of initiatives starting in 1942 to promote reading to aid the war effort. The council's "'Words at War' radio adaptation of books, its library events and celebrations, its recommended reading lists, and its short films," Kristin L. Matthews writes, "strove to arm America's citizens with a love of reading and democracy, preparing them to engage with both the physical world and the world of ideas."[12] Perhaps the council's most lasting contribution to reading for the war effort was its creation of the Armed Services Editions. "In their readable pocket form," these mass-produced paperback books "became battle comrades of our front-line soldiers."[13] The ASEs had a lasting effect on American reading culture, paving the way for the increased consumption of books in the postwar era. In this way, not only did reading and books affect the war, but so too did the war touch everything about reading, books, and the publishing industry—from the topics readers demanded to how books were produced, how they were designed, and how they were marketed and sold to readers.[14]

In addition to being bound up with the greater cause of preserving democracy, reading was also positioned as a crucial source of entertainment, distraction, and morale for servicemen on the front lines. Althea Warren, the Victory Book Campaign's first director, wrote of books' important therapeutic value: some "are medical plasters to extract pain," she averred; "others are tourists' tickets out of boredom or loneliness to exhilarating adventures, still others are diplomas for getting promotion and drilling ideas into a quickstep."[15] For servicemen in particular, books and reading were essential for overall wellness. In the words of John M. Connor, the second VBC president: "Our men are giving us their best. We cannot afford to do anything less than our best for them. Let's give them also along with their 'bacon, beans, and bullets' good books to make their hours of recreation and relaxation more enjoyable and refreshing."[16]

Reading was also used to recruit Black Americans into the war effort. In the powerful opening scene of *The Negro Soldier* (1944), a propaganda film created by the War Department to encourage African Americans to enlist, an African American minister reads passages from *Mein Kampf* to his congregation as a way to illustrate the high stakes of the war. After finishing a section of the book in which Hitler describes the achievements of the Negro race as "truly a sin against all reason ... criminal madness," the minister reiterates to his congregation, "The liberty of the whole earth depends on the outcome of this contest."[17] Reading Nazi propaganda, as the film illustrated, provided one way for the United States to motivate Black Americans to join the war effort. Once enlisted, Black servicemen, like many others, turned to reading as an important pastime. Indeed, the *Chicago Defender* reported that Black soldiers had a higher rate of literacy than white servicemen and that reading materials ranked high on Black soldiers' lists of desired items. "If you want to know what Negro soldiers in the Southwest Pacific want most for Christmas, here's the answer," a *Defender* war correspondent reported in 1943. Such items as newspapers, magazines, and books all made the top ten list of the "most desired items," ranking alongside photos of wives, pen and paper, as well as essentials such as wristwatches and toilet kits.[18] Rather than a luxury, books were considered essential to the well-being of Black servicemen.

In some ways, Black servicemen had access to books and other reading material. Soldiers at Fort Benning in Georgia, for instance, enjoyed a portable library staffed by a "lovely miss to look at," who kept business "quite brisk."[19] A library at Fort Sheridan in Illinois, where many Chicago servicemen trained, enjoyed various activities, including reading. A feature in the *Defender* pictured Private Homer Oliver "just curled up in a corner with a book . . . get[ting] in a little relaxation."[20] In Ohio, a book service for Black soldiers and members of the navy was created by the Ohio Negro Chamber of Commerce, providing "free books, newspapers and cigarettes" to "men and women in the armed forces at home and at the war fronts."[21] Soldiers stationed in North Africa, meanwhile, enjoyed "good books" at a Red Cross Club library.[22] At Camp Lee in Virginia, 4,500 Black soldiers welcomed two thousand books as well as current newspapers and magazines to the "library wing in the new Jim Crow Service club of the post" during Christmastime in 1941.[23] The next year, the camp's librarian, Georgia Holloway, compiled "a bibliography of all books by or about Negroes," which was "sent to each company of soldiers" in celebration of Negro History Week.[24]

But many Black soldiers and servicemen experienced this national scene of wartime reading very differently. For one thing, the conditions under which Black troops served were far inferior to those for white soldiers—and this included tenable access to books and magazines. Many Black soldiers were provided insufficient reading materials, or deprived of access altogether. One Chicago serviceman observed, for instance: "There is a pathetic difference between the accommodations for the Negro and the white soldiers. There is no library in the Negro section of the camp. All library and recreational facilities are paid for by outside agencies. Our group is not contributing to the welfare of our own soldiers. We took out some copies of the Chicago Defender and other magazines and they were gobbled up famishedly." In response, some community leaders and organizations resolved to "rall[y] our churches and civic organizations to send papers and magazines to our boys in the various camps to supplement other recreational and intellectual facilities, and to give them the same aid and comfort that is being given other boys by powerful groups of people."[25] In a similar vein, the African American sorority Delta Sigma Theta held a national Victory Book Drive of their own in May 1943 "to augment the recreational facilities of training centers all over the country where Negro men in the armed forces are stationed." The sorority aimed to collect fifteen thousand books by the end of the month, each of which bore a "specially designed" bookplate marking it as "thus presented by Delta Sigma Theta sorority."[26] If the government would not ensure equal access to books and other reading materials, then local Black communities would.

Such uneven access to books was a sore reminder of the inequality that accompanied Black soldiers into the war, which was often an experience of segregation, discrimination, abuse, and violence. Through the *Pittsburgh Courier*'s Double V campaign, Black Americans gave voice to the disparity and racism within the war effort. In February 1942, the *Courier* launched the campaign in response to a letter from a reader, James G. Thompson, who suggested the concept. "The first V for victory over our enemies from without," he explained, "the second V for victory over our enemies from within. For surely those who perpetrate these ugly prejudices here are seeking to destroy our democratic form of government just as surely as the Axis forces." In this way, Thompson concluded, "America could become united as never before and become truly the home of democracy." Linking racial justice to victory in the war, Thompson envisioned that with a successful Double V campaign, "colored Americans will come into their own, and America will eventually become the true democracy it was designed to be."[27]

A special wartime issue of the *Defender* later that fall reiterated the need to address democracy at home in the war effort. Its Victory Edition, which ran one hundred pages, included dozens of articles and visual propaganda that called for victory through racial unity. "Realizing that in these crucial days, the unity of the people—of all the people—is an essential, and inescapable requirement for winning the war and the peace," a note to readers declared, "the Defender seeks through the pages of this edition to acquaint Negroes and whites alike with a realistic pattern of thought that should hasten the removal of the misgivings and misunderstandings that impair race relations."[28] The issue also featured images of war posters "being turned out in volume these days at the South Side Community Center despite WPA curtailments" by local artists like Eldzier Cortor. One such poster, by Vera Donoghue, depicted white and Black hands clasped in a handshake as a show of peace and unity. Five words reiterated the message: "UNITE ALL OUT ... FOR VICTORY."[29] Other articles in the special issue penned by Du Bois, A. Philip Randolph, Alain Locke, and Charles S. Johnson, as well as a number of governors, mayors, senators, and other national leaders, encouraged readers to pledge national unity in the fight for democracy. Indeed, readers could turn to the centerfold and take "Our Pledge of Allegiance," which read in part:

> We the Negro people of America, pledge allegiance to the United Nations, and to the principles for which they are fighting. Democracy, international amity, and the right of every person to work so that he may live with dignity and enjoy a standard compatible with human decency are the basic requirements for world harmony and lasting peace....
>
> We pledge ourselves to fight to save civilization. No nation has the right to live which denies the dignity of any race. No race has the right to exist which fastens the yoke of oppression upon the necks of the unfortunate, the poor, and the meek.
>
> We pledge ourselves to fight segregation, discrimination and all forms of racial bigotry and Hitlerism which impede our war effort, and give aid and comfort to the enemy.[30]

To this end, the issue encouraged readers to do their part to ensure democracy abroad, specifically linking reading to the war effort. The editors even promised that reading and sharing the Victory Edition "can be your own contribution to building healthy racial relations as part of the task of winning the war."[31]

Other articles in the Victory Edition reiterated reading as a crucial tool in making the Double V campaign successful and urged Black writers and publishers in particular to take the lead by producing literature that built such "healthy racial relations as part of the task of winning the war." The historian and writer L. D. Reddick argued that racism is "a deterrent to our successful prosecution of the war."[32] Enemies realize that America "is incapable of victory because she is disunited. Every incident of racial conflict is refined and magnified as it is flashed over the ether to our friends and allies in an attempt to show them our perfidy and insincerity in the principles for which we are fighting." White Americans are misinformed about Black Americans because they "get their conception of the Negroes ... from the home, the school, the newspaper, the movie, the radio and other agencies which disseminate our ideas," he continued. "The results of this slander pouring forth from the radio, the comic strips, the press, the history textbooks, the historical novels, the plays and what have you," he argued, "are to educate white America to look upon the Negro as inferior. It is difficult for people who imbibe such propaganda not to believe that Negroes are worthless, if not vicious. This idea even permeates the thinking of some Negroes." What are needed during wartime, Reddick concluded, are realistic representations rather than caricatures. He thus called for an "absolute ban on all derogatory terms concerning the Negro" and efforts toward the "developing of a positive program of diffusing the truth about Negroes and Negro life" so that "a true appreciation of Negroes can develop throughout the nation."[33] In a similar way, Langston Hughes linked racial prejudice, the war effort, and reading in a full-page article, which concluded with a stern directive to readers:

> Our white fellow citizens must be made to realize that Jim Crow and all it symbolizes—meager educational facilities, discrimination in industries, lynchings—is not decent. It is an anachronism in American life that, especially for the sake of the war effort, must be gotten rid of—and soon. After all, this is a war for freedom. It's [sic] logic must be straight for it to be successful. It is not logical to speak of freedom for Poland and forget Georgia.
> These things Negro writers must tell America.[34]

And tell they did. *Negro Story* in particular led the cause, waging a battle of reading and books both on the home front and abroad. In doing so, the little magazine joined Reddick, Hughes, and others in using reading to win the war by exposing racial injustices and promoting racial unity in the service of global democracy.

VICTORY ON THE HOME FRONT: READING "A MAGAZINE FOR ALL AMERICANS"

On the home front, *Negro Story* launched three strategies to fight racial injustice through reading. First, the magazine provided reading opportunities that promoted positive representations of Black Americans. Second, Browning had a direct hand in building an infrastructure to support those reading experiences and opportunities—thus expanding the Black publishing industry and supporting current and upcoming periodicals to form a tight-knit network. Third, she brought new readers into the marketplace for Black literature—namely, white readers. In these ways, *Negro Story* responded to Reddick's directive to "diffus[e] the truth about Negroes and Negro life" while training the public to become socially conscious readers and consumers of printed texts in wartime.

From its inception, *Negro Story* focused its efforts on renovating the public image of Black Americans through fiction. "We want to present real live characters," Browning and Gayden wrote in the magazine's second issue.

> If writers can present these characters in various phases of Negro life, as vividly, for example, as Richard Wright gave us Bigger Thomas and William Attaway gave us his characters, the stories will help to eradicate the stereotypes in American thinking, concerning the Negro. In this way, concepts of a Negro who can live in America as a fine upstanding citizen will replace these old beliefs. Fiction has always played an important part in forming the attitudes of the public. Just so long as the Negro is shown in the movies and in fiction as a menial or buffoon, he will be seen in this light in the eyes of the public.[35]

This marked a significant change from previous decades, Jaime Harker writes, when "African American writers were constantly drafted to confirm or contradict cultural stereotypes.... Their race precluded them from being seen as active creators in the larger culture."[36] With *Negro Story*, Browning and Gayden charted a different path. Their second issue lays out the magazine's five aims:

1. To publish stories by and about Negroes in a realistic manner and to afford the Negro writer a creative outlet.
2. We welcome and encourage white writers who treat the Negro subject honestly and objectively.
3. To aid in discovering new writers.
4. To give the reading public fiction free from the old stereotypes that have passed for true characterization of the Negro.
5. To stimulate and create an interest in the Negro theme.[37]

Moreover, Browning and Gayden positioned their racial and gender identity as central to this mission. "We, the editors, as Negro women, not only welcome the opportunity to participate in the creation of a better world, but feel that we have an obligation to work and to struggle for it," they state in the first issue. "We sincerely believe that we can make our best contribution in this field."[38]

The literature that Browning selected to publish thus reflected this mission.

The majority of the magazine's stories and poems depict racial discrimination experienced by Black Americans, highlighting the lack of democracy at home. Indeed, the very first story the magazine published, "I Had a Colored Maid," by Margaret Rodriguez, links racial discrimination and the war explicitly. The story centers on Miss Merryweather (white) who accuses her colleague Connie (Black) of stealing an important report that has gone missing. "Colored people just naturally steal," Miss Merryweather angrily says to another colleague, Mrs. Martin, an older white woman. "I guess they can't help it." After Miss Merryweather screams racial epithets at Connie, who has just arrived with tears in her eyes, a security guard appears to inform the women that the report has been located, absolving Connie of any wrongdoing. The realization renders Miss Merryweather immobile: "She could not harness her mind, nor could she do anything at all but remain as she was, caught in a pattern too old for Connie and enmeshed in another pattern too new for Miss Merryweather." Connie then reveals that she has just been informed of tragic news: "My brother Jimmie was killed in the South Pacific. He was part of a landing crew." Immediately, sentimental identification moves Mrs. Martin to tears: "She put her arms around Connie and patted the girl's shoulder with a thin-veined hand. 'Don't I know, my child,' she said. 'Don't I know so well how it is. Two of my boys were taken, too. Twins, they were, and such fine boys.' The old woman's grief mingled with the girl's as they clung together, comforting each other." Meanwhile, Miss Merryweather "looked at them clinging in common grief . . . suddenly assailed by a thousand emotions, too baffling and too tremendous for her austere self to grasp at one time."[39] The story concludes with Miss Merryweather experiencing her own sentimental epiphany while the dead family members parade through her mind. The story thus models the possibilities for racial unity through shared empathy during wartime, suggesting that war might offer an opportunity, finally, to break the "old pattern" that has structured race relations throughout the nation's life.

Another story, "Justice Wears Dark Glasses" by Grace W. Tompkins (music editor for the *Defender*), similarly recounts the story of a Black woman, Mamie, wrongly accused of stealing from a store called Manson's. Her lawyer makes a valiant attempt to prove her innocence, arguing in court: "This woman is respectable. Her reputation is unimpeachable as these three witnesses will affirm. It is quite obvious that Manson's is trying to intimidate the Negroes who insist upon trading in the store when their publicized policy is not to wait upon colored people."[40] Despite his best efforts, Mamie is found guilty by an unsympathetic judge, who is depicted in an illustration that accompanies Tompkins's story with a gavel emblazoned with a swastika (see Figure 9). The image frames the injustice to Mamie as a threat to democracy akin to the Nazi threat. Story and image here link racial injustice to the war, reminding readers that democracy abroad cannot be secured if the threat to democracy at home goes unchecked too. If these stories did not compel readers, Browning further linked racism at home to war abroad with more direct comments throughout issues of *Negro Story*, such her as her plea in 1945 that "these un-American Nazi-like killings of innocent Negroes must stop. Adequate punishment of offenders should do the trick, don't you think. Let's fight for justice."[41]

In addition to publishing stories that offered lessons about the persistence of racial injustice, Browning compiled and published lists of recommended books by Black authors, much as Vivian Harsh did with her Hall Branch pamphlets, to encourage reading habits and values that would promote racial unity on the home front. In the magazine's second issue, Browning and Gayden listed seven texts (five by African American authors and two by white authors) under the banner "We Recommend These Books": Lillian Smith's *Strange Fruit*; Randolph Edmonds's *The Land of Cotton and Other Plays* (1942); Rackham Holt's biography *George Washington Carver* (1943); Langston Hughes's latest book of poems, *Shakespeare in Harlem* (1942);

FIGURE 9. Illustration by Elton Fax in *Negro Story* 1, no. 2 (July–August 1944): 11, facing Grace Tompkins's story "Justice Wears Dark Glasses."

Zora Neale Hurston's autobiography, *Dust Tracks on a Road* (1942); Roi Ottley's *New World A-Coming* (1943); and Florence Murray's *The Negro Handbook* (1942). This collection of texts emphasizes contemporary Black stories and/or writers dealing with the lives, history, and experiences of Black America.[42] Browning would go on to publish other, similar lists in the magazine, including several created by Black librarians, among them Catherine Latimer, research librarian at the Schomburg Library in New York City, and the Bronzeville librarian Marcella Ricks of the Oakwood Branch. Published in the third issue of *Negro Story*, Latimer's list includes familiar selections by Langston Hughes, Zora Neale Hurston, Charles S. Johnson, Florence Murray, and Roi Ottley. Walker's *For My People* also makes the cut.[43] Meanwhile, Ricks organizes her list into categories such as "The Negro in American History," "Race Trends and Race Relations," and "Records of Personal Achievements."[44] Again, these lists promoted reading habits that center literary and historical accomplishments "of the race." The magazine even facilitated the growth of local book collections: its first issue includes an ad soliciting book donations for Forestville Elementary (where Browning taught), where a "Special Collection" of books "Pertaining to the Negro" was being built. Curiously, though their interest in creating lists and collecting books within the community overlapped, Browning never mentions Vivian Harsh or the Hall Branch Library in *Negro Story*.[45]

The magazine communicated what audiences should read to promote racial pride and unity in other ways, too. In reviews, ads, and miscellany columns, Browning boosted such books as *An Anthology of Negro American Literature* ("This book is a fine collection and should be read by everyone," Browning and Gayden note),[46] Rayford Logan's *What the Negro Wants*, and Wright's *Black Boy*. It published favorable reviews of a variety of books, including Howard Fast's *Freedom Road* (1944), Brooks's *A Street in Bronzeville* (1945), and Ann Petry's *The Street* (1946). It also frequently listed current bestsellers, noting those by Chester Himes and Frank Yerby, and celebrated the achievements of contemporary Black writers such as Era Bell Thompson and Willard Motley—two Chicago-based writers who received Newberry fellowships.[47]

Negro Story also instilled pride in African American literary history by including features on nineteenth-century Black authors. One on William Wells Brown declared, "Brown's *Clotel* is only historical in importance but Brown should be lauded as a pioneer, the father of the American Negro novel, and as such is an example of a patriotic courageous man, whose life should be a symbol of accomplishment and hope for the American Negro writer of the future."⁴⁸ In a similar way, the magazine lauded Charles Chesnutt, declaring him "the best Negro novelist up to the year 1940." Chesnutt "pushed Negro fiction ahead," the piece continues. "It is certain, with gifted writers like Chesnutt and the moderns, there is to evolve gradually a brilliant literature for the American Negro of the future."⁴⁹ Browning even promoted the reading of slave narratives and offered to distribute them, announcing to her readers in 1945 that "*slave narratives* are to be found in the *Library of Congress*. Write in for a copy if you want to learn more about the history of America."⁵⁰

As Browning worked to provide reading experiences that dismantled racial stereotypes while building racial pride on the home front, she also worked to expand the infrastructure of Black publishing. To this end, she situated *Negro Story* in a growing network of Black magazine publishing of which she considered Bronzeville to be the epicenter, explicitly pursuing connections to Black publishers, editors, distributors, and other figures in the literary and print culture industry. Locally, Browning teamed up with the *Defender*, which had a strong relationship to *Negro Story*. Grace Tompkins, who contributed both short stories and poems, also served as associate editor for *Negro Story*, while Myrtle Sengstacke, wife of John H. Sengstacke (president of the *Defender* after his uncle, the founder, Robert Abbott, died in 1940), also served as an associate editor and then assistant.⁵¹ In addition, Browning promoted Ben Burns's book review column "Off the Book Shelf," highlighting it as "one of the most popular review columns."⁵² The *Sunday Chicago Bee* was also a close peer, offering readers "interesting tidbits about authors in every issue," Browning advised readers, while praising its editor, Olive Diggs, who "is winning fame as a speaker."⁵³ The first issue of *Negro Story* even ran a full-page ad for the *Bee*, which pitched the weekly as "THE ONLY PAPER EDITED BY WOMEN FOR THE ENLIGHTENMENT OF ALL."⁵⁴

Browning also built connections to periodicals across the country, such as *The Crisis* and *Negro Digest*.⁵⁵ But she spent much of her time throwing her editorial power behind lesser-known and up-and-coming periodicals. *Color*, published by I. J. K. Wells in West Virginia, "is a fascinating addition to Negro periodicals," Browning and Gayden wrote in the third issue. "It contains news of the world in pictures and stories."⁵⁶ Elsewhere Browning noted that "two new Negro fiction magazines have recently appeared: *Bronze Confessions*, published in Miami, Florida by Sam B. Solomon and *Town and Stories*, Pioneer Music Publishers Inc., New York City."⁵⁷ She also featured

Letter, "edited by Ada McCormick and published quarterly in Tucson, Arizona [which] has given us $75.00 in war bonds for prizes"; *Headlines*, edited by Louis Martin in Detroit, which "gives a complete and interesting condensation of the news from Negro newspapers"; and *PEP*, the "Negro newspaper trade journal [which] is edited now by the Lincoln School of Journalism."[58] There was also *Manuscript*, "a Washington News Letter," and, auspiciously, "two new magazines, *Ebony* and *Bronze* [which] are scheduled for release soon," she wrote in the August–September issue of 1945.[59]

Browning took a particular interest in featuring publications edited or otherwise led by Black women. "Mrs. Ora West is creating a magazine called *Expression*," she announced in the magazine's second year. "It looks as if Negro Chicago is trying to be the literary center of America. Look out New York!"[60] Later, Browning would note that "*Expression* is a fine magazine of discussion which should receive the support of all. More power to all women who are doing things in this world today."[61] She would also promote women in other fields, including music and entertainment, who "keep you reminded that women are really *scoring*." Those specifically named "in the newspaper field" included Connie Curtis (*Amsterdam News*); Toki Schalk, Elaine Graham, and Connie Nichols Curtis (*Pittsburgh Courier*); Mrs. Hortense Young (*Louisville Defender*); and Mrs. Gertrude Martin (*Headlines and Pictures* and the *Michigan Chronicle*). Browning follows this list with another catalog of Black women in music and entertainment, as well as a notice that "Mrs. Alone Feaman and Mrs. Lillian Proctor are giving a grand magazine, *The Chicago Circuit*, to Chicagoans. It is greatly needed, and there should be one similar in every locality. More about *The Circuit* later, as we intend to feature a magazine each issue."[62]

As Browning mapped out this network of Black publishers, editors, and publications, she also facilitated readers' access to this marketplace by regularly featuring Black distributors in an attempt to make Black books, magazines, and newspapers available to her readers. To this end, she promoted various Black-owned distribution companies throughout the pages of *Negro Story*. One, Carroll Ellis, "distributes all Negro publications in Chicago through his efficient organizations, National News Service, and is taking over a National Circulation of Negro Material," Browning and Gayden informed their readers; Ellis also served as an agent for *Negro Story*.[63] Another, the New York–based Great Eastern News Corporation, provided "Distribution of the World's Greatest Negro Publications," including *Negro*

Story.⁶⁴ Run by *Negro Story* agent Leroy M. Brannic, the company served as "one of the leading organizations for distributing Negro reading material," including "fourteen Negro publications and one white."⁶⁵ Browning noted: "He [sees] no reason why distributors should be hampered by race. He has developed a fine, flourishing business."⁶⁶ Through directing readers to these sources for the consumption of Black literature and print culture, Browning used *Negro Story* as a means of building a marketplace and a community of readers invested in reading about Black lives, experiences, and histories.

Rather than competing against these publications, editors, and other leaders within the Black publishing industry, Browning imagined them working together as a collective for readers. "There is room in the magazine field for *all* types of Negro magazines," she wrote in the magazine's May–June 1945 anniversary issue. "Look on the newsstands throughout America to see many kinds of magazines of similar form and even similar contents. There's room for all. This is a creative age—let's give the public what they want."⁶⁷ Toward the end of the magazine's run in 1946, she still continued to insist that "magazines and newspapers should work together in a unified front for the Negro." To facilitate this collaboration, Browning took a leadership role in the publishing industry. That year she helped form the National Negro Magazine and Publishing Association and served as its first president. Bringing together "Negro Magazine publishers and editors from all over the country," Browning's "brain-child" first met to discuss the treatment of "civil liberties, housing, individual health, socialized medicine, and fascism—native and foreign" in various forms of Black print from fiction to journalism. But the purpose of the group was not just political. During the gathering, "a very important sub-unit set up within the organization was the Editorial Bureau, formed for the purpose of raising the literary standard of Member publications."⁶⁸

Through her activity with the association, Browning worked to expand the growing community of Black readership, publishing, and literary marketplace that would make reading materials for and by Black Americans more accessible. Moreover, this collective of Black publishers did their work in the service of causes related to the war, such as the eradication of "fascism—native and foreign." In this way, Browning coordinated industry efforts to promote democracy at home for Black citizens. Others in the Black press took notice. Earl Conrad announced in his *Defender* column "Yesterday and Today" that "NEGRO MAGAZINES have sprung up and are doing a historic job. Such vehicles as Negro Digest, Headlines, Negro Story, Color, Newspic, Journal of Negro Education, the Negro History Bulletin, Crisis, Opportunity, and many others reach hundreds of thousands of all color." Moreover, he notes, "it reflects the desire and need of America for a great social advance; and it contributes to that drive toward social change. All hail the cultural renaissance! Tell us of the Negro—and the coming of true democracy!"[69]

Perhaps Browning's most revolutionary contribution to the Black publishing industry, however, was working to expand its reach to white readers. By subtitling *Negro Story* "A Magazine for All Americans" and then later "Short Stories by or about Negroes for All Americans," Browning expanded the market about "Negro stories" to non-Black audiences and beyond, recruiting a multiracial community of readers invested in Black stories and experiences. By inviting non-Black readers (and writers) into *Negro Story*'s imagined community, Browning sought to increase the cultural and intellectual value of literature by and about Black Americans and to renovate it as culturally valuable and desirable on a national level. In this way she also sought to funnel more money into the Black literary and publishing industry that she was helping to build. To this end, the magazine also courted white authors within this expanding publishing infrastructure. "We are aware of the increasing number of white fiction writers who portray the Negro sympathetically and honestly," Browning and Gayden write in the magazine's first issue. "We want stories from these writers. In fact, we do not wish to restrict this magazine to experiences seen only through the eyes of Negroes."[70] Browning even diversified the magazine's content to recruit more readers into the Black magazine industry, announcing in 1945 that she was expanding topics to go beyond Black experiences and representations. "*Negro Story* is announcing a broader policy," she wrote in the 1945 anniversary issue. "We will accept for publication a limited number of any type of story about or by any nationality."[71] In an effort to meet various interests of its expanding reading base, as well as to boost sales, Browning also diversified the magazine's genres, adding more poetry, a drama section, and a music section in the magazine's second year. In this way the magazine worked to make *Negro Story*, and the Black publishing industry it served, appeal to a wide base of readers.

In previous decades, sustaining Black magazines—for any audience— had been a difficult task. The Depression thinned what was already a small national market for Black magazines, literary or otherwise. Writing in 1936 for the Negro Writers' Guild in the *New York Amsterdam News*, the African

American columnist and novelist O'Wendell Shaw opined: "'The Negro race needs a successful magazine of the popular type.' In effect, this declaration sums up the dozens of letters that have reached this column during the past two years. It seems to be true that a popular magazine is needed, but past experience in connection with Negro magazine efforts raise serious doubt, in my mind, as to whether the rage is sufficiently advanced in the way of literary appreciate to pay for a magazine of this variety." He continued: "Save for two exceptions, (The Crises [sic] and Opportunity—sponsored by organizations), there has never been a known successful Negro magazine."[72] True, *The Crisis* and *Opportunity* had been more successful than other recent literary magazines such as Dorothy West's *Challenge* and *New Challenge* (1934–1937), and others such as *Fire!!* (1926), all of which folded after short runs. As *Tide* magazine stated in 1947: "The history of Negro magazines is another story. Until the war it had only one characteristic—failure."[73]

At the local level, popular magazines like *Abbott's Monthly* (1931–1933) and *The Bronzeman* (1929–1933) dominated Black readership in Chicago during the 1930s, offering fiction, gossip, sports, fashion, and other features geared for popular audiences aiming to cultivate a more sophisticated palate. (Indeed, *The Bronzeman* was modeled in part after *The Chicagoan*, which was itself modeled after *The New Yorker*.) For instance, Chester Himes's first short stories appeared in these magazines, as well as the *Defender*, among other local publications, in 1932.[74] Despite their popularity, in the end, these too folded as the Depression descended. When *Negro Story* appeared in 1944, then, the market for Black literary magazines was still in its infancy, leaving the magazine with "few peers," Bill Mullen notes.[75] Browning similarly claims in her fourth issue that the magazine was filling a lack in the market. "Until the advent of *Negro Story*," she writes, "*Opportunity* and *The Crisis* were the main outlets for the Negro creative writer and white writer interested in the Negro."[76]

But the market seemed to be shifting by early 1944—for Black readership in general (as the previous chapter demonstrated) as well as for the Black magazine marketplace expressly. *Negro Digest*—John H. Johnson's first venture into publishing—appeared in November 1942 and was showing promise. Browning's editorial sensibility and know-how thus led her to sense that the time was ripe for a magazine like *Negro Story* that used fiction to these ends—one that met the demands of an ever-growing Black readership alongside a growing general interest in Black life and letters among non-Black readers. In the same manifesto outlining their vision for the magazine as cultivating a space for Black authors, Gayden and Browning note that they see a demand to create a publication to satisfy the growing "market" for "short stories by and about Negroes for all Americans." Indeed, "there must be thousands of you hungering for stories about Negroes who are real people rather than the types usually seen in print," they write. "Our men overseas and in camps have been begging for them, judging from some of their letters."[77] During the magazine's second year, Browning continued to remind readers that "today the Negro is in the limelight. Both the fiction and non-fiction already released and that in preparation reflects a growing concern about the Negro."[78] Accordingly, she proclaimed in the magazine's second year, "we are trying to create a lucrative market for writers."[79] An ad in the first issue of the magazine even features O'Wendell Shaw's revision service, through which he promised to help writers tailor their work for this growing market:

> ATTENTION WRITERS! The market for stories and articles by and about Negroes is now greater than ever, and it continues to expand. Light, entertaining fiction stories and interesting feature articles (the latter dealing with outstanding Negro activities and personalities) are the new formulas wanted.
>
> Send us your manuscripts for a criticism and revision service that will help you slant them quickly for this new market.[80]

Others in the literary field sensed this national shift in reading habits, tastes, and audiences, too. Noted *Defender* columnist S. I. Hayakawa praised Browning and Gayden's timing:

> Obviously the time is ripe for such a magazine. The Negro reading public is expanding as more and more people become aware that ideas are weapons in the long, hard struggle for equality. Also there is an increasing white reading public for literature dealing with Negroes. The rapid success of "Negro Digest" is an indication of how strong national curiosity is now about all matters relating to the Negro. It is to be hoped that "Negro Story" will have an equally rapid success. . . . I strongly urge my readers to subscribe to "Negro Story" and get in from the beginning.[81]

Nick Aaron Ford, a writer and scholar who would serve as adviser to the magazine alongside Hughes, Ellison, and Himes, weighed in on *Negro Story*'s significance within the growing marketplace. "Of course a multitude of magazines are published each month. There are so many that people have difficulty choosing between them since no one can read more than a few of the monthly output," he noted. "Nevertheless, *Negro Story* is different from every one of them," argued Ford.

There is no other magazine that is devoted entirely to the experimental treatment of Negro life in fiction and poetry. There is no other national magazine so completely open to the contributions of young and daringly original writers. . . .

A magazine with such a program is bound to grow. It is fulfilling a need that has been apparent to some of us many years.[82]

Publishing a magazine that "fulfill[ed] a need" for Black literature and culture in turn promoted democracy at home for white and Black readers alike. But Browning's mission also appealed to a group of new readers on the national reading scene: Black soldiers.

VICTORY ABROAD: SOLDIERS AS READERS

Browning used *Negro Story* to support Black troops overseas as a kind of literary ammunition akin to the national discourse about books, democracy, and reading. Specifically, the magazine positioned soldiers as readers and their reading practices abroad as an extension of the Black publishing infrastructure Browning was building back on the home front. Further, she supported their work as authors, as many of them were directly related to Bronzeville and the Black Chicago Renaissance. In doing so, she gave voice to the experiences of Black Americans in the war, reinforcing the link between the fight for democracy at home and abroad.

Negro Story remained preoccupied with the war itself throughout its run. Browning devoted dozens of pages to stories and poems about it, featured soldier-authors, and regularly provided news and updates about individual soldiers and the war effort in general overseas in miscellany columns. The magazine included news about authors-turned-servicemen (such as Ralph Ellison and William Attaway), a piece about a newly formed unit of "the first Negro Wacs trained for overseas service," and items that updated readers on the whereabouts of servicemen overseas or in training.[83] It promoted war propaganda like *The Negro Soldier*, asserting that the film "show[s] what the Negro has really achieved in the army. It is skillfully and beautifully presented," adding, "We need more of this type of film."[84] It partnered with the regional offices of two unions—the United Auto Workers, CIO, and the United Electrical, Radio, and Machine Workers, CIO—to offer two writing awards, a short story prize and a poetry prize, each of which gave the winner a twenty-five-dollar war bond.[85] The back cover of its first issue urged readers to buy war bonds. The magazine even acted as a kind of "Green Book," informing readers about a Salvation Army Servicemen's Club in Harlem, for instance, that was "the largest canteen in the country for men and women in uniform" and was notably "open to all races and creeds."[86] *Negro Story* soon became so closely associated with news about Black servicemen that in 1944, Lieutenant Marshall E. Newton of the War Department wrote to tell the editors, "We have placed your publication on our mailing list for receipt of news releases on the Negro in the army."[87]

Browning also positioned Black servicemen as readers, perhaps the nation's most important readers at the time. Servicemen were a prominent part of the magazine's identity and were featured in every issue Browning edited and published. Indeed, servicemen are the first readers Browning and Gayden name in *Negro Story*. Recall the first issue, in which "A Letter to Our Readers" frames soldiers as an audience that fuels the growth of the literary marketplace: "There must be thousands of you hungering for stories about Negroes who are real people rather than the types usually seen in print. Our men overseas and in camps have been begging for them, judging from some of their letters."[88] And indeed, servicemen regularly wrote to the magazine, offering their reactions to individual stories as well as general thoughts about literary matters. "Lt. William Randolph has written us, sent a contribution, interested several of his friends and with a number of other soldiers, sailors and marines has expressed his joy at the success of our magazine," Browning informed readers in 1945.[89] That same year she reported that among soldiers, Himes's "stories have been our most popular. After all, people like to laugh, in these nerve-trying times. Soldiers write that Himes' stories have everyone in the camps in 'stitches' so to speak, which is certainly good for morale."[90] Other servicemen wrote to praise the magazine for enabling writers to "move forward with fresh vim, with courage," to donate "a few pennies from a poor soldier," and to criticize stories that provoked their "ire."[91] The magazine even prompted responses from white soldiers serving overseas. For instance, Browning included this note in the magazine's fifth issue: "A *Private* sends us a poem from somewhere overseas and writes, 'I am a member of a white tank destroyer unit here. In my opinion it would be very much to the interest of the war's end and of America were there not separate units and divisions.' He read about *Negro Story* in his union paper."[92]

Browning envisioned such soldiers who read and wrote for *Negro Story* as connecting the war effort to the literary marketplace that she was building in Bronzeville. This relationship relied on commercial consumption of the magazine—of literature by and about Black identity and experiences. Again and again, Browning exhorted her readers to purchase subscriptions for servicemen abroad, or to send their own copies overseas after finishing them. In its first issue, the magazine included two ads, set side by side, one encouraging readers to "SEND Negro Story To men in the Armed Forces for the 'duration'" and the other likewise urging, "SERVICE MEN Give Subscriptions To Your Friends At Home." Notably, both requests were to be sent to the magazine's own "Military Editor."[93] In subsequent issues, Browning reminded readers to "pass your copy of *Negro Story* along to a friend or a member of our armed forces," adding: "Soldiers overseas are sending gift subscriptions of *Negro Story* to friends and relatives in America. We would greatly appreciate such cooperation from our friends here in America."[94] In this way, the purchasing, circulation, and consumption of the magazine were all framed as being part of the war effort, with the magazine cast as an object that connected readers in the United States to servicemen abroad. Reading *Negro Story* thus became a collective effort: by purchasing and reading *Negro Story*, readers were doing their part to help win the war.

Black servicemen were also prominent among writers for the magazine. Supporting Black servicemen-authors was important to Browning, and she regularly lauded their literary accomplishments. She included notices about Sergeant Josiah E. Greene and Staff Sergeant Spencer Logan, for instance, who won the fiction and nonfiction prizes, respectively, in the Macmillan Centenary Awards for the Armed Forces of the United Nations.[95] She also featured the case of Private Bruce McMarion Wright from Harlem, who "traveled several thousand miles to have his first book of poems published by a British quarterly *The Welsh Review*."[96] Not surprisingly, many of the servicemen Browning published in the magazine were involved in the Black Chicago Renaissance; recurring names of contributors included Alden Bland, William Couch Jr., and Robert Davis. Each had important ties to the South Side's literary world. Bland was a noted local figure whose poem "South Chicago, May, 1937" appeared in the first and only issue of *New Challenge* in fall 1937, an issue that included Wright's "Blueprint for Negro Writing" as well as poetry by Margaret Walker, Frank Marshall Davis, and Sterling Brown. Bland also published "Let's Go Visiting," a story about a young Black couple's experience with racism in Chicago, in *Negro Story*'s first issue.[97] Bland's brother Edward, who died in Germany during the war on March 20, 1945, is the subject of Brooks's epigraph and elegy "Memorial to Ed Bland," which opens *Annie Allen*. Bill Couch was another topic of Brooks's work; he was rumored to be the inspiration for a love interest in *Maud Martha* (1953). Couch published poems throughout *Negro Story*, regularly participated in the Hall Branch Library Book Review and Lecture Forum, published poetry in "Lights and Shadows," and would go on to become a professor of literature. Meanwhile, Lieutenant Robert Davis, who contributed autobiographical pieces about the war to *Negro Story*, "was one of the original members of the *Chicago Poets' Class* and . . . a member of the *Negro Peoples Theatre* and *Posey Flowers Dance Group*."[98] He was close with the Renaissance writers discussed here and would serve as godfather to Margaret Walker's daughter Marion.[99] Couch and Davis, alongside Edward Bland, were also members of the Visionaries, a poetry group formed in 1941 by Inez Cunningham at the South Side Community Art Center. Other members included Gwendolyn Brooks and her husband, Henry Blakely, as well as Walker, Gayden, and Margaret Taylor Goss.[100] Other authors published in *Negro Story* serving abroad included Owen Dodson and Corporal R. E. Claybrooks, a Chicago native whose poem "Chicago's Black Belt" appeared in the 1945 anniversary edition.[101]

Though the literature that servicemen published in *Negro Story* was diverse, displaying their range of interests and writing styles, Browning most often published stories that offered Black soldiers' perspective and validated their experience of the war. In this way, she used the pages of *Negro Story* to showcase the fight for democracy abroad from Black perspectives. In all, about one third (31 percent) of the stories and poems published during the magazine's two years focus on the war or some aspect of it: Black soldiers training in the American South, waging combat in the South Pacific and Italy, writing letters home to loved ones, and, finally, returning home to Jim Crow America. Roughly sixty-three war-related pieces were published in the magazine's nine issues, with every issue including at least two, for an average of 32 percent war-related pieces per issue. Every issue in the magazine's first year included a poem by Couch (six of the magazine's nine total issues), while all of the poetry of an entire issue (issue 2, number 2, December 1945–January 1946) was dedicated to "Negro soldiers" for winning the war. A two-page spread from the magazine's second issue illustrates *Negro Story*'s preoccupation with the war (see Figure 10). Here, readers reach the conclusion of Margaret Goss's story "Private Jeff Johnson," which emphasizes the importance of racial unity for the war effort. After a fight nearly breaks out between Black and white soldiers, the narrator reminds readers, "To win this war, black and white ought to be fighting Hitler, not each other."[102] Readers move next to an oddly mournful poem by Couch (possibly reacting to a wartime breakup) before then taking in another war-related illustration by Elton Fax—this one a full-page image of a Black soldier in combat. These two pages alone immerse readers in the fight abroad and, most importantly, do so from Black perspectives.

Many of the pieces by soldiers were even narrated or otherwise focalized through Black soldiers, bearing witness to a particular kind of injustice while educating and informing readers about the realities of fighting the war while Black. The magazine's very first issue gives voice to this experience with Nick Aaron Ford's poem "The Negro Soldier Speaks," which recounts the presence of Black soldiers throughout American history before reminding readers of their own battle within the war:

FIGURE 10. Two-page spread from *Negro Story* 1, no. 2 (July–August 1944): 30–31, featuring a short story by Margaret Goss ("Private Jeff Johnson"), a poem by William Couch Jr. ("Epitaph"), and an illustration by Elton Fax.

> There is one right they hope to win
> Before they face the battlefield,
> The right to voice a last appeal
> For equal chance to fight like men:
> To pilot planes, ships, and tanks
> And earn a place in topmost ranks.[103]

Alongside Ford's verse on the same page sits Couch's poem "To a Soldier"—a more avant-garde depiction of the war in Europe:

> Here
> > where the cock sounds his synchronized song
> > in a sunless morning
> > and the caravans of young move towards the
> > battlefronts, leaving behind the degraded
> > cities wild-eyed and dim-lit like an old man
> > fallen ...
> > where flowers and time accumulate to dust
> > and the barbarous weed grows in the night
> > night taller than a child's reach
> > (O, brother say!)[104]

Browning took this attempt to show things as they were one step further and, as was common during the Black Chicago Renaissance, incorporated a documentary eye on the subject matter, placing the reader in servicemen's shoes. To do so, she dedicated pages of *Negro Story* to full-page features on the war and Black servicemen. Three appeared in the magazine's second issue. One of these, a photo feature titled "Ground Crewman—Their Work Is Important Too," consisted of four photos that provided a glimpse of what life was like in the war while honoring the labor of mechanics and other essential workers who perhaps did not get the same accolades and attention that soldiers did. In the same issue, Robert Davis contributed "Sketches from the Army," an autobiographically inflected story that illuminated the emotional difficulty of leaving for war, garnering sympathy for servicemen on the front lines. "This is the way it was for him—a great need to say something and no words alive enough or strong enough to express what he felt. How does one communicate association and feeling, accepted togetherness, immediacy or loss?"[105] At the end of the story, the dejected protagonist departs for the war abroad: "He looked back only once—after he had crossed the street—shifted the overnight bag to his left hand, waved quickly and turned away. There were tear streaks on his face when he reached the office of his local board. For some, it was different. But for him and for many others, it was like this."[106] This story, among other pieces Browning published, offered a window into the psychology and inner lives of Black soldiers, validating their emotional complexity. *Negro Story* thus humanized Black servicemen fighting for democracy abroad for white readers.

In line with this mission of documenting the war experience as it really was, many of the pieces *Negro Story* published also exposed the violence and discrimination Black soldiers endured, reinforcing that success in the war abroad was intimately linked to success in the battle for racial justice at home. Davis Grubb's "Rest Stop," for instance, recounts the killing of a Black serviceman by whites in a small Mississippi town.[107] The Black protagonist of Edward Rutan's "Johnnie Cull" wants to serve in the war but is wrongfully killed by a police officer. "If only he had been killed fighting for his country!" the narrator laments. "Instead he got murdered—yes that's the right word—murdered because of the color of his skin."[108] Langston Hughes's one-act play "Private Jim Crow" recounts a whole host of acts of discrimination against Black soldiers and concludes with a rallying cry: "Jim Crow car ahead! It can't be ahead on the Freedom Train, can it, America? Not if we want to go forward—there can't be any Jim Crow car on our Freedom Train!"[109] The Black soldier in Chester Himes's story "A Penny for Your Thoughts" is nearly lynched but is saved at the last moment by his uniform, while the Black soldiers in Stanley Richards's one-act play "District of Columbia" are refused service at a bar in the nation's capital. "Maybe what we been goin' through ain't all for nothin,'" one character surmises in the play's final lines. "Maybe all this fightin' and shoutin' about liberty and equality ain't just idle talk. Anyway, I like to think so."[110]

Browning balanced these stories of racial discrimination with pieces that honored the courage of Black soldiers. Dozens of prayers and salutes grace the pages of the magazine. Lucia Mae Pitt's poem "A WAC Speaks to a Soldier" expresses the solidarity of the Women's Army Corps with men on the front lines: "We send you forth, / And as you go marching in never ending files, / With our hearts and the work of our hands / We salute you."[111] The speaker of Mrs. Anne M. Harper's poem "A Colored Soldier's Prayer" confesses, "But I've a strong conviction / This is Our fight," and envisions at the war's end a time when "my people in that day may stand / In our great united land / And know a new day's begun."[112] Roberta I. Thomas's "Battle for Two" honors the sacrifice of Black servicemen while echoing the Double V campaign:

> Somewhere on the ocean, on the fields tonight,
> Black boys are fighting along with the White.
> They too, have come to defend Freedom's name
> For the color of skin won't falter the aim.
> But what shall be offered when the battle is won
> And Negro mothers mourn for their sons?
> I bid for your answer, O Land of the Free
> A one, or two-sided Victory!

Despite the valor with which the Black men fight "along with the White," Thomas's poem suggests a degree of ambivalence about Black soldiers risking their lives for the "Land of the Free."[113]

Gwendolyn Brooks's "Gay Chaps at the Bar," which Browning reprinted from the November 1944 issue of *Poetry* before it appeared in *A Street in Bronzeville*, likewise questions such sacrifice from Black men. The poem is prefaced by a quote from Couch about Black soldiers returning home uncelebrated: "and guys I knew in the States, young officers, return from the front crying and trembling. Gay chaps at the bar in Los Angeles, Chicago, New York." The poem develops this irony, exposing the disconnect between the scripts Black servicemen learned in order to survive the war—they "Knew white speech," for instance, "How to make a look an omen"—and those they lack once home:

> But nothing ever taught us to be islands.
> And smart, athletic language for this hour
> Was not in the curriculum. No stout
> Lesson showed how to chat with death. We brought
> No brass fortissimo, among our talents,
> To holler down the lions in this air.[114]

As the returning soldiers wrestle with such existential questions as "chat[ting] with death," they also face more grounded conflicts at "this hour" and in "this air" of Jim Crow America upon their return. In the end, the war has taken their bravery and reduced many to "crying" and "trembling," as Couch reveals.[115]

As these stories and poems circulated on the home front and overseas throughout the expanding publishing infrastructure that Browning helped develop, they answered Reddick's call to renovate the image of Black

Americans while encouraging racial unity and thus supporting Black servicemen and their fight for democracy abroad. *Negro Story* educates Browning's "All American" readers, bearing witness to and legitimizing the experiences of Black servicemen. It also honors their writing itself, providing a venue in which their experiences gained cultural value. In the process, the magazine renders Black servicemen as complex subjects, humanized by their war experiences. In these ways, *Negro Story* carried out its battle for racial equality on both fronts while cultivating new reading habits and tastes at mid-century. Further, as it centered African American literature, the magazine made the argument that such literature had value, literally—that it should be purchased and displayed in one's home as a marker of distinction and that reading it could lead to social change. Indeed, Browning believed, it could even help win the war by revealing the truths Black servicemen lived overseas and at home.

When Alice Browning began urging readers to form *Negro Story* book clubs, she knew she was on to something. Book clubs—both formal and informal—constituted an essential part of Bronzeville's reading ecosystem. Not only did they encourage the purchasing of books, thus supporting local businesses (and sometimes even the library), but also they provided the opportunity for readers to—as Browning wrote of Bronzeville's longest-running book club, the Book Circle—"set their own standards for good literature."[116] Featured by Browning in *Negro Story* as a central part of literary life in Black Chicago, the Book Circle met regularly at members' homes to discuss popular literature of the day. At the forefront of their reading habits was the discussion of postwar racial politics. To enable this discussion, they turned to a new literary taste—one that does not immediately conjure social consciousness: the middlebrow. The next and final chapter documents the reading habits and values of the Book Circle and in turn shows how these readers used the middlebrow to fashion "their own standards for good literature" as well as for good lives.

CHAPTER 5

The Book Circle
Black Women Readers and Middlebrow Taste in Bronzeville

In June 1945, Clara Green, a member of a Bronzeville Black women's reading group, the Book Circle, concluded her review of Richard Wright's *Black Boy* (1945) by asserting, "TRULY I FOUND NOTHING OF TEMPORARY OR LASTING LITERARY VALUE IN 'BLACK BOY.'" Indeed, "there is not the first vestige of human kindness or family affection shown throughout the book." Moreover, she judged, "the 'I' in this book is not endowed with any positive or pleasant attributes." Disgusted by Wright's self-portrayal, Green predicted "that the average readers [sic] sense of decency is so shocked by the reading of this unusually frank statement of the early years of the author's life that he will immediately declare there is no good in the book." While she recognized that Wright's memoir "might arouse the attention of an apathetic public to notice that the stoic endurance of a people does not reveal a lack of ambition or desire to better conditions"—as she acknowledged *Native Son* had done five years earlier—she could not see past *Black Boy's* "glaring baldness of obscenity!!!" and therefore concluded that it offered "nothing of a constructive nature—by and about the Negro."[1]

In her book review, which views literary value through the lens of racial politics, Green exemplifies another culture of reading in Bronzeville in addition to those discussed in previous chapters: readers who participated in middle-class book clubs to intervene in social debates. Indeed, when the Book Circle formed in December 1943, it continued the legacy of Black literary societies in the previous century that used reading and writing to demonstrate the race's fitness for inclusion in the national scene. To be sure, the Book Circle met on the city's South Side as a social club with the purpose of reviewing popular books, discussing the day's current events, and bonding with one another. At the same time, as scholars of book clubs and reading circles note, these organizations also provided members the opportunity to engage with social issues and develop or hone a political consciousness. These groups, like those that flourished in the previous century, "recognized that reading was a potentially transformative activity, not only for individuals but for society as a whole," Elizabeth McHenry tells us. Therefore, "rather than [engaging in] direct political or economic protest, middle-class black Americans saw their literary work as a means of instilling pride in their own community." They "believed that the acquisition of the skills and habits associated with high culture and refinement would" in turn "transform them into people worthy of recognition and respect."[2] Members thus invoked the uplift ideology of the nineteenth century—what Kevin K. Gaines has described as "an emphasis on self-help, racial solidarity, temperance, thrift, chastity, social purity, patriarchal authority, and the accumulation of wealth," which allowed African Americans to "striv[e] for bourgeois respectability in the absence of rights or freedom." Their hope "was that rights and freedoms would accrue to those who had achieved the status of respectability."[3]

By linking reading with respectability, the Book Circle continued the tradition of respectable reading that the *Chicago Defender* advocated for so avidly in the decades leading up to the postwar era of Morrow's book club. As I argued in chapter 2, this pressure to engage in respectable reading was especially important for Black women, on whom the burden of embodying Black middle-class norms of respectability often fell disproportionately. In the streets of Chicago during the early twentieth century, Black girls and women were charged with the task of providing moral instruction amid a strange and unwelcoming urban setting. During the height of the Migration, from 1910 to 1940, Marcia Chatelain writes, reformers and community leaders in Chicago "believed that girls, through their self-presentation and success, could ... carry the weighty responsibilities of race progress." What lay "at the heart of this strategy and ideology," Chatelain explains, "was the concept that the race needed strong women and strong mothers to address their needs," specifically "by limiting their expressions of sexuality and desire and displaying the values of the black middle class."[4] These "displays" included, as Anne

Meis Knupfer documents, acts of reading and the reception of literature by Black clubwomen in particular, which, she argues, "reflected race pride and progress."[5] As Gwendolyn Brooks already understood, it was the task of the Black woman to pull the Black family out of the poverty of the South and modernize Black identity—and to do so, oftentimes, with the knowledge and refinement she had achieved through the reading of books.

This chapter illustrates how Black women readers in Bronzeville—like Clara Green—lobbied for racial uplift through their participation in reading groups such as the Book Circle. While I demonstrate how the group continues the legacy of nineteenth-century literary societies that McHenry and others document, I argue that this Bronzeville reading community signals a shift in reading practices of the Black middle class—from an approach that courted highbrow culture through a politics of respectability (as McHenry's nineteenth-century readers did) to one that courted middlebrow American culture by participating in popular consumerism. This is not to say that a politics of respectability—or respectable reading—was not central to the Book Circle's identity (it was), but instead that this respectability was achieved through mainstream rather than elite American culture and consumption. In turn, the story of the Book Circle tells a larger story of the growth of Black readers as a consumer base to be taken seriously, one that helped fuel the burgeoning Negro market at mid-century. As I show at the end of this chapter, the Book Circle offers a bridge between nineteenth-century African American literary clubs and late-twentieth-century Black feminist readers, bringing Black women's legacy of agitating for racial equality through literary reception full circle.

THE "SPLENDID PROJECT" OF THE BOOK CIRCLE

On November 20, 1943, a small, unassuming notice ran in the *Defender* announcing the founding of a new book club in Bronzeville. The unnamed group formed at the home of a local teacher, Oneita Ferrell—70 East 48th Street—the *Defender* reported, while Ora G. Morrow, another local teacher, "was unanimously elected president."[6] A few weeks later, on December 4, Morrow wrote to Ethel Pritchard, a charter member named in the *Defender* notice, setting the date of the group's first meeting, sketching out a rough agenda for the event, and stating the group's "objectives," which she defined as: "(1) The highest cultural attainment possible. (2) Knowledge of as many books as possible, both fiction and non-fiction in the Literary field."[7] In pursuing these objectives, the Book Circle set out to use literature and reading, as many had before them, to cultivate respectability, self-improvement, and economic advancement so as to transcend restrictive social conditions—and it continues to do so today.[8]

The group's respectable identity was marked first and foremost by the social and economic positions of its members. The charter group was composed entirely of Black professional women: six elementary school teachers, Joy Braddan, Oneita Ferrell, Mabel Hancock, Eloise Paris, Ethel Pritchard, and Morrow herself; four librarians, Clara Green, Charlemae Hill Rollins, Mary Whitfield, and Beatrice Willis; and two social workers, Lera Harris and Elizabeth Maney (see Figure 11).[9] The members' occupations provided disposable income which allowed them to participate in a steady pattern of consumption, spending three dollars on membership fees, for example, to cover the cost of the books they read and reviewed, which often were acquired through subscriptions to the Book-of-the-Month Club and the Literary Guild. Their professional positions within Bronzeville, moreover, granted the club a degree of legitimacy in Chicago's cultural scene. As teachers, librarians, and social workers, the women occupied a respected place in the community. Such economic privilege also allowed members to enjoy a variety of programming and cultural opportunities across the city.

FIGURE 11. Members of the Book Circle in an undated photograph. Ora Morrow is standing on the far right. Courtesy Chicago State University Archives.

Indeed, social events accounted for the overwhelming majority of the group's spending. A high-profile event in their first year—a talk by Professor John T. Frederick of Northwestern University at the South Side Community Art Center, titled "Qualities Which Make a Book Good Literature"—cost the group $45.32 for programs, corsages, napkins, cups, ginger ale, and other items.[10] There were also expenses for Annual Founder's Day celebrations, gifts for "Secret Pals" at the annual Christmas party, teas, theater outings, flowers for sick members, and contributions to the NAACP, the Southern Christian Leadership Conference, and the Midwestern Writers' Conference. The group even raised money (fifty-five cents each) to send flowers—"twelve beautiful roses"—"to brighten the hospital hours" of the father of member Joy Braddan in the fall of 1944.[11] Through their conspicuous consumption, the group demonstrated an economic power that marked them as respectable within Bronzeville and the larger cultural scene in Chicago.

The women of the Book Circle also pursued intellectual rigor as a way to legitimize their group. Morrow in particular cultivated a professional, academic identity for the group.[12] Meetings followed a strict format designed by Morrow, who emphasized punctuality above all. In a letter to Ethel Pritchard she writes, "I believe you will agree that punctuality is one great attribute inherent in any cultured group—and the paramount characteristic of our organization—further that you will co-operate to the fullest extent in forming and perpetuating that desired attainment with which we wish to distinguish the Book Club."[13] In preparation for the group's second meeting, Morrow requested of members, "Wont [sic] you please be in your seat at 7:55 so that we may retain that most excellent record which we have already established—that of beginning on time? Our program calls for more books to be reviewed than before which makes it very necessarythat [sic] we do assemble at the appointed time."[14] Morrow also crafted agendas down to the minute and distributed them to members ahead of time so they could arrive prepared; she also encouraged members to bring the agenda to the meeting so they could take notes on its reverse throughout the evening's proceedings. To ensure a productive discussion, Morrow asked members to "make a desperate effort to make the discussion period a most profitable one" and to "respond to roll call with a Literary Quotation, citing the author."[15] Though the group hosted many social events, Morrow positioned its formal meetings as serious, even professional sessions. The group even created its own seal and letterhead (see Figure 12).

FIGURE 12. The Book Circle letterhead and seal, undated. Courtesy Chicago State University Archives.

In the group's first few years, meetings began promptly at 8:00 p.m. and lasted more than two hours. The first order of business was roll call, when each member presented her chosen interesting or meaningful quotation to the group. The meeting then turned to the group's business of approving past minutes and reviewing the bylaws, the reports of committees, new business, and details of the next month's meeting. At about 8:30 the group would turn its attention to the book (or books) at hand for the evening's discussion, led by assigned reviewers. Time was allotted for both a formal review of each book plus a group discussion. Refreshments were served afterwards.

Morrow was able to keep the group focused because she established a meticulous methodology of reviewing literature from the beginning. In her guide "Notes on How to Review a Book," she "advise[d] three readings" of the text—one "to understand the books [sic] structure," a second "to analyse the book in detail," and a third "for criticism—supported by evidence." Reviewers, Morrow directed, should "time" themselves and use note cards, conduct "background reading if subject warrants it," and structure their review in three parts: the author's biography, the text itself, and the reviewer's general critique. Reviewers should be sure to note the book's "Strength" and "Weaknesses"; "compare [it] with other works of same author" as well as "with other authors on same subject"; and evaluate whether the text is "good or valueless." Members were also instructed to follow "Specific Criteria":

1. Show wherein the author is informed.
2. Show wherein the author is misinformed.
3. Show wherein the author is logical.
4. Show wherein the author is illogical.
5. Show wherein the analysis is complete or incomplete or the account is complete or incomplete.

Rather than merely reporting on the book's content, Morrow wanted members to distill the text, providing an analysis that would spur discussion. Doing so also meant a good deal of research by the reviewer of the author, the author's previous work, and other reviews of previous work. Still, Morrow emphasized that the women of the Book Circle should form their own analysis based on textual evidence. "Do not quote extensively from the books," she directed them. "Base your opinions on the understanding of what the author has said." In the end, Morrow did not explicitly advise members on what constitutes a so-called good book, though her guidelines instruct members to evaluate the degree to which the author is "informed" or "misinformed," "logical" or "illogical," and whether the text itself is "complete or incomplete." She did make sure to note, however, that "even though your reaction may be uncomplimentary," reviewers should nevertheless "tell enough to make the audience want to read the book."[16] In this way, Morrow emphasized the value of reading itself.

Throughout this review process, Morrow enforced a strict code of conduct based on middle-class norms of propriety, evidenced in handouts, memos, and reminders for the group that read like the *Defender*'s "advice" for new migrants to the city. In one 1944 letter, for example, she wrote, "Please do not forget that we have, during our social period, the discussion of the vital and fine things that come to our knowledge of our people, to share with the group—never the lesser nor lighter material chats which tend to destroy the deep cultural effect that each reviewer leaves with us."[17] Indeed, members looked to Morrow for direction and instruction; in a compendium of their second year, the group noted that "it was [Morrow] who steered the course astutely through the beginning months and skillfully guided us away from the common exchanges of harmless gossip and meaningless chatter about clothes and fashions. It was she who not only by example but by encouragement and reminders set a record of punctuality and constant attendance that we are proud of." When she stepped down that year as president, the group noted that she "leaves us with a legacy of culture and literary taste wish [sic] we are deeply grateful for. May we continue to keep the Book Circle on a plane where we may all be as proud of it as we are at this moment."[18] Years later, for their twenty-fifth anniversary celebration, members feted Morrow, praising her "ability to organize, guide and stimulate in us the highest standards for good books and a good life."[19] To be sure, Morrow garnered deep respect and appreciation from Book Circle members. In her Christmas card from 1944, a member named Mae (most likely

Charlemae Rollins) wrote to Morrow: "I have enjoyed our association together in the Book Circle and out. It is an honor to be a member of an organization with so distinguished a president. No phooey—you've made a very successful president and I think all the members feel the same way—you should know it and this is a good time to tell you."[20]

By discouraging idle chatter and gossip and by establishing standards for reviewing books based on evidence and analysis, the Book Circle situated itself as a cultural authority on Chicago's South Side, a gatekeeper of taste in the community. Indeed, Morrow's "Notes on How to Review a Book" includes a note indicating that the list is "presented in compliance with many requests." Further, many of its members were called on as arbiters of taste and culture throughout the city. Throughout the 1940s, for instance, Oneita Ferrell, daughter of Morrow, authored a book review column, "Browsing with Books," in the *Sunday Chicago Bee*. Charlemae Hill Rollins, children's librarian at the Hall Branch Library, was invited to speak at the University of Chicago on subjects such as "the Criteria for selecting books for children," "Books for Building Respect" (for junior and senior high school students), and "books to break the stereotype."[21] During the summer of 1945, "new member" Ollye Marr Coffin, who succeeded Vivian Harsh as the head of Hall Branch Library upon Harsh's retirement in 1958, participated "at Kimball Hall in 'An Interracial Hour,' of dramatic readings."[22] After his 1945 lecture "Qualities which Make a Book Good Literature," John Frederick commended the group on its seriousness and engagement, writing that on his lecture circuit, "in most cases I take some time for funny stories, or digressions for entertainment. I did not feel that I needed to do this to hold attention with your group."[23] In November 1949, the group was asked to send members to the Midwestern Writers' Conference annual meeting to represent the interests of Black women readers,[24] and in 1955, the group held a short story competition—the Book Circle "Short Story Hunt"—for local high school students. Because of their status in the community, members were granted access to Chicago's literary social scene. In April 1952, Ferrell, then president of the group, was invited to a private dinner at the Cordon Club for the writer Arthur Meeker. The intimate group of guests included members of Chicago's literary elite, including Fanny Butcher, a well-known socialite and literary critic for the *Chicago Tribune*.[25] The group also corresponded with Roi Ottley, Claude McKay, and Gwendolyn Brooks, often inviting writers to their meetings, teas, and public talks.

The club even inspired satellite groups that dispersed the organization's rules, methodology, and ideology beyond Bronzeville. A guest at the April 1944 meeting, Mrs. Lucian Morrow (possibly Ora Morrow's daughter-in-law), "was so impressed with the BOOK CIRCLE procedures and scope of material that upon her return home she interested her friends in Murfreesboro Tennessee and organized a group of ten," the group's first-year report documents. "Constitution, By-Laws and Steering Committee reports were supplied and the same program as the parent body is enjoyed by them each month."[26] By 1968 the Book Circle could count four satellite groups operating at different times as branches of Morrow's original franchise: Murfreesboro, Evanston (in suburban Chicago), Gary (Indiana), and a "Preteen Group."[27] Morrow was thrilled with this development. In June 1944 she wrote to Mrs. Lucian J. Morrow: "THE-BOOK-CIRCLE is delighted to know that one of its dreams is about to be realized; that the desire to read more and more would spread into all corners of the globe, especially with our group. It makes for better understanding, broadens one's outlook on life and gives a cultural background otherwise unattainable.... [I]nasmuch as we want THE-BOOK-CIRCLE to become a national organization, we are anxious to have you give us the pleasure of making you part of that organization."[28] As the Book Circle garnered recognition and praise, Rex Goreleigh, a member of the board of directors of the South Side Community Art Center, wrote to Morrow to commend the club on a recent event. "It was most delightful and delovely and every moment was a supreme enjoyment and pleasure," he assured her. "My heartiest congratulations on the splendid project of the 'Book Circle.'"[29]

As a "splendid project," the Book Circle engaged the uplift ideology of the nineteenth century—aligning reading with a vision of respectability and self-improvement that aimed to showcase the "best" of the race. To be sure, the group "saw their literary work" much as their nineteenth-century counterparts did: "as a means of instilling pride in their own community." This was especially important for African Americans living in Bronzeville, considered by many to be one of the city's "slum neighborhoods."[30] By "elevating" the neighborhood through their literary taste and middle-class norms, the members of the Book Circle positioned themselves as models of refinement and respectability on the city's South Side. The Book Circle's connections to the Hall Branch Library in particular grounded the group in legitimate local reading practices and institutions. Though their regular meetings were open only to members, the group often invited the public to their annual teas as a way "of sharing with their friends the many pleasant literary moments that they enjoy together throughout the year."[31] Publicly they were recognized on multiple occasions for their work in the city to promote both culture and positive race relations.[32]

Yet, despite the Book Circle's purpose of achieving—in Morrow's words—the "highest cultural attainment possible," *why* they read, *what* they read, and *how* they read were decidedly middlebrow. McHenry's nineteenth-century reading groups invested themselves in the so-called great works of Western literature, from Homer, Milton, and Shakespeare to Browning, Emerson, Hawthorne, and Whitman.[33] In doing so, these groups, in McHenry's words, "wished to consume those texts that had traditionally been defined as high culture, thus associating themselves with the prestige identified with genteel society."[34] But the same cannot be said of the Book Circle, whose aspirations aimed at the world of the intellectual and the cultural elite, but whose literary taste landed them squarely with the middlebrow.

READING THE MIDDLEBROW

Often understood as normalizing, comforting, and reinforcing the status quo, the middlebrow would hardly seem to inspire social change. After all, at best, the middlebrow's complicity with capitalism, according to Joan Shelley Rubin, renders it inert. "As middlebrow popularizers accommodated consumer priorities," she argues, "worthwhile aesthetic commitments were also lost in the bargain."[35] At its worst, writes Janice Radway, the middlebrow becomes an arm of the capitalist machine itself, commodifying cultural production and lulling audiences into false consciousness. Middlebrow institutions such as the Book-of-the-Month Club, Radway explains, "were threatening to the extent that they foregrounded the connections between culture and the market and to the extent that they threatened to obliterate the distinction between those who were cultured and those who were not." In other words, "what was troubling" about middlebrow institutions was their "failure to maintain the fences cordoning off culture from commerce, the sacred from the profane, and the low from the high."[36] Although its meaning has always been somewhat ill-defined, the middlebrow is typically associated with being "middle-class, reverential towards elite culture, entrepreneurial, mediated, feminized, emotional, recreational and earnest," Beth Driscoll observes.[37] In any event, the term is often aligned with bad taste. Virginia Woolf famously shunned the middlebrow as "betwixt and between"; it is "the man, or woman, of middlebred intelligence," she wrote in 1942, "who ambles and saunters now on this side of the hedge, now on that, in pursuit of no single object, neither art itself nor life itself, but both mixed indistinguishably, and rather nastily, with money, fame, power, or prestige."[38]

And yet reading middlebrow literature can offer readers the potential for individual and social change. In her study of white women's book clubs, Elizabeth Long describes a variety of attributes associated with reading middlebrow literature (specifically novels) that "can lead to deep personal insights and to critical reflection about literature and the social order." Through reading and discussing middlebrow literature, readers may engage in "complex processes of self-definition" as they investigate their relationship to characters and the worlds they inhabit. This process of "personal identification" can, in turn, facilitate inward processes of reflecting on "the meaning of [readers'] own life situations," as well as causing readers to "question their own values" and even "clarify [their] own aspirations." But the middlebrow can incite outward-looking processes as well, "spur[ring] critical self-reflection about social activism." Identifying with characters and/or experiencing empathy for others, much as sentimental writers of the nineteenth century believed, has the potential to connect individuals across different class, racial, and gender identities. "Discussions of character provide an especially powerful basis for challenging critical authority," Long contends; as readers locate their own authority in the reception process, they become "confident in their expertise in 'reading' and judging characters in the world beyond books."[39] In turn, this gives readers opportunities to investigate the relationship between social roles and their own position within the social order.

Indeed, at the larger, societal level, as Gordon Hutner and Jaime Harker argue, engagement with the middlebrow may be more than just individually transformative. Throughout the twentieth century, popular, accessible books that "were mostly about the challenges that middle-class Americans face," Hutner contends, offered readers the ability to engage in valuable reception practices:

> [Such books] represent a rudimentary vision of some relative cohesiveness of American life, a shareable set of values and questions about the world in which middle-class Americans live. Rather than get lost in them, readers found themselves through them. These readers were attracted to this literature, I suggest, for its potential, not for escape, but for re-creation—the

opportunity for refreshing themselves and their understanding of society, their civic identities as readers. . . . To this end, such novels are social objects; reading them signified a citizen's interest in the general life going on outside of or shaping the private sphere.[40]

In a similar way, Harker writes, the middlebrow is capable of advancing progressive politics through emotion—guiding readers to feel a certain way, much like the sentimental identification with nineteenth-century fiction by women writers. Through a "combination of activism and middlebrow [that] came through an emphasis on emotion," Harker argues, "a progressive strand of women's middlebrow authorship thrived in the interwar period."[41] For both Hutner and Harker, the middlebrow may not incite revolution, but it most certainly can engender social reform, producing thoughtful and engaged "citizen-readers."[42]

It is the middlebrow's potential to shift the social order through catalyzing both personal and social improvement that becomes central to the Book Circle's strategy of, to use Amy Blair's term, "reading up"—the belief that the "right books" can help readers "achieve wealth and elevated status." As "upwardly mobile readers" themselves, the Book Circle's members were poised to benefit from such reading practices.[43] Indeed, the middlebrow had much to offer Black readers in the postwar era—the possibility, it seemed, to envision rising within the ranks of postwar American society through the consumption of popular mass culture. Yet this strategy, as I go on to show, is less about "reading up" than it is about "reading into the middle" for the Book Circle—that is, reading to join mainstream popular culture rather than the intellectual and cultural elite.

The full potential of middlebrow reading is often limited, however, by race. As Radway notes, "There were limits, apparently, to the kinds of identification middlebrow personalism could promote." Take the case of *Native Son*, dramatically altered by Book-of-the-Month editor Dorothy Canfield Fisher, who omitted passages that would offend the propriety of (white) middle-class readers. In this way, Radway explains, "the industry and the club may have acted to normalize certain experiences and a familiar range of legible emotions [and experiences] as appropriate to the professional-managerial class."[44] The middlebrow inhabited the white (heterosexual, cisgender, able bodied) national imaginary; it represented the national default setting of what apparently all middle-of-the-road Americans assumed, valued, and believed to be true. "Middlebrow readers may have been exposed to writing about African Americans, even to writing that advocated for them, but they didn't embrace, or didn't have access to, African Americans depicted as one of 'us,'" writes Harker. "However miscegenated actual American culture might be, middlebrow readers inhabited a fictional land of Jim Crow."[45] Perhaps by definition, then, the middlebrow could offer the members of the Book Circle only so much. And yet, whether or not reading middlebrow literature actually yielded the members of the Book Circle any material or social privileges, the group's *belief in*—indeed, its *social use of*—the middlebrow emerged as a strategy to advocate for economic and social equality on Chicago's South Side in the postwar era.

THE BOOK CIRCLE'S "PURPOSEFUL READING"

Unlike the readers McHenry documents in the nineteenth century—who immersed themselves in the Western canon—the Book Circle consumed popular mainstream literature. A survey of the books the group read in its first ten years—from December 1943 to December 1953—reveals a fascinating mix of best-selling and now forgotten texts, including fiction, nonfiction, biographies, self-help guides, romances, and memoirs.[46] Of the 106 titles the group reviewed during this period, sixty-four were fiction (60 percent) and thirty-nine were nonfiction (36 percent).[47] Almost all the books, regardless of subject matter or genre, were contemporary. Of the fiction, Pearl Buck's novel *A House Divided* (1935) was the oldest, and of the nonfiction, the oldest (not including the Bible) was Alfred Adler's *Understanding Human Nature* (1927). Twenty-eight of the 106 were bestsellers (26 percent), seven were Book-of-the-Month Club selections (7 percent), and at least five were Literary Guild picks (5 percent).[48] The most popular genre of fiction the group read was historical fiction (twenty of the sixty-four, 31 percent), followed by international stories (fifteen, 23 percent), religious fiction (eight, 12 percent), and novels about war (seven, 11 percent). Of the thirty-nine nonfiction titles, biographies composed the majority (23 percent), followed by memoirs (seven, 18 percent), American history and politics (seven, 18 percent), social studies (six, 15 percent), self-help and pop psychology (six, 15 percent), global history (four, 10 percent), and war (three, 7 percent).

Of the 106, only thirty-two (30 percent) explicitly dealt with Black and white race relations. A mere twelve (11 percent) were penned by Black authors, including Richard Wright, Gwendolyn Brooks, Ann Petry, and Ralph Ellison. In its first decade, the members of the Book Circle also read popular Black writers such as Willard Motley and Frank Yerby, as well as Bronzeville authors such as Era Bell Thompson and Alden Bland. They were not, however, drawn to what we might consider classics of the African American canon, such as slave narratives or literature of the Harlem Renaissance. They read no Phillis Wheatley, for instance, no Charles Chesnutt, no Frances E. W. Harper, no Jessie Fauset, no Zora Neale Hurston, and, surprisingly, considering his ties to Chicago, no Langston Hughes.[49] Moreover, despite their correspondence with Claude McKay, there is no evidence that they read and reviewed any of his work in an official capacity. The Book Circle also did not indulge in middle-class novels by African Americans in the 1940s of the kind that Gordon Hutner documents in *What America Read*. Of Hutner's list, the Book Circle reviewed only Ann Petry (*The Street*), Ellison (*Invisible Man*), Ottley, and Wright (*Black Boy* but not *Native Son*) in its first decade.[50] Instead, by and large, the Book Circle read popular middlebrow literature or general interest nonfiction that did not take up "the race problem."

The group's interest in this range of middlebrow and nonfiction books speaks to its mission of self-improvement through exposure to topics outside the so-called Black experience. Indeed, the group was explicit about this intent: "The purpose of this organization shall be to bring together once a month persons deeply interested in literature, in order to promote cultured development, exchange ideas, criticism and personal reactions," its constitution read. "Opportunities are hereby given for personal growth and group consciousness in observing a wider scope of human relationships."[51] Member Gertrude Rogers attested to the personal benefits she gained from her membership in the group. "To have taken my turn as a reviewer was a most satisfying experience toward developing self confidence," she writes; "to have assisted with the organization of a satellite group of interested adults while a resident of Gary was a fulfillment of purpose."[52] In a similar way, Ester L. Towles explained: "Growth through shared reading is exemplified through many facets. By sharing the ideas and understandings which have been gained, the group takes on new perspectives, and intellectual curiosity is increased as well as more critical thinking. Spiritual, moral, and aesthetic values are improved."[53] Years later, Mabel Hancock appreciated being part of "an organization that has gained so much national prominence, that develops [sic] an analytical minds [sic] and helps to acquaint the reader with new trends in the literary world."[54]

Reviews by Book Circle members reflect this ethos. In their written reports, members emphasize the educational value of a text, particularly its potential for self-improvement. For instance, Morrow praised Walter Lippman's *U.S. Foreign Policy*—a history of American foreign policy since the nineteenth century—as "an exceptionally well written treatise, not only because of the historical information it imparts, but the clarity and brevity with which the author expresses himself makes one absorb and enjoy as well as THINK seriously about the great isolationists and their seeming short sightedness."[55] In a similar way, Morrow lauded *Undercover*—an exposé of fascist organizations in the United States—as "an eye opener and revelation. Since reading [John Roy] Carlson I have been more prone to study all groups more thoroughly. Every American citizen should read UNDERCOVER."[56] In response to a biography of George Washington Carver, the group offered "a brief pause of silence, a reverent silence in appreciation for one of our group . . . who had contributed so much to humanity. All agreed that the author had treated the subject to the satisfaction of the most critical."[57] Offering her reaction to Joseph Grew's memoir *Ten Years in Japan*, "one reviewer says that this book is necessary reading for a clear understanding of the Japanese Militaristic mind"; she concludes, "This is a must for all, especially those who believe that war with Japan could have been avoided."[58]

The group also read middlebrow novels for self-improvement rather than solely for pleasure or entertainment. In response to *Indigo*, Christine Weston's novel of four friends in India, members noted that "the reading is slowed up somewhat by the assumption that the reader has a background knowledge of information concerning India"; this characteristic of the book "made reference reading essential for an appreciation of the novel." Therefore, reviewer Mary Whitfield concluded, "quite a bit of research was done by the reviewer and all agreed that the reading and reviewing of the book proved to be an educational experience of value."[59] Lera Harris praised the popular bestseller *The Apostle*—a novel based on the life of Saint Paul—as "a book that one should read and have in his hone [sic] library to increase his knowledge of the great phenomenal [sic] of Christianity." She also noted the author's attempt "to develop a greater understanding and appreciation of the meaning of Christianity." The group agreed that "THE APOSTLE is thought provoking and a masterpiece of literary skill."[60] Similarly, reviewer Joy Braddan enjoyed Pearl Buck's novel *The Promise* "not only because it was an interesting love story, but it gives much food for thought. Pearl Buck has the distinctive art of giving facts a fictional setting and through her characters arises such vital and pertinent drama that one does not question what is fact and what is fiction."[61]

Because members of the Book Circle read middlebrow books to educate themselves about the world that existed beyond Bronzeville, they thus used them as "social objects" to engage national and even international affairs. Middlebrow novels like *The Apostle* and *Indigo* as well as popular nonfiction such as *Undercover* and *U.S. Foreign Policy* offered Book Circle members the opportunity to reflect on their identities and values while situating themselves within a larger global context. They thus engaged such reading material, to return to Hutner's words, "for its potential, not for escape, but for re-creation—the opportunity for refreshing themselves and their understanding of society, their civic identities as readers." In addition to facilitating individual improvement and education, the Book Circle importantly exposed members to issues outside a local scope. Indeed, Book Circle testimonies repeatedly note the usefulness of reading such books because they engaged the group in external global issues.

Members routinely noted the group's "high purpose of bettering the conditions of all of us through our love for good books."[62] For the Book Circle's twenty-fifth anniversary celebration, for instance, member Esther L. Towles reflected that "by sharing the ideas and understandings which have been gained, the group takes on new perspectives, and intellectual curiosity is increased as well as more critical thinking. Spiritual, moral, and aesthetic values are improved," and "hugeness in thinking replaces the small." In this way, she continued, "new understanding of those different cultural backgrounds and values are [sic] gained. The group becomes better informed, and as thoughts and ideas are shared we help one another find some degree of exhilaration, happiness, satisfaction, and fulfillment in our lives."[63] Albertine Gray praised Morrow's "high purpose of bettering the conditions of all of us through our love for good books."[64] Ruth M. Williams similarly attested that "we're inspired to look outside ourselves and our daily pursuits and positively be concerned about and work for the enrichment of the larger society," while Lucille Boysaw recalled:

> It was thrilling indeed to enter the Book Circle and become a part of this warm, accepting and intellectually stimulating circle of friends. The Book Circle steadily pushes one's mind to seek answers of information through reading. The challenge of sharing ideas, the rebuttal of opinions through well-rounded reading selections all help to give enriched dimensions to my life. Finally, the Book Circle gave me renewed discipline to read and share other reading outside the narrow confines of my interest. All of this continued development is a part of the circle of friends—The Book Circle.[65]

To this end, Dorothy Curry remembered, the group provided "the enjoyment of good and purposeful reading."[66] Similarly, "to say it has been a great pleasure is putting it mildly indeed," wrote another member upon taking a leave from the group. "I appreciate to the fullest the added knowledge and experience I have acquired in this association with you." Moreover, "I know what the Book Circle stands for both in purpose and expression. I think it magnanimous and noble."[67] Rather than retreating into the private sphere, then, members found that their experience with reading middlebrow novels and popular nonfiction with the Book Circle solidified for them an identity as "citizen-readers"—reading as a way to become educated about and involved in current affairs.[68] As Mabel Hancock reminded members: "Knowledge is power. Read and learn and grow."[69]

Yet the Book Circle's use of middlebrow and general interest nonfiction to engage social issues as "citizen-readers," particularly issues concerning race, came into great tension with another purpose of reading these books: the transmission of genteel culture. As Joan Shelley Rubin has argued, various institutions of popular culture—including book clubs—became a means to "strengthen genteel definitions of character and culture."[70] The same is true for the Book Circle, who, in turning to reading for self-improvement, cultivated middle-class norms through literary practices as well as social events, as detailed in the previous section. To be sure, how the group reviewed books—the taste they used to establish literary value—very much reflected middle-class norms of respectability. In a letter reminding members of their May 1950 meeting, for instance, Oneita Ferrell warned the group that their next selection, Nelson Algren's novel *The Man with the Golden Arm*, "is a sordid book, different from any we have read this year. You may not want to own it."[71] When reviewing *In Bed We Cry*—a romance concerning a love triangle—Mary Whitfield excoriated the book's immoral characters: "The supporting characters are creatures of instincts, sophisticated by civilization but incapable of resisting the call of the flesh as a bird is of resisting the temptation to fly." In the end, Whitfield dismissed the book itself as "the bad girl of the forties."[72]

For women who considered themselves in the cultural vanguard of Bronzeville, the Book Circle unsurprisingly did not value books that threatened middle-class norms of decency—those that acted, in the gendered language of Mary Whitfield, like a "bad girl" (remember Brooks's scolding by William Henry Huff for her own poetic transgressions). But their fidelity to a politics of respectability at times created tension with their commitment to racial justice. Recall how Clara Green's objection to *Black Boy*'s "glaring baldness of obscenity!!!" led her to dismiss the possibility of any "TEMPORARY OR LASTING LITERARY VALUE IN 'BLACK BOY.'" Here her rejection did not stem from literary or stylistic preferences, nor did she fault character development or plot; instead, she rejected the book because it did not advance the proper *taste* for racial progress. Yet other Book Circle members felt differently. In her review of the book for the *Chicago Bee*, Morrow also bristled at Wright's violation of middle-class norms but ultimately found underneath the book's "utter disregard for decency" an important message. "Certainly only the willfully blind reader can ignore the fact," she concludes, "that the author of Black Boy has made one think.—Can America thrive as life Half slave and Half Democrat?"[73] For Morrow, the social function of the text, its ability to make readers "think" about race relations, outweighs the text's indecency.

A summary of responses to the book during the June 1945 meeting suggests that members could not come to a consensus about Wright's text. The group recorded that "reactions were typical of those found in any group where the book is discussed; some of the members agreed with the reviewer whose personal reaction ... was one of distaste for the obscenity so prevalent throughout. Clara Green believes that although the book will achieve widespread acclaim, it contributes nothing to the field of literature—nothing of a constructive nature—by and about the Negro. Other members disagreed heartily and cited specific incidents within the scope of their experiences to support the thesis of the book."[74]

A similar split had occurred two years earlier within the Book Circle over Roi Ottley's *New World A-Coming: Inside Black America*, a contemporary study of Black life in Harlem that the group read for its inaugural December 1943 meeting. Reviewer Ethel Pritchard praised the book for its "valuable factual material which will stimulate race pride and race solidarity. It gives an insight into current negro problems, the causes and effects of which are caustically expressed but without bitterness. A copy should be in every home."[75] Yet another, unsigned review in the Book Circle's archive insisted that the book "does not reflect Black America." It continues, "As one reads it nausea becomes a preferable disease to the contempt that [Ottley] has for a Negro who so incoherently parades the short comings of his people to the exclusion of the many great things accomplished." The reviewer concludes, "I make this indictment that the book was either written by a white person or to appease a white group or for pecuniary reasons."[76]

The debate that *New World A-Coming* and *Black Boy* elicited demonstrates a divide in the group about the proper means—or literary taste—for achieving racial uplift. Though middle-class respectability was not included in Morrow's "Notes on How to Review a Book," it nevertheless often dictated how members responded to the books they read. Indeed, the debate over decorum as literary taste itself illustrates the seriousness with which the group considered (middlebrow) reading an act of—or threat to—racial progress. In many ways, middlebrow reading extended certain privileges to Black readers: for one, the opportunity to participate more fully in the national scene through the consumption of mass consumer culture. It also, as Harker writes, allowed Black women writers such as Jessie Fauset a way to counter "the sexual stereotyping of African Americans with ... images of a thoroughly conventional black middle class."[77] But as the debate within the Book Circle illustrates, there was also a powerful tension between the seemingly placid middlebrow and the ugly realities of racial injustice. Sean McCann writes, "For a time, in the early 1940s, in short, there was a moment when writers as unlike each other as Richard Wright and Dorothy Canfield Fisher could meet on the ground of the middlebrow, collaborating to publish books that would meld a radical vision of proletarian anger to a liberal project of literary enlightenment." Such a collaboration was possible for this brief moment because writers and cultural institutions coming out of the New Deal shared "a vision of literature as civic discourse with a politics of activism and uplift." As McCann explains, "Middlebrow culture, in short, made middle-class aspiration and social reform seem harmonious and consistent with an economy built on private property." And yet many Black writers coming out of a tradition of social protest, such as Margaret Walker, "struggled to maintain that belief" because "they saw the middlebrow promise of upward mobility and cultural refinement grow increasingly distant."[78]

Rather than resolving this tension between the middlebrow and social reform, the Book Circle sits at its center. Whether or not members believed that reading such books could directly resolve social problems, they repeatedly returned to the middlebrow to work through and debate them. Indeed, the examples of *Black Boy* and *New World A-Coming*—and of solidly middlebrow novels, as I go on to show—demonstrate that the group consistently read race through the lens of the middlebrow. Yet so too did they read the middlebrow through the lens of race. The fact that seventy-four (or 70 percent) of the 106 books that the Book Circle reviewed in its first ten years did not explicitly engage race relations might suggest that the group read to escape the realities of racial discrimination. Nevertheless, the way the group reviewed middlebrow fiction and general interest nonfiction demonstrates how they in fact explicitly used popular and mainstream books to confront white supremacy in the postwar era.

READING THE MIDDLEBROW AGAINST WHITE SUPREMACY

Again and again, Book Circle members interpret and evaluate texts based on how directly they relate to contemporary race relations in the United States. In the group's discussion of Pearl Buck's novel *The Promise*, "similarities between the situation of the darker races in the East and the Negro group in the United States were stressed particularly in relation to the Caucasians. Appreciation was voiced for the wonderful work Pearl Buck had done and is doing to bring about a better understanding between peoples."[79] In response to Lin Yutang's *Between Tears and Laughter*, a meditation on the Second World War, Oneita Ferrell emphasized the book's message "that all men have a right to keep intact the human dignity of the soul. Herein lies a challenge to the white man that the darker races can no longer be ignored." She concludes by asserting that the book "is significant in that it presents a point of view, a philosophy for post war planning. There is no doubt that before a lasting peace is achieved, we must adopt this philosophy but here is a question as to when man will be ready to accept this evidence of faith in the inherent goodness of his fellowmen."[80] Reading in *Earth and High Heaven* about conflicts between various ethnic groups in Canada, Lera Harris similarly linked the struggle for racial equality in the United States to a global cause: "Books of this nature are interesting because they create an alertness to prejudice and intolerance as they effect [*sic*] every race."[81] Finally, though the book is set in India, Mary Whitfield praised the "thesis" of *Indigo*: "that there is very little difference between people of different races."[82]

Rather than assimilating into or accommodating white America—a charge often leveled at the Black middle class—the Book Circle's middlebrow reading habits afforded its members a means to mobilize their economic and intellectual privilege to petition for racial equality. In this way, the Book Circle's middlebrow reading habits answer McHenry's call for a more nuanced understanding of the Black middle class. "Against the backdrop of the 'authentic' actions of their less-privileged counterparts," she writes, "the perspectives of the black middle and upper classes, their activities, and their actions have been considered as indicative of one of two things: the desire to assimilate into the white middle class, or the passive acceptance of white domination and accommodation to racial segregation. This limited vision of the black middle and upper classes as assimilationist or accommodationist oversimplifies the complexity of the experience of black Americans in the United States."[83]

From a distance, the Book Circle's choice to read many supposedly "raceless" texts would lead some to have such a limited "assimilationist or accommodationist" vision of the group and its members; yet the ways that members like Lera Harris and Mary Whitfield read and reviewed these texts offer a more complex understanding of Black audiences. Middlebrow taste afforded not a retreat from the realities of white supremacy but instead a direct confrontation with them. Indeed, middlebrow literature gave Book Circle readers the opportunity to discuss perhaps the most common mainstream aspect of American culture: racial discrimination. The women of the Book Circle saw in their reading, therefore, a means to engage both the legacy and the current moment of the nation's racial politics. It even allowed members to look forward. In reflecting on her years as a member, Lucille Boysaw wrote in 1968, "Our readings have certainly helped to prepare us for a greater understanding of the Black Revolution."[84] In a similar way, Morrow urged members that same year to make an "INVESTMENT, HERE AND NOW—a greater, deeper and more serious involvement in the struggle with our Black Youths as they seek to find the **identity of real men and women** which belongs to them.... Book Circle you have the tools. Use them—NOW."[85]

The Book Circle's reading practices—which focus so heavily on mainstream, middlebrow books—suggest that reading for racial uplift had, by the postwar era, become aligned with American consumerism and the consumption, via books and reading, of a particular middlebrow taste. That is to say that, while middle-class Black Americans still saw "their literary work as a means of instilling pride in their own community," as McHenry writes of nineteenth-century reading practices, they did so less by "consum[ing] those texts that had traditionally been defined as high culture" to "transform them [and their entire race] into people worthy of recognition and respect" than by consuming mainstream books through newfound purchasing power. At the same time, the Book Circle revealed that this new strategy of racial uplift and empowerment for middle-class Black Americans in the postwar period was necessarily in tension with the individualist and capitalist underpinnings of mainstream middlebrow culture.

As they read and discussed popular books, then, the women of the Book Circle participated, in the words of Elizabeth Long, "in a collective working-out of their relationship to the contemporary historical moment and the particular social conditions that characterize it. This activity is quite literally productive," Long continues, "in that it enables women not merely to reflect on identities they already have but also to bring new aspects of subjectivity into being."[86] Through their reviews of bestsellers like *The Apostle* and popular nonfiction such as *Undercover*, as well as important "race books" like *Black Boy*, the Book Circle engaged their historical moment, critiquing, speaking back to, and attempting to shape the "particular social conditions that characterize[d]" their lives. In this way, while middlebrow reading practices in the postwar years often induced *anxiety* for white readers (about taste and class), they alternatively symbolized *opportunity* for many middle-class Black readers. To be sure, reading middlebrow literature did not end the restrictive covenants or any other form of racism and white supremacy that African Americans faced in Chicago; it did, however, give the women of the Book Circle a new way to advocate for equality in their community through their participation in mass consumer culture. As their reviews and personal testimonies show, the members of the Book Circle conceived of their reading as a means to transform themselves as well as their historical moment. After all, as Jacqueline Bobo writes, "As part of an interpretive community, black women cultural consumers are not simply viewers and readers but cogent and knowledgeable observers of the social, political, and cultural forces that influence their lives."[87] The story of the Book Circle illustrates such an interpretive community in the twentieth century and, in doing so, makes visible the everyday acts of reading and reception that fulfill the personal, political, and social needs of Black women.

Sometime in late 1970 or early 1971, Charlemae Hill Rollins, a founding member of the Book Circle, wrote to the group announcing her retirement:

> *Dear Ora and Members of The Book Circle,*
>
> *It is with sincere regret that I must resign from our*

> Beloved Book Circle.
>
> Believe me it is because my health (my memory really) has become so impaired (with age I guess) that it is impossible for me to function successfully. It's best that I face this and try to learn to accept it.
>
> It has been one of the most enjoyable and stimulating experiences of my life.
>
> I have certainly enjoyed each and every one of you and also everything we did together.
>
> These wonderful memories will sustain me as I adjust to "the aging process."
>
> Bless you—all of you,
>
>> Lovingly,
>> Mae[88]

Rollins's moving tribute to her time with the Book Circle—a nearly twenty-eight-year relationship—speaks to the deeply personal experience it provided her. The feeling was clearly mutual. An undated document in the Book Circle records includes lyrics, set to the tune of "God Bless America," for a song titled "All Praise to Charlemae":

> All Praise to Charlemae
> Pal We Admire
> Keep Books Beside Her and Cheer Her
> Thru the Years with a Love All Afire
> From Book Circle, to the Library
> To the Children Who Fill the Room
> All Praise to Charlemae
> To Us She's a Boom![89]

Rollins's letter echoes sentiments from other members cited here who also describe their time with the Book Circle as profoundly meaningful, both formative and transformative. As Esther L. Towles testified, within the Book Circle, "the common goals, the closeness, the true friendships improve the art of getting along with each other and fosters [sic] good relations." Thus, because of the Book Circle, "we are better fortified to face day-to-day responsibilities and challenges."[90]

Members' "closeness" and "true friendships" with one another echo throughout their reviews and other records. Reviews in particular demonstrate members' mutual affection and delight. "Ethel Pritchard's reviews are always well prepared and delivered with perfect diction and beautiful choice of words," one report noted.[91] Another documented that Ora Morrow "is one of our most reliable reviewers. She prepares her material carefully and her statements are weighted before offered. Her quiet dignified manner is seldom ruffled. Her reviews are anticipated with pleasure."[92] Beatrice Willis was lauded as "one of the most popular reviewers of the Book Circle. She injects so much of her personality into the telling of her story."[93] Another attested, "Mary Whitfield gives the most entertaining reviews," adding: "There is never a dull moment. This review [of *Indigo*] was particularly spicy; so much so that one of the members decided to reread the book in search of some of the interesting features emphasized by Mary."[94] Perhaps Ruth M. Williams summed up the group dynamics best in her reflection. "Within the group, one gets a feeling of genuine warmth and concern for the well-being of all members," she confides. "Certainly one feels that the Book Circle CARES."[95]

Such testimonies underscore a final importance of the Book Circle's reading practices: joy. That members of the Book Circle found pleasure, comfort, and belonging in their participation in the group is clear in the letters and reflections they left behind. Though the group took their reading and reception practices seriously, to be sure, they also had fun. During the May 1944 meeting, members enjoyed special book-themed food, as the group's report reads: "While the main interest of the Book Circle pertains to food for the mind. Members were delighted with the ice cream molds which were served in the form of books."[96] At annual Christmas parties, members exchanged gifts and viewed "slides of past Book Circle events," Mary Whitfield recounted. "Quizzes, games and laughter are the threads running through this tapestry of fun."[97] And that fun proved to be perhaps the most enduring and motivating factor of the group's reading practices—what kept them coming back together over the span of decades all the way up to this day, having celebrated their eightieth anniversary in 2023. During a February meeting in 1944, not even bad weather could deter the group. "The worst blizzard of the year began one hour before the scheduled time for the meeting," the group later recorded. "At eight o'clock it had reached its peak. But the eight members who faced the elements were unanimous in stating that this meeting at the home of Harriette Keys was most enjoyable."[98]

If the women of Bronzeville—and this new role of middlebrow reader—continued the tradition of Black women's literary groups in the nineteenth century, which turned to reading as "a potentially transformative activity," then they also looked ahead, anticipating the "personal is political" ethos that would come to define Black feminism by the end of the century. Indeed, as a deeply personal experience that "sustained" and "fortified" members through the reading and reception of literature, the Book Circle anticipated Black feminists later in the century who positioned activists as readers—and, alternately, readers as activists. Indeed, when Barbara Smith, Sonia Sanchez, Barbara Christian, and many others created syllabi, formed reading groups, and shared books, they imagined reading as a strategy of consciousness-raising—of sustaining and fortifying themselves to face day-to-day responsibilities and challenges. The following chapter, this book's conclusion, expands this discussion to illustrate how Bronzeville's reading communities bridge Black reading circles of the nineteenth century and the late twentieth to form a powerful legacy of Black women's reading practices in the United States.

CONCLUSION
Legacies of Black Women's Reading

In the final decades of the twentieth century, Gwendolyn Brooks, Alice Browning, and Margaret Walker all "reemerged" as important figures on a new national scene of reading and Black politics.[1] Though they were invested in reimagining methods and purposes of reading, their earlier work struck a chord with the radical energy of the late century, inspiring a new generation that in turn sparked new receptions of the women's work. In 1967, Brooks left the Second Annual Black Writers' Conference utterly changed, fortified with a new vision of poetry. The previous year, Margaret Walker published *Jubilee* and then in 1968 founded the Institute for the Study of the History, Life, and Culture of Black People at Jackson State University. She continued this important work at the beginning of the Black studies movement by organizing the 1971 National Evaluative Conference on Black Studies and the 1973 Phillis Wheatley Poetry Festival. In the midst of this activity, in 1970 Browning founded the International Black Writers Conference, an annual event in Chicago that she directed until 1984, which encouraged the reading and discussion of Black art, literature, and culture. At the end of the twentieth century, then, these women continued to provide infrastructures for reading and reception as radical tools of self- and social transformation. In particular, such initiatives by Brooks, Walker, and Browning helped galvanize nascent Black women's studies, a movement that necessitated the reading of Black women's cultural traditions.

Alice Walker's foundational essay "In Search of Our Mothers' Gardens" (1974) views literary history through a Black feminist lens by paying tribute to creative production—stories, songs, poems, even gardens—by anonymous Black women. For Walker, Black women's creative work has meant, above all, survival. For her mother, Walker writes, "so hindered and intruded upon in so many ways, being an artist has still been a daily part of her life. This ability to hold on, even in very simple ways, is work black women have done for a very long time." But if *writing* has symbolized Black women's agency, so too has *reading*. In her essay, Walker recognizes that the listening to and indeed reception of creative work have been just as important as the production of the creative work. "Yet so many of the stories that I write, that we all write, are my mother's stories," she confesses. "Only recently did I fully realize this: that through years of listening to my mother's stories of her life, I have absorbed not only the stories themselves, but something of the manner in which she spoke, something of the urgency that involves the knowledge that her stories—like her life—must be recorded."[2] Here, in an essay read for its theorization of Black women's cultural production, Walker also conceptualizes the centrality of reception practices themselves—listening, bearing witness—to the lives of Black women. Of course, Black women's purposes for reading, as well as what they read, vary by time, geography, class, and other sociocultural factors. But their reading practices nevertheless contributed to the legacy of survival that Walker speaks of—a legacy that has been neglected, systematically erased from national literary and cultural histories. Like the stories of Walker's mother, this history "must be recorded."

This association of survival with Black women's reading and reception practices echoes throughout Black feminist literary scholarship inspired by Walker and the recovery projects of the 1970s to today. As a new wave of Black feminism emerged out of the 1960s, the reading, sharing, and discussing of key texts—such as the Combahee River Collective's manifesto "A Black Feminist Statement" (1977)—became a way to use reading in the name of social justice and identity politics. Readers were thus imagined as activists and activists were imagined as readers—or, it is perhaps more accurate to say that this relationship was reimagined, since Black feminism positioned reading to be social, political, even revolutionary from its inception. By the late twentieth century, reading literature specifically by and about Black women emerged as an urgent political and collective act of survival. Indeed, the Collective itself used reading in its own consciousness-raising endeavors. Not long after forming, the Collective recounts:

> We decided ... to become a study group. We had always shared our readings with each other, and some of us had written papers on Black feminism for group discussion a few months before this decision was made. We began functioning as a study group and also began discussing the possibility of starting a Black feminist publication.... Currently we are planning to gather together a collection of Black feminist writing. We feel that it is absolutely essential to demonstrate the reality of our politics to other Black women and believe that we can do this though [sic] writing and distributing our work. The fact that individual Black feminists are living in isolation all over the country, that our own numbers are small, and that we have some skills in writing, printing, and publishing makes us want to carry out these kinds of projects as a means of organizing Black feminists as we continue to do political work in coalition with other groups.[3]

In an era when "the personal is political," sharing texts that spoke to Black women's lives did what Gertrude Mossell and Pauline Hopkins had done for Black women readers at the beginning of the century with their lists of notable race women: it reflected Black women's experiences back to them in written form, validating and then dispersing them to the wider public—a tradition that Harsh continued well into the twentieth century. As Barbara Smith would write in her foundational essay "Toward a Black Feminist Criticism" (1977), "I want most of all for Black women and Black lesbians somehow not to be so alone." For Smith, reading provides a means of theorizing Black feminist work while building community. She goes on to admit "how much easier both my waking and my sleeping hours would be if there were one book in existence that would tell me something specific about my life. One book based in Black feminist and Black lesbian experience, fiction or nonfiction. Just one work to reflect the reality that I and the Black women whom I love are trying to create. When such a book exists then each of us will not only know better how to live, but how to dream."[4]

Black feminists soon produced many such books. Those in academia began recovering "lost" works by Black women writers; making reading lists, syllabi, and anthologies; and circulating them both in and outside of the classroom. Indeed, the birth of Black women's studies both emerged from and was shaped by this effort to make Black women's work visible and accessible to other Black women—efforts that depended on acts of reading and consuming written texts. As Aisha Peay attests, "the genesis of Black Women's Studies" was located "in a burgeoning black feminist critical community, marked by the publication of journals and collections that were foundational for the field."[5] Anthologies such as Toni Cade Bambara's *The Black Woman: An Anthology*

(1970); Mary Helen Washington's *Black-Eyed Susans* (1975); Cherríe L. Moraga and Gloria E. Anzaldúa's *This Bridge Called My Back: Writings by Radical Women of Color* (1981); Barbara Smith's *Home Girls: A Black Feminist Anthology* (1983); Mari Evans's *Black Women Writers (1950–1980)* (1984); and, of course, *The Norton Anthology of African American Literature* co-edited by Nellie McKay (1996) validated Black women's writing as serious and important work, and legitimized Black women's studies as a valid academic discipline. The recovery and reissuing of monographs, too, such as the Schomburg Library of Nineteenth-Century Black Women Writers editions (1988) made the reading of Black women's writing possible for future generations.

In particular, Gloria T. Hull, Patricia Bell Scott, and Barbara Smith's *All the Women Are White, All the Blacks Are Men, but Some of Us Are Brave* (1982) facilitated this process and possibility. As detailed in chapter 1, this foundational text included political, theoretical, and personal treatises, in addition to providing readers a series of bibliographies and syllabi. These include, for instance, Joan R. Sherman's "Afro-American Women Poets of the Nineteenth Century: A Guide to Research and Bio-Bibliographies of the Poets"; Rita B. Dandridge's "On the Novels Written by Selected Black Women: A Bibliographic Essay"; Frances Foster's "Black Women Writers" spring 1976 course syllabi; as well as similar ones by Gloria Hull, Barbara Smith, and Alice Walker. Such bibliographies and syllabi are important tools of Black feminist intervention, Hull and Smith write in their introduction. "The variety of multidisciplinary bibliographies are meant to encourage integrated work and lively classroom teaching and are a uniquely useful gathering of resources on Black women. The course syllabi (perhaps the most valuable part of the book for many readers) should begin to suggest some possibilities."[6] These possibilities centered the reception of Black women's literature, directing readers to important source materials. As Smith reiterates in "Toward a Black Feminist Criticism," "It is important to remember that the existence of a feminist movement was an essential precondition to the growth of feminist literature, criticism, and women's studies, which focused at the beginning almost entirely upon investigations of literature." Moreover, "a Black feminist approach to literature that embodies the realization that the politics of sex as well as the politics of race and class are crucially interlocking factors in the works of Black women writers is an absolute necessity."[7] *But Some of Us Are Brave* thus positions reading as a necessary act of personal, political, and academic reform.

Its doing so would pave the way for future Black feminist anthologies such as *The Crunk Feminist Collection* (2017), edited by Brittney C. Cooper, Susana M. Morris, and Robin M. Boylorn, which similarly rely on blending oral, textual, and visual literacies and legacies of Black women. "Through our written and spoken words, our activism, our collective work, and our support of one another," they proclaim in their hip hop manifesto, "we will act up, turn it out, set it off, bring wreck, talk back, go off, or get crunk whenever and wherever necessary."[8]

This academic emphasis on reading—much like the activist uses of reading documented by the Combahee River Collective—was very much born out of a personal need to represent, recover, and (re)connect (with) Black women. Though writing and the production of texts that represented Black women were essential to the Black feminist movement, both in and outside of academia, it was the *reading* and circulation of those texts that produced a movement. In this way, the personal fueled the political as well as the academic. Mary Helen Washington remembers that it was reading Zora Neale Hurston's *Their Eyes Were Watching God* (1937), after all, that inspired her to make a career out of reading, anthologizing, and sharing Black women's creative work. Reading Hurston, she writes,

> set me on the task which would engage me, passionately, for the next twenty years. I began to immerse myself in collecting the stories of black women, and I realized that I had not been able to commit myself to my work because in the literature I had been taught and in the world I was expected to negotiate, my face did not exist. I know that I felt an immediate sense of community and continuity and joy in the discovery of these writers as though I had found something of my ancestry, my future, and my own voice.[9]

Washington's testimony here reiterates the fundamental connection between reading and Black feminist politics. As Alice Walker has said of collectively reading women's literature, particularly Black women's writing, "If you're not a feminist already, you become one."[10]

THE CONSUMERISM OF BLACK WOMEN'S READING

In the final decade of the century, the revolutionary power of Black women's reading and reception practices would become marketed, sold, and consumed in unprecedented numbers. The commercial success of Terry McMillan's stories about middle-class Black women which dominated Black women's popular reading in the 1990s was dubbed "the McMillan Phenomenon." Novels such as *Waiting to Exhale* (1992) and *How Stella Got Her Groove Back* (1996) made McMillan a best-selling author and caused publishers to reconsider Black readers, especially women, as a profitable consumer base. McMillan's great appeal—and sales numbers—stemmed from her ability to voice Black women's lives and experiences in US popular culture. "McMillan knew that a black book-buying public and a black readership existed, and that they were hungry to see their own creativity, aspirations, and experiences reflected in literature," Elizabeth McHenry explains.[11] Just like Black women writers before her, McMillan allowed Black women readers to see themselves in literature. As Patricia Hill Collins has written of *Waiting to Exhale* and *How Stella Got Her Groove Back*, these books "can be read as companion pieces that advise Black middle-class women how to emerge."[12] Moreover, McMillan's female characters were readers too. In the opening paragraphs of her narrative, Stella confesses, "I've got about a hundred books I've been meaning to read since last year and I figure now I can probably read them all."[13] Though by no means a new market, Black women readers were seemingly singlehandedly transformed by the McMillan Phenomenon into a demographic that publishers aggressively courted. Movies based on McMillan's work soon followed, making Black women's stories of independence both mainstream and marketable products.

Oprah Winfrey harnessed this energy in the fall of 1996, when she began her now ubiquitous Book Club. Though it appeals to many female readers of various racial identities, it joined—and even incited—a wave of Black book clubs in the final years of the twentieth century. With selections as challenging as Toni Morrison and William Faulkner, the Book Club promotes reading to a wide swath of the American public; it also speaks in unique ways to Black readers, most of whom are women. "One of Oprah's intentions in presenting herself as a reader and conducting a television book club is to augment the public's understanding of African Americans, their culture, and the possibilities open to them," McHenry writes. "Like earlier reading societies, she is intent on creating and spreading positive images of black people."[14] In this way, Winfrey continues the legacy of Black women readers—like Alice Browning—who used reading and the publishing industry to circulate positive images. At the same time, Oprah's Book Club functions much as the Book Circle and Black feminist anthologies did: it brings Black women together, uniting them in a shared literary practice. Moreover, by using her Book Club to promote Black women's writing, Winfrey also continues the legacy of Vivian Harsh, carefully curating texts for the general public, setting the standard for stories, literary tastes, and texts that matter. As Cecilia Konchar Farr has argued, "The Book Club placed Oprah in the role of cultural critic and arbiter of taste," whether critics (and academics) like it or not.[15]

TWENTY-FIRST-CENTURY READING COMMUNITIES

The new century has witnessed the emergence of online book clubs, forums, and other virtual spaces for readers to discuss and review books with one another. Online book clubs specifically for Black women proliferated, starting with the Go On Girl! Book Club, which began offline in 1991 and whose papers are housed in the Vivian G. Harsh Research Collection of Afro-American History and Literature. Such book clubs became even more popular in the second decade of the twenty-first century. These included, in part, Mocha Girls Read (2011), Black Chick Lit (2016), The Sistah Girl Next Door (2016?), and Book Girl Magic (2017). Through Black BookTock, Twitter, online forums, blog posts, Instagram accounts, and even podcasts, these groups continued the work of previous Black women readers and societies by addressing the needs and interests of their reading base while building community through reading. A play on the popular cultural phenomenon and hashtag #BlackGirlMagic, Book Girl Magic (BGM), for instance, began hosting group discussions of books on Facebook Live in addition to posting online reviews on its website. Its creator, Renee, described BGM as "a space created [to] empower women of color while celebrating authors of color in our monthly book club picks. We bond in sisterhood by discussing and sharing ideas about the books we read."[16] In a similar way, the founder of Mocha Girls Read (MGR), Alysia, formed the online book group after growing frustrated that most online book forums she joined had few, if any, women of color. Longing for such a community, Alysia began MGR as "a group of black women who love to read, want to read more and meet like-minded women. The books we read range from fiction, self-help, historical romance, best sellers, good ol' short stories and basically anything we can get our hands on. *Mocha Girls Read* brings black women in the community together to read great literature, online and in person chit chatting about the monthly selection and a whole lot more."[17]

More recently, Glory Edim's *Well-Read Black Girl* (2018) took center stage as *the* resource for Black women readers. What started in 2015 as an Instagram post soon became a wildly popular online (and in-real-life) book club, Twitter account, book (published by Penguin), and even a literary festival. Throughout these various virtual and real spaces, Edim framed reading as a powerful act connecting Black women, past and present. Memories of reading, she writes, "pull Black women toward one another and solidify our unspoken sisterhood. Reading highlights the intersection of narrative and self-image to create compelling explorations of identity. Reading allows us to witness ourselves. Being a reader is an incredible gift, providing me with a lens to interpret the world. Most important, it has invigorated my imagination and allowed me to choose which narratives I want to center and hold close."[18]

In a similar way, digital efforts such as #CiteASista, #CiteBlackWomen, and #SisterPhD have looked to "center and hold close" Black women's scholarly work and reception in academia. Such hashtags and digital spaces promote and circulate the intellectual work of Black women, much as the anthologies of Black feminists did in the late twentieth century. "As a once monthly twitter chat that serves as a space to uplift and center the voices and contributions of Black women in the U.S.A. & abroad," Brittany Williams and Joan Collier launched #CiteASista in 2016 "to give credit and thanks for all of the often used but rarely credited hard work by Black women" as well as to discuss "ways to support and uplift of [sic] Black women in daily life."[19] At the same time, these groups, much like reading groups of previous eras, give Black women a space, as #SisterPhD put it, in which to "facilitate friendships and sisterhood through talking out research, connecting about life experiences, allowing room to vent, and problematize opportunities for growth of self and the group."[20] These forums thus create communities of Black women readers who continue to theorize and validate the lived experiences of Black women in academia.

Notwithstanding the popularity of these online forums, perhaps nothing demonstrated the enduring legacy of Black women's relationship to reading in the second decade of the twenty-first century like the reception of Michelle Obama's *Becoming*. Published in the fall of 2018, the book was buoyed by a sophisticated marketing campaign, including a book tour, a televised interview with Oprah, a segment on Ellen DeGeneres's popular talk show, and even a website that offered a reader's guide as well as apparel and accessories bearing the *Becoming* brand. Highly anticipated by general audiences, the memoir was met with an especially enthusiastic response by Black women readers when it was released. In a feature for *Essence* magazine, Erica Armstrong Dunbar recalled a roundtable held some weeks in advance of the book's release with "a small group of Black women writers, scholars, and legal experts" as well as Obama herself. Dunbar reported that "all of the women at the roundtable felt a deep connection to this memoir." Indeed, she writes, "at its heart, *Becoming* is a celebration of ordinary Black womanhood through an extraordinary story." In this way, "the memoir follows in the tradition of other groundbreaking work that tells the stories of Black women. From Phillis Wheatley's poetry, to Harriet Jacobs's narrative that highlighted the moral bankruptcy of slavery, to more modern memoirs and biographies of women such as Ida B. Wells, Fannie Lou Hamer, and Ella Baker, *Becoming* contributes to a growing field of Black women's history, a history that is still riddled with gaps and holes that need to be filled."[21]

But if *Becoming* helped fill in those gaps and holes by contributing an extraordinary story to Black women's history—of becoming the nation's first lady—then it also did so by honoring Black women's reading practices. In bringing together *Essence*'s group of successful Black women professionals— and *readers*—Obama continued the tradition of reading to unite Black women. She did so with millions of other Black women readers, too, who, like Winfrey, chose *Becoming* as their book club's next selection. Moreover, part of the book's promotion included highlighting Obama's own identity as a Black woman reader. In a feature for the *New York Times*, Obama described at length her reading habits, preferences, and practices, confessing that she had read *Song of Solomon* "three times" and would often read *The Grapes of Wrath* and *Life of Pi* with her daughters, Malia and Sasha, when they were younger, constituting a kind of "Obama family book club," as she described it.[22] It is moving to imagine what Bronzeville's readers—especially the women discussed in this volume—would think about the nation's first lady, herself a native of Chicago, whose grandmother ran a bookstore on the city's South Side. The release of *Becoming* shows us, then, how Black women continue to look to reading as an act that validates the various identities and lived experiences they inhabit—as women, professionals, mothers, and even first lady.

If one is not born a woman but becomes one, then this legacy of Black women's reading and reception practices illustrates how one becomes a reader, too. This process of becoming, as the stories here show, is as rebellious as it is joyous—perhaps more so because the two are so intimately intertwined. The infrastructures of reading that Harsh, Brooks, Walker, Browning, and Morrow fashioned in the middle decades of the twentieth century constructed accessible, relevant reception practices that in turn midwifed future generations of Black feminist thought and practice. From Harsh's community reading, to Brooks's rebellion against respectable reading, to Walker's consumer reading, Browning's wartime reading, and, finally, the Book Circle's middlebrow reading, these women created spaces for collective practices of reflection and imagination. Though debates about respectability at times incited conflict within these reading communities, a consistent thread throughout all of them is their commitment to survival and transformation. Now more than ever—in a hostile climate of book bans, surges in white supremacy and anti-LGBTQ+ legislation, and the obliteration of affirmative action and reproductive justice by the Supreme Court—we need such commitments to reflection and imagination, survival and transformation that Black women's reading and reception practices make possible.

Notes

PREFACE

1 "American Library Association Reports Record Number of Unique Book Titles Challenged in 2023," *ALA News*, March 14, 2024, https://www.ala.org/news/press-releases/2024/03/american-library-association-reports-record-number-unique-book-titles.
2 Recent scholarship on Black memory work includes the scholarship and activism of The Blacktivists, "a collective of trained Black archivists who prioritize Black cultural heritage preservation and memory work." See www.theblacktivists.com; and Ashley D. Farmer et al., "Toward an Archival Reckoning," *American Historical Review* 127, no. 2 (June 2022): 799–829. Also see the special issue, "Black Archival Practice," of *The Black Scholar* 52, no. 2 (2022), ed. Tonia Sutherland and Zakiya Collier.

INTRODUCTION

1 Even after Wright departed Chicago in 1937, his connections to Gayden remained firmly in place. In 1940 he purchased a house for his mother two doors down from the home on Vincennes Avenue where Browning and Gayden published *Negro Story*. This proximity proved fruitful for the pair, who were able to secure the rights to Wright's most famous story, "Almos' a Man," for their first issue of the magazine. Bill V. Mullen, *Popular Fronts: Chicago and African-American Cultural Politics, 1935–46* (Urbana: University of Illinois Press, 1999), 107–8.
2 Richard Wright, *Black Boy*, 60th anniversary ed., restored text (New York: HarperCollins, 2005), 31.
3 Horace Cayton to Richard Wright, April 2, 1945, Horace R. Cayton Papers, box 15, folder 11, Vivian G. Harsh Research Collection of Afro-American History and Literature, Carter G. Woodson Regional Library, Chicago Public Library.
4 Sterling A. Brown, "The Negro Author and His Publisher," *The Negro Quarterly* 1, no. 1 (Spring 1942): 17, 20, originally published in the Johnson C. Smith University *Quarterly Review of Higher Education among Negroes* 9, no. 3 (July 1941): 140–46.
5 St. Clair Drake and Horace R. Cayton, *Black Metropolis: A Study of Negro Life in a Northern City* (1945), rev. and enlarged ed. (Chicago: University of Chicago Press, 1993), 12. Michelle Obama writes that her paternal grandmother, LaVaughn Robinson, was "a sweet, soft-spoken woman and devout Christian," adding that "by day," she "expertly managed a thriving Bible bookstore on the Far South Side." Michelle Obama, *Becoming* (New York: Crown, 2018), 37.

6 Elizabeth Schroeder Schlabach, *Along the Streets of Bronzeville: Black Chicago's Literary Landscape* (Urbana: University of Illinois Press, 2013), 45.
7 Jacqueline Goldsby, "A Salon for the Masses: Black Reading Circles during the Chicago Renaissance," lecture delivered at James Madison University, Department of English, February 29, 2016.
8 Arna Bontemps, "Famous WPA Authors," *Negro Digest* 8, no. 8 (June 1950): 47.
9 Robert Bone and Richard A. Courage, *The Muse in Bronzeville: African American Creative Expression in Chicago, 1932–1950* (New Brunswick: Rutgers University Press, 2011), 8.
10 Mullen, *Popular Fronts*; Darlene Clark Hine and John McCluskey Jr., eds., *The Black Chicago Renaissance* (Urbana: University of Chicago Press, 2012). See also Adam Green, *Selling the Race: Culture, Community, and Black Chicago, 1940–1955* (Chicago: University of Chicago Press, 2007); Robert E. Weems Jr. and Jason P. Chambers, eds., *Building the Black Metropolis: African American Entrepreneurship in Chicago* (Urbana: University of Illinois Press, 2017); and Robert E. Weems Jr., *Black Business in the Black Metropolis: The Chicago Metropolitan Assurance Company, 1925–1985* (Bloomington: Indiana University Press, 1996). Of Christopher Robert Reed's many important histories of Black Chicago, see especially *The Rise of Chicago's Black Metropolis, 1920–1929* (Urbana: University of Illinois Press, 2011). See also two anthologies of Black Chicago literature: Richard R. Guzman, ed., *Black Writing from Chicago: In the World, Not of It?* (Carbondale: Southern Illinois University Press, 2006); and Steven C. Tracy, ed., *Writers of the Black Chicago Renaissance* (Urbana: University of Illinois Press, 2011).
11 Anne Meis Knupfer, *The Chicago Black Renaissance and Women's Activism* (Urbana: University of Illinois Press, 2006), 2. For a rich discussion of how women, both Black and white, reorganized institutions of print on a national scale in this era, see Christine Pawley, *Organizing Women: Home, Work, and the Institutional Infrastructure of Print in Twentieth-Century America* (Amherst: University of Massachusetts Press, 2022).
12 Richard Courage, introduction to *Roots of the Black Chicago Renaissance: New Negro Writers, Artists, and Intellectuals, 1893–1930* (Urbana: University of Illinois Press, 2020), 6. Here Courage is discussing work by Christopher Robert Reed.
13 Stephanie Brown, *The Postwar African American Novel: Protest and Discontent, 1945–1950* (Jackson: University Press of Mississippi), 33.
14 Janice A. Radway, *Reading the Romance: Women, Patriarchy, and Popular Literature* (1984; Chapel Hill: University of North Carolina Press, 1991); Joan Shelley Rubin, *The Making of Middlebrow Culture* (Chapel Hill: University of North Carolina Press, 1992); Janice A. Radway, *A Feeling for Books: The Book-of-the-Month-Club, Literary Taste, and Middle-Class Desire* (Chapel Hill: University of North Carolina Press, 1997); Jaime Harker, *America the Middlebrow: Women's Novels, Progressivism, and Middlebrow Authorship between the Wars* (Amherst: University of Massachusetts Press, 2007); Gordon Hutner, *What America Read: Taste, Class, and the Novel, 1920–1960* (Chapel Hill: University of North Carolina Press, 2009); Kristin L. Matthews, *Reading America: Citizenship, Democracy, and Cold War Literature* (Amherst: University of Massachusetts Press, 2016); Frank Felsenstein and James Connolly, *What Middletown Read: Print Culture in an American Small City* (Amherst: University of Massachusetts Press, 2015).
15 Elizabeth McHenry, *Forgotten Readers: Recovering the Lost History of African American Literary Societies* (Durham, NC: Duke University Press, 2002), 4.
16 For an indispensable study that considers twentieth-century Black readers, see Shawn

Anthony Christian, *The Harlem Renaissance and the Idea of a New Negro Reader* (Amherst: University of Massachusetts Press, 2016).

17 McHenry, *Forgotten Readers*, 3.

18 McHenry, *Forgotten Readers*, 225. For more on the practice of reading white canonical authors, see Katherine West Scheil, *She Hath Been Reading: Women and Shakespeare Clubs in America* (Ithaca, NY: Cornell University Press, 2012), especially chap. 4, "Shakespeare and Black Women's Clubs."

19 McHenry, *Forgotten Readers*, 68, 67; and for more on nineteenth-century literary societies and Black women specifically, see 67–79.

20 Jacqueline Jones Royster, *Traces of a Stream: Literacy and Social Change among African American Women* (Pittsburgh: University of Pittsburgh Press, 2000), 110.

21 P. Gabrielle Foreman, *Activist Sentiments: Reading Black Women in the Nineteenth Century* (Urbana: University of Illinois Press, 2009), 77.

22 Benjamin Fagan, "Harriet Jacobs and the Lessons of Rogue Reading," *Legacy* 33, no. 1 (2016): 20, 21.

23 Darlene Clark Hine, introduction to Hine and McCloskey, *The Black Chicago Renaissance*, xxi, xx, xxi.

24 Olson, *Chicago Renaissance*, 25–26.

25 Hutner, *What America Read*, 4.

26 For more on readers as friends, see Barbara Hochman, *Getting at the Author: Reimagining Books and Reading in the Age of American Realism* (Amherst: University of Massachusetts Press, 2001). For other strategies and practices of Black women readers, see Jacqueline Bobo, *Black Women as Cultural Readers* (New York: Columbia University Press, 1995); Elizabeth Long, *Book Clubs: Women and the Uses of Reading in Everyday Life* (Chicago: University of Chicago Press, 2003); and Elizabeth Long, "The Chat-an-Hour Social and Cultural Club: African American Women Readers," in *A History of the Book in America*, ed. David Paul Nord, Joan Shelley Rubin, and Michael Schudson, vol. 5 (Chapel Hill: University of North Carolina Press, 2009), 459–71.

27 Harker, *America the Middlebrow*, 62.

28 Frances Smith Foster, "Genealogies of Our Concerns, Early (African) American Print Culture, and Transcending Tough Times," *Early American Literature* 45, no. 2 (2010): 347–59; Marcia Chatelain, *South Side Girls: Growing Up in the Great Migration* (Durham, NC: Duke University Press, 2015); Koritha Mitchell, *From Slave Cabins to the White House: Homemade Citizenship in African American Culture* (Urbana: University of Illinois Press, 2020). See also Nazera Sadiq Wright, *Black Girlhood in the Nineteenth Century* (Urbana: University of Illinois Press, 2016); Noliwe M. Rooks, *Ladies' Pages: African American Women's Magazines and the Culture That Made Them* (New Brunswick: Rutgers University Press, 2005); Kim Gallon, *Pleasure in the News: African American Readership and Sexuality in the Black Press* (Urbana: University of Illinois Press, 2020); *Legacy* forums "Where Are the Women in Black Print Culture Studies?," *Legacy* 33, no. 1 (2016), and "Recovery and Democracy," *Legacy* 36, no. 2 (2019); the special issue "African American Print Cultures," *MELUS* 40, no. 3 (Fall 2015), edited by Joycelyn Moody and Howard Rambsy II; Aria S. Halliday, "Centering Black Women in the Black Chicago Renaissance: Katherine Williams-Irvin, Olive Diggs, and 'New Negro Womanhood,'" in *Against a Sharp White Background: Infrastructures of African American Print*, ed. Brigitte Fielder and Jonathan Senchyne (Madison: University of Wisconsin Press, 2019): 240–58.

29 Brigitte Fielder and Jonathan Senchyne, "Introduction: Infrastructures of African American Print," in *Against a Sharp White Background*, 14.
30 Stephanie Y. Evans, *Black Women in the Ivory Tower, 1850–1954: An Intellectual History* (Gainesville: University Press of Florida, 2007); Mia Bay et al., eds., *Toward an Intellectual History of Black Women* (Chapel Hill: University of North Carolina Press, 2015); Brittney C. Cooper, *Beyond Respectability: The Intellectual Thought of Race Women* (Urbana: University of Illinois Press, 2017). See also Shanna Greene Benjamin, *Half in Shadow: The Life and Legacy of Nellie Y. McKay* (Chapel Hill: University of North Carolina Press, 2021); Kristin Waters and Carol B. Conaway, eds., *Black Women's Intellectual Traditions: Speaking Their Minds* (2007; Waltham, MA: Brandeis University Press, 2022); Ann duCille, "The Occult of True Black Womanhood: Critical Demeanor and Black Feminist Studies," in *Female Subjects in Black and White: Race, Psychoanalysis, Feminism*, ed. Elizabeth Abel, Barbara Christian, and Helene Moglen (Berkeley: University of California Press, 1997), 21–56; Daina Ramey Berry and Kali Nicole Gross, eds., *A Black Women's History of the United States* (Boston: Beacon Press, 2020).
31 See "Appendix 1: Some Early African American Women Contributors, Editors, Publishers, and Owners of Periodical Publications," in Royster, *Traces of a Stream*, 289–93.
32 In addition to Knupfer's *Chicago Black Renaissance and Women's Activism*, see Liesl Olson, *Chicago Avant-Garde: Five Women Ahead of Their Time* (Chicago: Newberry Library, 2021).
33 Darlene Clark Hine et al., eds., *Black Women in the Middle West Project: A Comprehensive Resource Guide, Illinois and Indiana* (West Lafayette: Purdue Research Foundation, 1986), http://eblackcu.net/portal/archive/files/black_women_in_middle_west_9739e95526.pdf; Wanda A. Hendricks, *Gender, Race, and Politics in the Midwest: Black Club Women in Illinois* (Bloomington: Indiana University Press, 1998); Terrion L. Williamson, ed., *Black in the Middle: An Anthology of the Black Midwest* (Cleveland: Belt Publishing, 2020).
34 Evans, *Black Women in the Ivory Tower*, 21, 44. The Midwest and South soon outpaced other geographic regions in providing higher education for Black women, with states such as Iowa and Kansas emerging as key locations in the early twentieth century. Evans explains: "Although Pennsylvania had a strong history of women's literary societies and a large free black population, there was not an effective system of higher education for black women. By 1910, only 5 black women had graduated college in Pennsylvania, while 20 had graduated in Kansas and 23 in Texas. African Americans born in Pennsylvania were more likely than those born in any other state to get a college degree; however, they would get a degree in any other state than Pennsylvania" (44).
35 Hendricks, *Gender, Race, and Politics*, xiii, xviii.
36 Audre Lorde, "Poetry Is Not a Luxury," in *The Selected Works of Audre Lorde*, ed. Roxane Gay (New York: Norton, 2020): 3–7; Alice Walker, "In Search of Our Mothers' Gardens," in *In Search of Our Mothers' Gardens: Womanist Prose* (Orlando: Harvest, 1983): 231–43; Combahee River Collective, "A Black Feminist Statement," in *This Bridge Called My Back: Writings by Radical Women of Color*, expanded and rev. 3rd ed., ed. Cherríe L. Moraga and Gloria E. Anzaldúa (Berkeley: Third World Press, 2002): 234–44; Gloria T. Hull, Patricia Bell Scott, and Barbara Smith, ed., *All the Women Are White, All the Blacks Are Men, but Some of Us Are Brave: Black Women's Studies* (New York: Feminist Press, 1982).
37 Courtney Thorsson, *The Sisterhood: How a Network of Black Women Writers Changed American Culture* (New York: Columbia University Press, 2023), 5.
38 Laura Helton et al., "The Question of Recovery: An Introduction," *Social Text* 125 33, no.

4 (December 2015): 3. For an extended treatment of Black memory work and the archive, see Laura E. Helton, *Scattered and Fugitive Things: How Black Collectors Created Archives and Remade History* (New York: Columbia University Press, 2024).
39 Helton et al., "The Question of Recovery," 1.
40 Joycelyn Moody and Howard Rambsy II, "Guest Editors' Introduction: African American Print Cultures," *MELUS* 40, no. 3 (Fall 2015): 3.
41 Jill Lepore, "The Prodigal Daughter: Writing, History, Mourning," *The New Yorker*, July 1, 2013, 34–40.
42 Shanna Greene Benjamin, "Intimacy and Ephemera: In Search of Our Mother's Letters," *MELUS* 40, no. 3 (Fall 2015): 16–27; Laurel Thatcher Ulrich, *A Midwife's Tale: The Life of Martha Ballard, Based on Her Diary, 1785–1812* (New York: Vintage, 1991).
43 Carla L. Peterson, "Family History as Personal Narrative: Writing *Black Gotham*," *Legacy* 32, no. 2 (2015): 194. See also Carla L. Peterson, *Black Gotham: A Family History of African Americans in Nineteenth-Century New York City* (New Haven: Yale University Press, 2011).
44 Joanna Brooks, "Feminism, Theology, and the Personal in American Studies," *Legacy* 32, no. 2 (2015): 174.
45 Toni Morrison, "Unspeakable Things Unspoken: The Afro-American Presence in American Literature," Tanner Lectures on Human Values, delivered at the University of Michigan, October 7, 1988, 136, https://tannerlectures.utah.edu/_documents/a-to-z/m/morrison90.pdf.
46 Green, *Selling the Race*, 214.
47 Thomas Dyja, *The Third Coast: When Chicago Built the American Dream* (New York: Penguin, 2013); Eve L. Ewing, *Ghosts in the Schoolyard: Racism and School Closings on Chicago's South Side* (Chicago: University of Chicago Press, 2018), and *1919, Poems* (Chicago: Haymarket Books, 2019); Eve L. Ewing and Nate Marshall, dir. Sarah Fornace, *No Blue Memories: The Life of Gwendolyn Brooks* (Manual Cinema, 2017); Mariame Kaba and Essence McDowell, *Lifting as They Climbed: Mapping a History of Trailblazing Black Women in Chicago* (Chicago: Haymarket Books, 2023); Nate Marshall, *Wild Hundreds* (Pittsburgh: University of Pittsburgh Press, 2015); Ethan Michaeli, *The Defender: How the Legendary Black Newspaper Changed America* (Boston: Houghton Mifflin Harcourt, 2016); Natalie Moore, *The South Side: A Portrait of Chicago and American Segregation* (New York: St. Martin's Press, 2016); Reed, *The Rise of Chicago's Black Metropolis, 1920–1929*; E. James West, *A House for the Struggle: The Black Press and the Built Environment in Chicago* (Urbana: University of Illinois Press, 2022).

CHAPTER 1

1 Oscar De Priest to Carl Roden, June 5, 1931, Carl Roden Papers, Correspondence Series, box 1931, folder A–J, Special Collections, Chicago Public Library, hereafter Roden Papers, cited by box and folder. Roden answered De Priest's suggestion four days later, writing, "I consider [Harsh] in every respect, both by education and training, the best qualified person in our service for the position referred to." Carl Roden to Oscar De Priest, June 9, 1931, Roden Papers, box 1931, folder A–J. It is unclear whether Harsh knew that De Priest had recommended Shaw. Coincidentally, the Hall Branch Library installed a bust of De Priest in 1952 after his death—a process that Harsh herself oversaw. See "Hall Library to Get Bust of De Priest," *Chicago Daily Tribune*, March 9, 1952, S1.

2 Carl Roden to Andrew J. Kolar, August 7, 1931, 1, 2, Roden Papers, box 1931, folder K–O.
3 Carl Roden to Andrew J. Kolar, October 3, 1931, 1, Carl Roden Papers, box 1931, folder K–O.
4 Carl Roden to Andrew J. Kolar, October 30, 1931, 2, Roden Papers, box 1931, folder K–O.
5 Carl Roden to V. S. Gordon, December 11, 1931, Roden Papers, Correspondence, box 1931, folder A–J.
6 Laura Burt, "Vivian Harsh, Adult Education, and the Library's Role as Community Center," *Libraries & the Cultural Record* 44, no. 2 (2009): 243.
7 See the *Chicago Defender*'s obituary of Harsh: Adolph J. Slaughter, "Historian Who Never Wrote: The Vivian Harsh Story," *Daily Defender*, August 29, 1960, 9.
8 It has been theorized that Harsh's "absence" from the archive was intentional on her part, due perhaps to her characteristic self-effacement; she was known for being a private though not a reclusive person. Or perhaps, as Melanie Chambliss has suggested, Harsh was influenced by a culture of dissemblance that promoted modesty and discouraged self-promotion in African American women to preserve a sense of self in an often violent public sphere. It is also, no doubt, due to the fact that after she died, as Chambliss explains, Harsh's family members discarded her papers, correspondence, and other materials. "Vivian G. Harsh's Life and Legacy with Dr. Melanie Chambliss and Tracy Drake," *Loss/Capture* 2020, https://losscaptureproject.cargo.site/Loss-Capture-In-Conversation-Vivian-G-Harsh-s-Life-and-Legacy-with-Dr.

In some cases, Harsh seems to have been the victim of her own success. Quirks of various cataloging systems enter her under an institutional rather than an individual name. In both the Beinecke and University of Massachusetts special collections, correspondence by Harsh is cataloged under the author "Chicago Public Library," not Harsh herself (even though she signed the letters with her name); instead, she is preserved in the record as "contributor." Here, personal and professional identities merge; or one even eclipses the other, with Harsh becoming a synecdoche for the city's library system. In these situations, depending on the archive and its cataloging system—as well as the search capabilities of its database—locating Harsh can be extremely difficult unless one already knows where and how to look for her.
9 "Miss Vivian Harsh Gets Library Post," *Chicago Defender*, July 11, 1931, 4.
10 Michael Flug, "Harsh, Vivian Gordon," in *Women Building Chicago, 1790–1990: A Biographical Dictionary*, ed. Rima Lunin Schultz and Adele Hast (Bloomington: Indiana University Press), 359.
11 Ron Grossman, "Flashback: A Heroine to History: Vivian Harsh, Chicago's First Black Librarian Preserved Black History, Literature with Massive Collection," *Chicago Tribune*, January 31, 2020.
12 Donald Franklin Joyce, "Vivian G. Harsh Collection of Afro-American History and Literature, Chicago Public Library, *Library Quarterly* 58, no. 1 (January 1988): 68, 67. Joyce notes that "from 1935 through 1967, the various administrations of the Chicago Public Library System did not advocate the development of special research collections. Consequently, few or no special appropriations were made available for purchasing materials for the Special Negro Collection" (68).
13 Janet Peck, "Hall Library Noted for Its Negro Works," *Chicago Daily Tribune*, October 21, 1945, S1.
14 [Vivian G. Harsh], Hall Branch 1934 Annual Report, 4, George Cleveland Hall Branch Archives, box 1, folder 3, Vivian G. Harsh Research Collection of Afro-American History

and Literature, Carter G. Woodson Regional Library, Chicago Public Library, hereafter Hall Branch Archives, cited by box and folder.
15 [Vivian G. Harsh], Hall Branch 1933 Annual Report, 1, Hall Branch Archives, box 1, folder 2.
16 Vivian G. Harsh, "George Cleveland Hall Branch Library and Its Social Environment," 1957, 1–2, Hall Branch Archives, box 3, folder 20.
17 "Making the Most of Idle Moments," *Chicago Defender*, January 25, 1936, 19.
18 "Hall Library, Seven Years Old, Is Known from Wisconsin to Mississippi," *Chicago Defender*, January 28, 1939, 24.
19 Chicago Public Library, *The Negro and His Achievements in America: A List of Books Compiled for the American Negro Exposition*, 1940, 2, Hall Branch Archives, box 3, folder 13.
20 Peck, "Hall Library Noted," S1.
21 [Vivian G. Harsh], Hall Branch 1937 Annual Report, 2, Hall Branch Archives, box 1, folder 6.
22 Joyce, "Vivian G. Harsh Collection," 69. Joyce notes that the four-volume *Dictionary Catalog of the Vivian G. Harsh Collection of Afro-American History and Literature* was finally published in 1978. The definitive guide to Harsh's collection, the *Dictionary* serves as "an author, title, and subject catalog to all materials in the collection . . . [and] also includes specially prepared indexes to many of the manuscripts and book collections" (73).
23 Harsh, "George Cleveland Hall Branch Library and Its Social Environment," 1.
24 Laura E. Helton, "On Decimals, Catalogs, and Racial Imaginaries of Reading," *PMLA* 134, no. 1 (January 2019): 101–5.
25 Helton, "On Decimals," 105.
26 I take cataloging information about the contents of Harsh's collection in this paragraph and the next from *The Dictionary Catalog of the Vivian G. Harsh Collection of Afro-American History and Literature*.
27 Dorothy B. Porter, *A Catalogue of Books in the Moorland Foundation, Compiled by Workers on Projects 271 and 328 of the Works Progress Administration* (Washington, DC: Howard University, 1939), 149.
28 Helton writes: "At 326—'Slavery Serfdom Emancipation'—Porter turned Dewey's ten categories into a hundred. Borrowing some class divisions from the Library of Congress's competing arrangement and inventing other categories herself, she created locations in the taxonomy for 'Psychological aspects of slavery,' 'Mohammadism and slavery,' 'Fugitive slave laws,' 'Colonization debates,' and 'Insurrections.'" Helton, "On Decimals," 105–6.
29 Helton, "On Decimals," 107.
30 [Vivian G. Harsh], Hall Branch 1938 Annual Report, 6, Hall Branch Archives, box 1, folder 7.
31 [Vivian G. Harsh], Hall Branch 1941 Annual Report, 6, Hall Branch Archives, box 1, folder 11.
32 [Vivian G. Harsh], Hall Branch 1942 Annual Report, 6, Hall Branch Archives, box 1, folder 12.
33 "A wing adjoining the Adult Reading Room contains the Special Collection and the Reference Books, with the Lecture Room in a similar wing off the Children's Room." George C. Hall Branch Library 25th Anniversary pamphlet, 1957, Hall Branch Archives, box 5, folder 3.
34 [Harsh], Hall Branch 1938 Annual Report, 5.

35 [Harsh], Hall Branch 1942 Annual Report, 6.
36 Harsh, "George Cleveland Hall Branch and Its Social Environment," 1.
37 Emily Guss, "Cultural Record Keepers: Vivian G. Harsh Collection of Afro-American History and Literature, Carter G. Woodson Regional Library, Chicago Public Library," *Libraries & the Cultural Record* 45, no. 3 (2010): 361.
38 Charlemae Rollins, "Library Work with Negroes," *Illinois Libraries* 25, no. 2 (February 1943): 92–93. Her address was originally delivered in October 1942 in Chicago. A photocopy of the article is in the Hall Branch Archives, box 3, folder 30. The report—which includes lesson plans, short biographies of prominent African Americans, stories appropriate for each age group, and of course reading lists—was published that year. See *Supplementary Units for the Course of Study in Social Studies*, vols. 1–3 (Chicago: Bureau of Curriculum Board of Education, 1942).
39 "Library Exhibit Portrays Role of Negro in U.S.," *Chicago Tribune*, February 15, 1944, 9.
40 [Vivian G. Harsh], Hall Branch 1950 Annual Report, 1, Hall Branch Archives, box 1, folder 20. Other public exhibitions to which Harsh's collection contributed materials included the 1933 Century of Progress World's Fair for the Chicago Women's Club, the 1938 *Defender* Achievement Congress, and the 1940 Negro Exhibition. Harsh proudly notes in her 1938 annual report that "books from the Special Collection, posters were attractively arranged, lists and applications distributed" at the *Defender* Achievement Congress, adding, "Many persons visited the library exhibit." [Harsh], Hall Branch 1938 Annual Report, 2.
41 [Harsh], Hall Branch 1938 Annual Report, 4.
42 Arna Bontemps, "G. C. Hall Library Does Worthy Job of Enlightening Knowledge Seekers," *Chicago Defender*, March 29, 1941, 6. Langston Hughes was a particular favorite of readers. In 1936 Harsh wrote to him: "Your kindness, willingness and approachableness have endeared you with Chicago people, so that a hearty welcome always awaits you here. Women's clubs are asking for your books, high school students are copying your poems in notebooks, and readers, who had probably read nothing by you before have now gone through everything on file here at Hall Branch." Vivian G. Harsh to Langston Hughes, February 27, 1936, Langston Hughes Papers (JWJ MSS 26), box 44, folder 780, Langston Hughes Papers, James Weldon Johnson Collection in the Yale Collection of American Literature, Beinecke Rare Book and Manuscript Library, Yale University.
43 "Librarian Will Discuss Books for Negroes Today," *Chicago Daily Tribune*, February 13, 1953, A8.
44 [Vivian G. Harsh], Hall Branch 1949 Annual Report, 2, Hall Branch Archives, box 1, folder 19.
45 [Vivian G. Harsh], Hall Branch 1948 Annual Report, 1, Hall Branch Archives, box 1, folder 18.
46 "Interest in Race History Increases," *Chicago Defender*, March 2, 1940, 6.
47 "The Negro: A List of Books" [ca. 1930s], Hall Branch Archives, box 3, folder 13. The list is missing key works from the 1940s by Richard Wright and others that frequently appear on other Hall Branch lists; moreover, the latest book published on the list is the 1937–38 edition of *The Negro Year Book*.
48 "The Negro: A List of Books" [ca. 1930s], 1.
49 "The Negro: A List of Books" [ca. 1940s], 4, Hall Branch Archives, box 3, folder 13.
50 Readers' Bureau Chicago Public Library, *The Negro and His Achievements in America: A*

List of Books Compiled for the American Negro Exposition (1940), 2, Hall Branch Archives, box 3, folder 13.
51 "On These We Stand: A Selected List of Readings on the Negro" (ca. 1960), prepared by the staff of the George C. Hall Branch, 2, Hall Branch Archives, box 3, folder 13. It is worth noting that, of the extant bibliographies, the informal mimeographed lists, more likely to be used internally among Hall Branch readers, do not include call numbers; the glossy, more widely distributed brochures, however, do include call numbers—suggesting a certain familiarity or at least comfort on the part of Hall Branch readers with using the Special Collection that other readers did not experience.
52 [Harsh], Hall Branch 1938 Annual Report, 3.
53 "In November 1958, Harsh retired from Hall Branch Library. With her departure, many of the programs that characterized the library as a community institution, such as the Book Review and Lecture Forum, lapsed entirely. In a 1959 Chicago Daily News article, her successor, Ollye Marr Coffin, expressed a desire to further increase the impact of the library upon Bronzeville and resume the Book Review and Lecture Forum. However, she failed to fulfill her promises and, in fact, did just the opposite when she closed the Special Negro Collection to the public and retired it to the library's basement." Traci Parker and Chris Dingwall, "Guide to the Chicago Public Library, George Cleveland Hall Branch Archives, 1930–1975," Mapping the Stacks: A Guide to Black Chicago's Hidden Archives, https://mts.lib.uchicago.edu/collections/findingaids/index.php?eadid=MTS.hallbranch.
54 Slaughter, "Historian Who Never Wrote."
55 Joyce, "Vivian G. Harsh Collection," 69–71.
56 "Chicago Public Library Gets $2M Grant to Preserve Black History," ABC7 Chicago, April 17, 2023, https://abc7chicago.com/chicago-library-public-near-me-mellon-foundation/13144153/. The grant will allow the CPL "to digitize and process documents from the [Harsh] collection, including the records of the Illinois Chapter of the Black Panther Party, the National Alliance of Black Feminists, the papers of communist and civil rights and labor leader Ishmael Flory, the Chicago SNCC History Project, and a selection of Harold Washington's political papers." See Kit Ginzky, "Black Jewel of the Midwest," *South Side Weekly*, July 27, 2023, https://southsideweekly.com/black-jewel-of-the-midwest/.
57 Bontemps similarly wrote: "The George Cleveland Hall Branch Library serves a community covering more than one hundred city blocks. Within this area live more than one hundred thousand people, representing many levels of education and culture and every type of occupation." Bontemps, "G. C. Hall Library Does Worthy Job," 6.
58 Harsh, "George Cleveland Hall Branch Library and Its Social Environment," 1.
59 Harsh, "George Cleveland Hall Branch Library and Its Social Environment," 2. Harsh also notes in her annual reports the number of newspaper articles published, as well as posters produced and window displays created, promoting the Hall Branch Library.
60 Harsh, "George Cleveland Hall Branch Library and Its Social Environment," 3.
61 "Hall Library, Seven Years Old," 24.
62 Meredith Johns, "Library Honors Dr. George C. Hall," *Chicago Defender*, December 5, 1953, 9.
63 Harsh, "George Cleveland Hall Branch Library and Its Social Environment," 2, 3.
64 "Hall Library Forum Begins on Wednesday," *Chicago Daily Tribune*, October 5, 1952, S_A6.
65 Harsh, "George Cleveland Hall Branch Library and Its Social Environment," 2.

66 [Harsh], Hall Branch Annual Report, 1934, 3. Hurston enthusiastically accepted Harsh's invitation, writing to her: "I shall be very glad to meet with your club on the evening of November 7th. It gives me great pleasure to know that you included 'Jonah's Gourd Vine' on your program last year. Thanking you for your interest and kind letter." Zora Neale Hurston to Vivian Harsh, October 23, 1934, Hall Branch Archives, box 4, folder 27.

67 "Hall Library, Seven Years Old," 24.

68 [Vivian G. Harsh], "Report—Special Activities—Hall Branch Library—1937," Hall Branch Archives, box 1, folder 6. NYA stands for the National Youth Administration, a WPA program established in June 1935 to provide work for youths aged sixteen to twenty-four. In 1936, Mary McLeod Bethune was appointed director of the NYA's Division of Negro Affairs. See Jametta Davis, "Providing a New Deal for Young Black Women: Mary McLeod Bethune and the Negro Affairs Division of the NYA," *Rediscovering Black History*, National Archives, March 25, 2014, https://rediscovering-black-history.blogs.archives.gov/2014/03/25/providing-a-new-deal-for-young-black-women/.

69 The term was coined by Goldsby. See, for instance, Jacqueline Goldsby, "A Salon for the Masses: Black Reading Circles during the Chicago Renaissance," lecture delivered at Department of English, James Madison University, February 29, 2016.

70 This number is most certainly an undercount, considering that many other pamphlets and flyers—for Negro History Week and for the Book Review and Lecture Forum—as well as monthly branch bulletins for local teachers, also included reading lists of various sorts.

71 Melanie Chambliss, "A Vital Factor in the Community: Recovering the Life and Legacy of Chicago Public Librarian Vivian G. Harsh," *Journal of African American History* 106, no. 3 (Summer 2021): 419.

72 Vivian G. Harsh to W. E. B. Du Bois, April 28, 1925, 3, W. E. B. Du Bois Papers (MS 312), Special Collections and University Archives, University of Massachusetts Amherst Libraries, http://credo.library.umass.edu/view/full/mums312-b170-i190, hereafter Du Bois Papers, cited by URL.

73 Platt first appears in CPL records as a library assistant in 1887–88 through 1909–10. From there, she served in the Catalogue Division through 1914–15 and then as head assistant of the Reference Division in both 1915–16 and 1916–17. The trail ends here, when annual reports of the CPL board of directors cease listing staff in 1917–18. For the first reference to Platt in CPL records, see *Sixteenth Annual Report of the Board of Directors of the Chicago Public Library, June 1888* (Chicago: Public Library Rooms, City Hall, 1888), 4. To track Platt's subsequent years of employment, see *Seventeenth Annual Report* (1888–1889) through *Forty-Fifth Annual Report* (1916–17).

Most likely, Harsh would have met Platt when she began her own employment in the CPL system during 1909–10. Harsh first appears in CPL records under "Library Assistants and Pages, Central Library" in the *Thirty-Eighth Annual Report of the Board of Directors of the Chicago Public Library, 1909–1910* (Chicago: Chicago Public Library, 1911), 6. CPL annual reports do not begin to list the staff of individual branches until the *Thirty-Ninth Annual Report of the Board of Directors of the Chicago Public Library, 1910–1911* (Chicago: Chicago Public Library, 1912).

74 Louis Shores, "Public Library Service to Negroes: Existing Facilities for Training the Negro Compiled from Questionnaires Sent to Librarians of Over Eighty Cities," *Library Journal* 55 (February 15, 1930): 153. In a letter fragment from the CPL staff to *The Crisis* dated November 11, 1930, likely authored by Harsh herself, the writer references Shore's article by name, noting that "the figures given there in reference to colored assistants in

The Chicago Public Library are probably those of 1928 or 1929." See Chicago Public Library to *The Crisis*, November 11, 1930, Du Bois Papers, https://credo.library.umass.edu/view/full/mums312-b184-i389.

75 Marjorie Kemp, Chicago Public Library Report of February 1930, February 1931, Du Bois Papers, http://credo.library.umass.edu/view/full/mums312-b059-i092.

76 Marjorie Kemp to W. E. B. Du Bois, ca. April 1931, W. E. B. Du Bois Papers, http://credo.library.umass.edu/view/full/mums312-b059-i091. In April and May 1931, Du Bois and assistant librarian N. R. Levin exchanged correspondence regarding Black employment within the CPL system, specifically janitorial and other manual labor positions. On May 28, Levin sent the following information: "Our records show that we have 68 employees classed as Janitor, Janitresses. Window washers and Elevator operators. Of these 14 are colored and 54 are white." See Chicago Public Library to W. E. B. Du Bois, May 28, 1931, W. E. B. Du Bois Papers, http://credo.library.umass.edu/view/full/mums312-b188-i308.

77 Roden to De Priest, June 9, 1931.

78 Chambliss, "A Vital Factor in the Community," 419.

79 See *Forty-Fifth Annual Report of the Board of Directors of the Chicago Public Library, 1916–1917* (Chicago: Chicago Public Library, 1917), 8.

80 Du Bois would go on to reach out to at least one librarian on Harsh's list, Mildred Raymond, and ask her to contribute a photograph and biography to his *Crisis* feature. See W. E. B. Du Bois to Mildred Raymond, May 12, 1925, W. E. B. Du Bois Papers, https://credo.library.umass.edu/view/full/mums312-b171-i005. There is no response from Raymond extant in Du Bois's papers.

81 Additional correspondence between Du Bois and members of the CPL staff offers some clarification on Harsh's list. In the letter fragment from the CPL dated November 11, 1930, cited earlier, the author reports to *The Crisis* that "four colored branch librarians are in full charge of their branch libraries. Most of the colored assistants are located in various branches throughout the city, some few being assigned at Main Library." Though only the first page of the letter is extant, the author indicates that "at present I am librarian at Ogden Park Branch." Chambliss reports that Harsh became head of the Ogden Branch in 1929; she therefore most certainly is the author of this letter to Du Bois. Chicago Public Library to *The Crisis*, November 11, 1930. See also Chambliss, "A Vital Factor in the Community," 421.

82 W. E. B. Du Bois to Vivian G. Harsh, July 14, 1931, W. E. B. Du Bois Papers, https://credo.library.umass.edu/view/full/mums312-b188-i531.

83 See Pauline Young to W. E. B. Du Bois, January 6, 1936, W. E. B. Du Bois Papers, https://credo.library.umass.edu/view/full/mums312-b081-i035. See also Pauline Young to W. E. B. Du Bois, March 2, 1936, W. E. B. Du Bois Papers, https://credo.library.umass.edu/view/full/mums312-b081-i041.

84 W. E. B. Du Bois to Vivian Harsh, February 24, 1936, W. E. B. Du Bois Papers, https://credo.library.umass.edu/view/full/mums312-b077-i299. That same day, Du Bois wrote individually to Porter, Delaney, and Dunlop, requesting information for his *Encyclopedia*. For his correspondence from February 1936 with these three librarians, see W. E. B. Du Bois Papers, https://credo.library.umass.edu/view/collection/mums312.

85 Chicago Public Library to W. E. B. Du Bois, February 27, 1936, W. E. B. Du Bois Papers, https://credo.library.umass.edu/view/full/mums312-b077-i301.

86 Peterson presented a bust of him by Augusta Savage to the 135th Street Branch of the New York Public Library in 1923. See "The Horizon," *The Crisis* 25, no. 5 (March 1923): 225.

87 Fannie Barrier Williams, "The Club Movement among Colored Women of America," in Booker T. Washington, N. B. Wood, and Fannie Barrier Williams, *A New Negro for a New Century* (Chicago: American Publishing House, 1900), 382.

88 Jean Fagan Yellin, "Afro-American Women, 1800–1910: Excerpts from a Working Bibliography," in *All the Women Are White, All the Blacks Are Men, but Some of Us Are Brave: Black Women's Studies*, ed. Gloria T. Hull, Patricia Bell Scott, and Barbara Smith (New York: Feminist Press, 1982), 221, 222.

89 Fahamisha Shariat, "Blakwomen Writers of the U.S.A. Who Are They? What Do They Write?" (1979), in Hull, Scott, and Smith, *But Some of Us Are Brave*, 370, 374, 375.

90 Laura E. Helton, "Making Lists, Keeping Time: Infrastructures of Black Inquiry, 1900–1950," in *Against a Sharp White Background: Infrastructures of African American Print*, ed. Brigitte Fielder and Jonathan Senchyne (Madison: University of Wisconsin Press, 2019), 82.

91 Brittney C. Cooper, *Beyond Respectability: The Intellectual Thought of Race Women* (Urbana: University of Illinois Press, 2017), 26.

92 Harsh's 1925 list, as remarkable as it is, is ultimately still limited in its scope and does not encapsulate the entirety of the history of Black librarians in the CPL. It does not include, for instance, Regina Anderson Andrews, who served as an assistant in the CPL from 1921 to 1923 before becoming the first African American branch librarian in the New York Public Library system. While in Chicago, Andrews "became acquainted with" Harsh, later "cit[ing] Harsh as a mentor." Ethelene Whitmire, *Regina Anderson Andrews: Harlem Renaissance Librarian* (Urbana: University of Illinois Press, 2015), 5. See also the correspondence between Andrews and Du Bois in the W. E. B. Du Bois Papers, https://credo.library.umass.edu/view/collection/mums312.

93 Cooper, *Beyond Respectability*, 26.

94 See W. E. B. Du Bois to Vivian Harsh, February 24, 1936.

95 Chicago Public Library to W. E. B. Du Bois, April 16, 1936, W. E. B. Du Bois Papers, http://credo.library.umass.edu/view/full/mums312-b077-i302. Du Bois wrote to acknowledge his receipt of the bibliography on April 21, also housed in the online repository of his papers: http://credo.library.umass.edu/view/full/mums312-b077-i303.

96 [Harsh], Hall Branch 1933 Annual Report, 4.

97 "George C. Hall Branch of the Chicago Public Library," informational flyer, undated, Hall Branch Archives, box 2, folder 23. To my knowledge, Laura Burt was the first to note Annie Allen at the Hall Branch but does not mention *Annie Allen*. See Burt, "Vivian Harsh, Adult Education," 246.

98 Vivian G. Harsh and Annie L. Allen, "Fiction Leaders: 'The Promise,'" "Book Week," *Sunday Chicago Bee*, November 28, 1943, 24.

99 Burt, "Vivian Harsh, Adult Education," 246.

100 Harsh and Allen, "Fiction Leaders."

101 "Freedom Train Theme of Library Exhibits," *Chicago Defender*, July 3, 1948, 4.

102 Brooks's title is typically interpreted as a homage—ironic or sincere—to two Western classics, *The Iliad* and *The Aeneid*. By way of explaining her title, Brooks recounted in 1969: "Well, the girl's name was Annie, and it was my little pompous pleasure to raise her to a height that she probably did not have, and I thought of the *Iliad* and said I'll call this 'The Anniad.' At first, interestingly enough, I called her Hester Allen, and I wanted then to say 'The Hesteriad,' but I forget why I changed it to Annie." See "An Interview with Gwendolyn Brooks," interview by George Stavros in *Conversations with Gwendolyn*

Brooks, ed. Gloria Wade Gayles (Jackson: University Press of Mississippi, 2003), 46. In his biography of Brooks, George Kent devotes only one line to the name change, writing, "On August 24 [1948] she suggested 'Annie Allen' as a better title, a change enthusiastically accepted by Elizabeth [Lawrence]," Brooks's editor at Harper. George E. Kent, *A Life of Gwendolyn Brooks* (Lexington: University Press of Kentucky, 1990), 78. Certainly, these two meanings of *Annie Allen*—as a classical allusion as well as one that honors the Hall Branch, the heart of Bronzeville's reading culture—may coexist.

CHAPTER 2

1 Brooks is first mentioned as a member of the Lasers in the September 29, 1934, "Lights and Shadows" column. The next month Jones announced that a free Laser pin would go to the member voted most popular. Though Beatrice Abbott cast her vote for Brooks, the young poet did not win; instead, Abbott herself and fellow Laser C. C. Powell De Shong received the most votes. See Dewey R. [Jones], "And Here It Is!," "Lights and Shadows," *Chicago Defender* October 20, 1934, 14; and "Pin Winners," *Chicago Defender*, November 10, 1934, 2. Though the origins of the "Lasers" name is unclear, it is likely from an abbreviation of the column's title: LAS.
2 Ernestine Cofield, "William Henry Huff, Defender's Poet Laureate, Is Dead at 76," *Chicago Daily Defender*, November 19, 1963, 3; Gwendolyn Brooks, "Corner in a Portrait Gallery," "Lights and Shadows," *Chicago Defender*, June 1, 1935, 16, lines 25–26. It is unclear whether Brooks intended the six lyrical tributes under "Corner" to be separate stanzas of one poem or six different lyrics entirely. I have treated "Corner" as the former.
3 Gwendolyn Brooks, "Happiness," "Lights and Shadows," *Chicago Defender*, March 6, 1937, 16, lines 11–12.
4 William Henry Huff, "For Gwendolyn Brooks (Who Thinks There's No Hapiness [sic])," "Lights and Shadows," *Chicago Defender*, April 17, 1937, 17.
5 Brooks, "Happiness."
6 Robert S. Abbott, "Depression No Reason for Lack of Culture, Says Editor Abbott," *Chicago Defender*, April 28, 1934, 12. This article served as the eleventh installment of a series of articles Abbott published throughout 1934 on the importance of culture for the race.
7 Kim Gallon, *Pleasure in the News: African American Readership and Sexuality in the Black Press* (Urbana: University of Illinois Press, 2020), 17, 37, 9.
8 Catherine R. Squires, "Rethinking the Black Public Sphere: An Alternative Vocabulary for Multiple Public Spheres," *Communication Theory* 12, no. 4 (November 2002): 461.
9 Adam Green, *Selling the Race: Culture, Community, and Black Chicago, 1940–1955* (Chicago: University of Chicago Press, 2007), 98. Population data from James R. Grossman, *Land of Hope: Chicago, Black Southerners, and the Great Migration* (Chicago: University of Chicago Press, 1989), 4.
10 Letters to the editor of the *Chicago Defender*, May 1 and September 22, 1917, in Emmett J. Scott, "Letters of the Negro Migrants of 1916–1918," *Journal of Negro History* 4, no. 3 (July 1919): 297, 302.
11 Ethan Michaeli writes: "More than a dozen vendors and subscription agents of the newspaper were harassed and threatened with death throughout the South. . . . In Meridian, Mississippi, a town particularly depleted of its African American population, the chief of police ordered the confiscation of *The Defender*. None of these efforts to censor or ban

the newspaper were at all effective; ... if *The Defender* was simply inserted into a plain brown envelope, it generally arrived at its subscriber's home intact." Ethan Michaeli, *The Defender: How the Legendary Black Newspaper Changed America* (Boston: Houghton Mifflin Harcourt, 2016), 77.

12 "Overstepping the Bounds," *Chicago Defender*, August 4, 1917, 12. The newspaper also regularly complained that its audience did not read enough. One editorial contended that "our people read far too little, although they ought to read the most." See "Defender Suggests Good Reading List," *Chicago Defender*, October 23, 1926, 5. A feature for the newspaper's thirtieth anniversary in 1935 similarly exhorted: "PEOPLE MUST READ MORE.... If there ever was a time when the people must read, that time is NOW." Nahum Daniel Brascher, "Chicago Defender Now Nearing Its 30th Birthday," *Chicago Defender*, April 6, 1935, 9.

13 E. Franklin Frazier, *The Negro Family in Chicago* (Chicago: University of Chicago Press, 1932), 238. Frazier also notes, "But the very intensity of their pride in the small gains which they had made in civilization and sensitiveness concerning their status often kept them from seeing in the struggles of the ignorant masses the same painful steps by which their forefathers had achieved some small measure of culture" (238).

14 Bill V. Mullen, *Popular Fronts: Chicago and African-American Cultural Politics, 1935–1946* (Urbana: University of Illinois Press, 1999), 45.

15 Popular etiquette columns in the *Defender* of this era included "Every-Day Courtesies" by Geraldine Banks (beginning in May 1928 but running more regularly in the early 1930s) and "Advice to the Wise and Otherwise," penned by Princess Mysteria (starting in April 1923 and ending with her death in May 1930).

16 "Still They Come," *Chicago Defender*, February 10, 1917, 8.

17 Ben Baker, "A Few Do and Don'ts," *Chicago Defender*, July 13, 1918, 16. See also "Some 'Don'ts,'" *Chicago Defender*, May 17, 1919, 20; "Don'ts for Newcomers," *Chicago Defender*, July 14, 1923, 14; and "Advice to Migrants," *Chicago Defender*, May 9, 1925, 4.

18 "Book Review: Two Good New Books," *Chicago Defender*, April 2, 1921, 16; Zoe Trodd, "The Black Press and the Black Chicago Renaissance," in *Writers of the Black Chicago Renaissance*, ed. Steven C. Tracy (Urbana: University of Illinois Press, 2011), 450. It is important to note here that even in 1921, it is not just the reading of books but their *purchase* specifically that is linked to a "growing desire" to become respectable. I discuss this growing consumption of Black literature by Black readers in the next chapter. Such linking of reading to social mobility echoes the "upwardly mobile readers" Amy L. Blair describes in *Reading Up: Middle-Class Readers and the Culture of Success in the Early Twentieth-Century United States* (Philadelphia: Temple University Press, 2012), 19. I return to a discussion of Blair's "upwardly mobile readers" in chapter 5 on the Book Circle.

19 "Book Don'ts," *Chicago Defender*, May 18, 1912, 4.

20 Richard A. Courage, "Chicago's Letters Group and the Emergence of the Black Chicago Renaissance," in *Roots of the Black Chicago Renaissance: New Negro Writers, Artists, and Intellectuals, 1893–1930*, ed. Richard A. Courage and Christopher Robert Reed (Urbana: University of Illinois Press, 2020), 229.

21 Langston Hughes, "Here to Yonder," *Chicago Defender*, May 17, 1947, 14.

22 See, for instance, "George C. Hall Library Notes," *Chicago Defender*, March 30, 1935, 7.

23 The history of the *Defender*'s literary reception is complicated by the fact that editors and titles of columns changed frequently. Parsing out the columns' provenance thus proves tricky. According to Courage, "The Bookshelf" first appeared in 1922 under

the direction of A. L. Jackson, disappeared from March 1923 to November 1925, and then remained under Jones's control until July 1934. See Courage, "Chicago's Letters Group and the Emergence of the Black Chicago Renaissance," 227. Running parallel to that column was Gertrude Martin's "Book Reviews: Read More—Learn More," which began in January 1939 and continued until the column seems to have merged with "The Bookshelf" in December 1946. Martin continued "The Bookshelf" until October 1948, when the column suddenly lost its title and remained without one until November 1950, when it regained the "Book Reviews" title. Martin would continue the column until March 1955; Audrey Weaver then assumed the column on June 11, 1955, and carried it through December 22, 1956. After that, the column changed hands several times, perhaps enjoying the most consistency with Ernestine Cofield in the late 1950s and early 1960s.

"Book Chats" first appears on December 31, 1921, under Mary White Ovington, who also regularly wrote reviews for "The Bookshelf" while it was edited by Jones. But the column doesn't show up again until June 15, 1935, under V. Polly Harris (who added the V starting with her second column, which appeared June 22, 1935). Under Harris's direction, "Book Chats" was a mix of brief reviews, literary/book news, including local literary news, as well as literary gossip. Harris's first column, for instance, not only discussed recent books, such as Louis Zara's *Blessed Is the Man* and Louis Bromfield's *The Man Who Had Everything*, but also detailed the marriage plans of Pearl S. Buck.

24 William Kennison, "Boy Tells Why We Should Read Books," *Chicago Defender*, January 19, 1935, 15.
25 Early in its life, the column was also known by a shorter title, "This and That." See the ad "The Mouthpiece of 14 Million People," *Chicago Defender*, January 14, 1922, 16.
26 "This, That and T'Other: A Bit of News, Gossip, Fiction and Fun," *Chicago Defender*, September 17, 1921, 16.
27 On July 14, 1923, the column appears with the "Lights and Shadows" title and is signed FAY (Frank A. Young). The first "Lights and Shadows" column signed by Jones is dated December 1, 1923; he also signed the next two columns, December 8 and 15, possibly filling in for Young. Young resumed control of "Lights and Shadows" on December 22, 1923, and continued until September 6, 1924, when Jones announced his editorship. Early iterations of "Lights and Shadows" may have included another *Defender* column, "Have a Smile, Give a Smile." See Delaney Hall, "Lights and Shadows: Dewey Roscoe Jones and the *Chicago Defender*'s Poetic Legacy," *Poetry Foundation*, February 15, 2012, https://www.poetryfoundation.org/articles/69775/lights-and-shadows.
28 Tree Top Tall, "Introducing Me," "Lights and Shadows," *Chicago Defender*, April 9, 1927, A2.
29 Hall, "Lights and Shadows."
30 Miss Independence, "Watch Out, Langston, the 'Lasers' Are after You," letter to Dewey R. [Jones], "Lights and Shadows," *Chicago Defender*, March 6, 1926, A10.
31 Dewey R. [Jones], "Lights and Shadows," *Chicago Defender*, April 21, 1928, A2.
32 Dewey R. [Jones], "Defender Column Contributors Win High Honors," *Chicago Defender*, July 30, 1927, 9.
33 Robert Crawford, "Thank You, Sir," letter to the editor, *Chicago Defender*, October 10, 1925, A12.
34 John T. Hinton, "In the Mail Bag," letter to Dewey R, "Lights and Shadows," *Chicago Defender*, March 30, 1935, 14.
35 Lonnie Richard Garner, letter to the editor, *Chicago Defender*, August 4, 1962, 4.

36 Dewey R. [Jones], "Time's Up: An Open Letter to My Contributors," "Lights and Shadows," *Chicago Defender*, July 24, 1926, A2.
37 Dewey R. [Jones], "Lights and Shadows," *Chicago Defender*, September 6, 1924, 12.
38 S. I. Hayakawa, "Second Thoughts," *Chicago Defender*, August 28, 1943, 15. De Vries served as editor of *Poetry* from 1938 to 1944. Of Japanese descent, Hayakawa was one of the few non–African American columnists for the *Defender*. See Katherine Bishop, "S. I. Hayakawa Dies at 85, Scholar and Former Senator," *New York Times*, February 28, 1992, B6.
39 Wanda A. Hendricks, *Gender, Race, and Politics in the Midwest: Black Club Women in Illinois* (Bloomington: Indiana University Press, 1998), xi.
40 Anne Meis Knupfer, *Toward a Tenderer Humanity and a Nobler Womanhood: African American Women's Clubs in Turn-of-the-Century Chicago* (New York: New York University Press, 1996), 36.
41 Hendricks, *Gender, Race, and Politics in the Midwest*, 38.
42 Fannie Barrier Williams, "The Club Movement among Colored Women of America," in Booker T. Washington, N. B. Wood, and Fannie Barrier Williams, *A New Negro for a New Century* (Chicago: American Publishing House, 1900), 424, 426.
43 St. Clair Drake and Horace Cayton, *Black Metropolis: A Study of Negro Life in a Northern City*, rev. and enlarged ed. (Chicago: University of Chicago Press, 1993), 394–95.
44 Marcia Chatelain, *South Side Girls: Growing Up in the Great Migration* (Durham, NC: Duke University Press, 2015), 4, 10, 143.
45 Aria S. Halliday, "Centering Black Women in the Black Chicago Renaissance: Katherine Williams-Irvin, Olive Diggs, and 'New Negro Womanhood,'" in *Against a Sharp White Background: Infrastructures of African American Print*, ed. Brigitte Fielder and Jonathan Senchyne (Madison: University of Wisconsin Press, 2019), 254.
46 Women began appearing regularly in "Lights and Shadows" after Jones took over in 1924. He explicitly called on them to participate in his first column. "We need assistance," he admitted, encouraging readers to send in their verse. "And that applies to the 19th amendment causes also." Dewey R. [Jones], "Lights and Shadows," *Chicago Defender*, September 6, 1924, 12. Black women did not appear regularly in the column before that time because Frank A. Young wrote most of the columns himself when he was editor.
47 Holt wrote music columns for the *Defender* throughout the late teens and early twenties, and then published *Music and Poetry* from 1921 to 1922. Having sought advice from Harriet Monroe of *Poetry* magazine, Holt later wrote that "her business system was most complete for special magazine work and she permitted me to completely copy it." Nora Douglas Holt, "News of the Music World: Poetry's Birthday Party," *Chicago Defender*, September 30, 1922, 5.
48 Blanche Watson, "A Document of a Woman's Heart," "The Bookshelf," review of *An Autumn Love Cycle* by Georgia Douglas Johnson, *Chicago Defender*, March 16, 1929, A1. For the newspaper's twenty-fifth anniversary, Georgia Douglas Johnson wrote a letter to the editor congratulating Abbott "upon the anniversary number of the World's Greatest Weekly" and noting, "The poem, 'Easter Rain,' by Mr. Huff reads very nicely indeed." See "Defender Swamped by Congratulations: Messages Pouring in from America and Europe," letter to the editor, *Chicago Defender*, May 10, 1930, 3.
49 Dewey R. Jones, "The Bookshelf," review of *God Sends Sunday* by Arna Bontemps, *Chicago Defender*, August 8, 1931, 15.
50 Georgia Douglas Johnson, "A Song of Courage," "Lights and Shadows," *Chicago Defender*, January 22, 1927, A2; and "Hope," "Lights and Shadows," *Chicago Defender*, July 28, 1928,

A2. Johnson was so popular and well respected that she was solicited for contributions to "Lights and Shadows." In January 1924, for instance, Frank Young advertised, "This column is run by FAY, who will be glad to receive any first class squibs of witty nature or poetry of merit. Georgia Douglas Johnson and others please take notice." FAY [Frank A. Young], "Lights and Shadows," *Chicago Defender*, January 26, 1924, 12.

51 The *Defender* carried "Homely Philosophy" through April 1935.
52 Georgia Douglas Johnson, "Homely Philosophy: Good Books," *Chicago Defender*, February 9, 1929, A2.
53 Beatrice Abbott has no apparent relation to Robert Abbott.
54 See Beatrice Abbott, "Hymn of Humility," "Lights and Shadows," *Chicago Defender*, April 25, 1936, 16; "Belles Lettres," "Lights and Shadows," *Chicago Defender*, August 8, 1936, 16; and "Good Neighbor," "Lights and Shadows," *Chicago Defender*, December 12, 1936, 16.
55 Beatrice Abbott, "Contrast," "Lights and Shadows," *Chicago Defender*, December 26, 1936, 16.
56 George E. Kent, *A Life of Gwendolyn Brooks* (Lexington: University Press of Kentucky, 1990), 4.
57 Gwendolyn Brooks, "Interview," in *Conversations with Gwendolyn Brooks*, ed. Gloria Wade Gayles (Jackson: University Press of Mississippi, 2003), 111–12.
58 Quoted in Kent, *A Life of Gwendolyn Brooks*, 28. Though ambitious, this "revised" list is a simplified version compared to the twelve resolutions she originally set for 1934, which included drawing, singing, playing the piano, and composing original music (27–28).
59 Gwendolyn Brooks, "Wealth," "Lights and Shadows," *Chicago Defender*, May 4, 1935, 8, line 16.
60 Gwendolyn Brooks, "Selfish," "Lights and Shadows," *Chicago Defender*, October 30, 1937, 16; and "Life Is Too Short," "Lights and Shadows," *Chicago Defender*, December 29, 1934, 12, line 3.
61 Brooks, "Life Is Too Short," lines 5–8.
62 Gwendolyn Brooks, "Count No Day Lost," "Lights and Shadows," *Chicago Defender*, August 7, 1937, 16, lines 13–16.
63 Gwendolyn Brooks, "Genius," "Lights and Shadows," *Chicago Defender*, November 9, 1935, 16, lines 7–8 and 14.
64 Gwendolyn Brooks, "Shadows," "Lights and Shadows," *Chicago Defender*, May 11, 1935, 16, lines 17–20.
65 Gwendolyn Brooks, "A Song of Thanksgiving," "Lights and Shadows," *Chicago Defender*, December 1, 1934, 14, lines 17–20.
66 Gwendolyn Brooks, "A Christmas Story," "Lights and Shadows," *Chicago Defender*, December 22, 1934, 14, lines 7 and 11.
67 Gwendolyn Brooks, "One Little Quarrel," "Lights and Shadows," *Chicago Defender*, September 8, 1934, 14, lines 1, 3, 7.
68 "Some 'Don'ts,'" 20.
69 Gwendolyn Brooks, "Friend," "Lights and Shadows," *Chicago Defender*, July 3, 1937, 16, lines 11–12. See also Brooks, "Corner in a Portrait Gallery," "Lights and Shadows," *Chicago Defender*, June 1, 1935, 16; "Sonnets for Beatrice," "Lights and Shadows," *Chicago Defender*, January 4, 1936, 16; "For Semuel H. Randolph (Ima Twin)," "Lights and Shadows," *Chicago Defender*, September 26, 1936, 16; and "Two Songs for Friends," "Lights and Shadows," *Chicago Defender*, October 31, 1936, 18, which celebrates intimate friendships with Lavinia Brascher and Lucille Harris. "Corner in a Portrait Gallery," meanwhile, lauds six Laser friends: Jones, Abbott, C. Powell De Shong, Huff, Walter Stanton Fort, and King Jefferson.

70 Ima Twin, "Remember When They Said," "Lights and Shadows," *Chicago Defender*, June 6, 1936, 16, lines 55–56.
71 Beatrice Abbott, "For Gwendolyn Brooks (Appreciation)," "Lights and Shadows," *Chicago Defender*, March 16, 1935, 14, lines 1–2 and 5–6. The other poem Abbott dedicates to Brooks is "Onus Probandi (For Gwendolyn Brooks)," "Lights and Shadows," *Chicago Defender*, December 11, 1937, 16.
72 Gwendolyn Brooks, "To My Parents," "Lights and Shadows," *Chicago Defender*, May 18, 1935, 16, lines 2, 13, 19, 7–12, and 29–30.
73 Frazier, *The Negro Family in Chicago*, 74, 75, 147.
74 Green, *Selling the Race*, 151, 150.
75 Chatelain, *South Side Girls*, 39. For more on bias in Frazier's study, see Chatelain, *South Side Girls*, chap. 4.
76 Chatelain, *South Side Girls*, 4.
77 Janice A. Radway, *Reading the Romance: Women, Patriarchy, and Popular Literature* (Chapel Hill: University of North Carolina Press, 1991), 23.
78 Dale M. Bauer, *Nineteenth-Century American Women's Serial Novels* (Cambridge: Cambridge University Press, 2020), 1, 2.
79 Green, *Selling the Race*, 44, 45.
80 Brittney C. Cooper, *Beyond Respectability: The Intellectual Thought of Race Women* (Urbana: University of Illinois Press, 2017), 22, 3.
81 William Henry Huff, "The Ultra-Modern Wife," "Lights and Shadows," *Chicago Defender*, July 30, 1932, 14, lines 9–16.
82 William Henry Huff, "Womanhood Then and Now," "Lights and Shadows," *Chicago Defender*, June 12, 1937, 16, lines 1–5.
83 See William Henry Huff, "A Stitch In Time," "Lights and Shadows," *Chicago Defender*, March 7, 1936, 16; "O Mother Dear," "Lights and Shadows," *Chicago Defender*, May 9, 1936, 16; "Girls Should Neither Smoke Nor Drink!," "Lights and Shadows," *Chicago Defender*, October 24, 1935, 16; and "The Girl Who Answered No," "Lights and Shadows," *Chicago Defender*, July 13, 1935, 16.
84 In 2008 Moya Bailey coined the term "misogynoir" to describe "the uniquely co-constitutive racialized and sexist violence that befalls Black women as a result of their simultaneous and interlocking oppression at the intersection of racial and gender marginalization." See Moya Bailey, *Misogynoir Transformed: Black Women's Digital Resistance* (New York: New York University Press, 2021), 1.
85 Orient, "Handling a Woman Electrically," "Lights and Shadows," *Chicago Defender*, November 22, 1924, A14, lines 1–3.
86 Dan Burley, "Lights and Shadows," *Chicago Defender*, August 14, 1937, 16.
87 "Lights and Shadows," *Chicago Defender*, November 16, 1935, 16.
88 Kent, *A Life of Gwendolyn Brooks*, 41.
89 "Gwendolyn Brooks," interview by Roy Newquist, in Gayles, *Conversations with Gwendolyn Brooks*, 27.
90 Brooks, "To My Parents," lines 25–28.
91 I have been unable to track down extant responses to Brooks's poem to gauge how provocative this conflation of the Black family with "infirmity" and "debility" would have been to *Defender* readers. Regardless, the stark contrast between what would have been expected of Brooks as a Black female poet at this time and what she actually provided

readers suggests a much more radical approach to popular poetry in the Black press. Certainly Huff thought so.

92 Gwendolyn Brooks, "Music Is Not Music," "Lights and Shadows," *Chicago Defender*, February 9, 1935, 14, lines 1–4.
93 Gwendolyn Brooks, "Knowledge," "Lights and Shadows," *Chicago Defender*, January 5, 1935, 12, lines 9–12.
94 Kent, *A Life of Gwendolyn Brooks*, 30.
95 Gwendolyn Brooks, "Plaint," "Lights and Shadows," *Chicago Defender*, March 13, 1937, 18, lines 5–8.
96 Gwendolyn Brooks, "Gift," "Lights and Shadows," *Chicago Defender*, February 23, 1935, 14, lines 13–14.
97 Gwendolyn Brooks, "I Loved You Best," "Lights and Shadows," *Chicago Defender*, April 27, 1935, 14, lines 11–12.
98 Gwendolyn Brooks, "After Christmas," "Lights and Shadows," *Chicago Defender*, May 25, 1935, 16, lines 5–8.
99 Gwendolyn Brooks, "How Can I Keep My Mind Away," "Lights and Shadows," *Chicago Defender*, July 6, 1935, 16, lines 5–7.
100 Gwendolyn Brooks, "I Thank You for Your Kindness," "Lights and Shadows," *Chicago Defender*, April 9, 1938, 16, lines 6–10.
101 Gwendolyn Brooks, "The Smallest Things," "Lights and Shadows," *Chicago Defender*, May 2, 1936, 16, lines 13–14.
102 Gwendolyn Brooks, "You Say I Am in Love," "Lights and Shadows," *Chicago Defender*, December 12, 1936, 16, lines 1–2.
103 Gwendolyn Brooks, "Star Love," "Lights and Shadows," *Chicago Defender*, December 4, 1937, 16, lines 5–8.
104 Gwendolyn Brooks, "Bubbles," "Lights and Shadows," *Chicago Defender*, February 26, 1938, 16, line 16.
105 Gwendolyn Brooks, "Prayer," "Lights and Shadows," *Chicago Defender*, April 24, 1937, 17, lines 9–12.
106 Gwendolyn Brooks, "You Need Not Bring Me Roses," "Lights and Shadows," *Chicago Defender*, September 11, 1937, 16, lines 9–12.
107 Gwendolyn Brooks, "The Bright Star," "Lights and Shadows," *Chicago Defender*, September 21, 1935, 16, lines 12 and 14.
108 Gwendolyn Brooks, "Solace," "Lights and Shadows," *Chicago Defender*, December 11, 1937, 16, lines 6–7.
109 Gwendolyn Brooks, "Possession," "Lights and Shadows," *Chicago Defender*, September 1, 1935, 16, lines 6, 10–11.
110 Gwendolyn Brooks, "Sonnet," "Lights and Shadows," *Chicago Defender*, August 24, 1935, 16, lines 13–14.
111 Gwendolyn Brooks, "Kismet," "Lights and Shadows," *Chicago Defender*, December 7, 1935, 16, lines 7–8.
112 Gwendolyn Brooks, "Jingling Judy's Journal," "Lights and Shadows," *Chicago Defender*, January 18, 1936, 14.
113 Gwendolyn Brooks, "Never Enough," "Lights and Shadows," *Chicago Defender*, September 22, 1934, 14, lines 1, 13–16.
114 Gwendolyn Brooks, "Postscript to Suffering," "Lights and Shadows," *Chicago Defender*,

March 23, 1935, 14, lines 5–8; Gwendolyn Brooks, "Destiny," "Lights and Shadows," *Chicago Defender*, January 26, 1935, 14, lines 9–10, 25–28.

115 Chatelain, *South Side Girls*, 18.
116 One exception is Abbott's 1936 poem "Frustration," in which the speaker deals with infertility, lamenting the fact that

> Across the way, the Smiths have four—
> But none comes ever to my door.
> Yet—I could care for them so well,
> Too bad department stores don't sell
> Roly Poly Babies!"

Beatrice Abbott, "Frustration," "Lights and Shadows," *Chicago Defender*, November 7, 1936, 20, lines 1–5.

117 Beatrice Abbott, "Crocodile Tears," "Lights and Shadows," *Chicago Defender*, September 1, 1934, 14, lines 1–2, 9–16.
118 Gwendolyn Brooks, "Myself," "Lights and Shadows," *Chicago Defender*, March 19, 1938, 16.
119 Gwendolyn Brooks, "An Old Apartment Building," "Lights and Shadows," *Chicago Defender*, August 20, 1938, 16, lines 1–2, 5–13, 48.
120 Gwendolyn Brooks, "A Song in the Front Yard," in *Blacks* (Chicago: Third World Press, 1987), 28, lines 1–4. Originally published in Gwendolyn Brooks, *A Street in Bronzeville* (New York: Harper & Brothers, 1945), 10.
121 "*Black Books Bulletin* Interviews Gwen Brooks," interview by Haki Madhubuti, in Gayles, *Conversations with Gwendolyn Brooks*, 74.
122 "Gwendolyn Brooks," interview by Roy Newquist, 27.
123 "*Black Books Bulletin* Interviews Gwen Brooks," 74–76.
124 Brooks quoted in Don L. Lee, "Gwendolyn Brooks: Beyond the Wordmaker—The Making of an African Poet," preface to Gwendolyn Brooks, *Report from Part One* (Detroit: Broadside Press, 1973), 14.
125 "My People Are Black People," interview by Ida Lewis, in Gayles, *Conversations with Gwendolyn Brooks*, 61.
126 Brooks, "My People Are Black People," 56.
127 "Honored," *Sunday Chicago Bee*, [September? December?] 23, 1945, 15. In the only extant copy—hard copy or digital—of this issue that I have been able to find, the month is illegible. Since the date clearly reads the twenty-third, and there were only two Sundays after the book's publication in 1945 that fell on the twenty-third day of the month, one in September and another in December, this notice about Brooks must have appeared in one of those two months.

CHAPTER 3

1 Maryemma Graham, *The House Where My Soul Lives: The Life of Margaret Walker* (New York: Oxford University Press, 2022), 164.
2 Margaret Walker, "For My People," in *For My People* (New Haven: Yale University Press, 1942), 13 and 14, lines 3 and 9.
3 Margaret Walker, Journal 17, February 6, 1940, 48, Margaret Walker Alexander Personal Papers [AF012] Series 2: Journal and Diary Material, Margaret Walker Center, Jackson State University, Margaret Walker Center Digital Archives Project, https://margaretwalker.jsums.edu/digital/collection/uy/id/2608/rec/16. Courtesy the Margaret Walker Center.

4 Stephen Vincent Benét, foreword to Walker, *For My People*, 5.
5 For notice of the book's second printing, see "Book Notes," *New York Herald Tribune*, March 17, 1943, 23. For announcement of its third printing, see the advertisement for Yale University Press, *New York Herald Tribune*, May 6, 1943, F19.
6 "Margaret Walker," Poetry Foundation website, http://www.poetryfoundation.org/bio/margaret-walker.
7 George Bradley, introduction to *The Yale Younger Poets Anthology*, ed. George Bradley (New Haven: Yale University Press, 1998), xlviii, l. The sixth printing with Yale University Press was published in 1968.
8 Kate Orazem, "The Rhyme and Reason behind the Yale Series of Younger Poets," *Yale Herald*, November 12, 2010, http://yaleherald.com/homepage-lead-image/cover-stories/the-rhyme-and-reason-behind-the-yale-series-of-younger-poets/ (no longer available); Bradley, introduction, xlviii. For comparison, "Michael Casey's *Obscenities* (1971) sold 117,500 copies," Orazem writes, exceeding "the number of any of the series' previous bestsellers."
9 "*Native Son* was the first novel by an African American to be selected as a book-of-the-month. It sold 200,000 copies in under three weeks and was number one on the *New York Times* bestseller list for several weeks. A significant number of its sales were attributable to its designation as a main selection. Book-of-the-Month Club members numbered over 500,000 in 1940, nearly half of whom regularly bought the book-of-the-month." Mark Madigan, "Book-of-the-Month Club," in *The Richard Wright Encyclopedia*, ed. Jerry W. Ward Jr. and Robert J. Butler (Westport, CT: Greenwood Press, 2008), 53. Gene Jarrett reports that within three years of publication, Yerby's novel *The Foxes of Harrow* (1946) "had sold over two million copies." Gene Jarrett, *Deans and Truants: Race and Realism in African American Literature* (Philadelphia: University of Pennsylvania Press, 2007), 162.
10 David Streitfeld, "A Writer for Her People: Margaret Walker Found These Truths to Be Self-Evident," *Washington Post*, December 2, 1998, D01.
11 George E. Kent, *A Life of Gwendolyn Brooks* (Lexington: University Press of Kentucky, 1990), 167.
12 Bradley, introduction, xlvi, xlviii. *Publishers' Weekly* reported in the spring of 1944 that *Theory of Flight* had reached "3 printings, totalling almost 2,000 copies." See "Yale Younger Poet Series Reaches Forty-Second Volume," *Publishers' Weekly*, April 15, 1944, 1524.
13 Davarian L. Baldwin, *Chicago's New Negroes: Modernity, the Great Migration, and Black Urban Life* (Chapel Hill: University of North Carolina Press, 2007), 52.
14 William Scott, "Belonging to History: Margaret Walker's For My People," *MLN* 121, no. 5 (December 2006): 1084.
15 Benét, foreword, 5–6.
16 Margaret Walker, "We Have Been Believers," in *For My People*, 17, line 8.
17 Walker, "Delta," in *For My People*, 21–23, lines 31–32, 52–53, 93–94.
18 Margaret Walker, "The Struggle Staggers Us," in *For My People*, 58, lines 9–14.
19 Margaret Walker, "Our Need," in *For My People*, 57, lines 9–14.
20 Margaret Walker, "People of Unrest," in *For My People*, 27, lines 1, 6–7.
21 Margaret Walker, "For My People," in *For My People*, 13 and 14, lines 1 and 10.
22 Margaret Walker, "Since 1619," in *For My People*, 26, lines 15–16.
23 Margaret Walker, "Lineage," in *For My People*, 25, lines 1 and 7.
24 Margaret Walker, "Today," in *For My People*, 28, line 4.
25 Margaret Walker, "Dark Blood," in *For My People*, 15, lines 1 and 3.

26 Walker, "Delta," 20, lines 8–10.
27 Margaret Walker, "Sorrow Home," in *For My People*, 19, line 5.
28 Margaret Walker, "Southern Song," in *For My People*, 18, lines 1 and 4.
29 Graham, *The House Where My Soul Lives*, 241.
30 Mary E. Burton, "A Promising Negro Poet," review of *For My People* by Margaret Walker, *Louisville Courier-Journal*, August 20, 1944, sec. 3, 10.
31 Pearl Strachan, "The World of Poetry," review of *For My People* by Margaret Walker and other books, *Christian Science Monitor*, November 14, 1942, WM10.
32 MAS, "New Poetry Selections," review of *For My People* by Margaret Walker and other books, *Hartford Courant*, December 20, 1942, SM14.
33 B. T. A., "'My People' in Verse and a Novel," review of *For My People* by Margaret Walker and *River Bottom Boy* by Harold Matthews, *Louisville Courier-Journal*, December 6, 1942, sec. 3, 8.
34 Graham, *The House Where My Soul Lives*, 164.
35 Nelson Algren, "A Social Poet," review of *For My People* by Margaret Walker, *Poetry* 61, no. 5 (February 1943): 634–36.
36 "A Guide to the Outstanding Fall Books: Selected by the Reviewers and Editors of BOOKS from Titles Published since August 1," *New York Herald Tribune*, December 6, 1942, G8.
37 Arna Bontemps, "Let My People Grow!," review of *For My People* by Margaret Walker, *New York Herald Tribune*, January 3, 1943, G3.
38 Frank Marshall Davis, "'For My People' Termed Best Poetry," review of *For My People* by Margaret Walker, *Atlanta Daily World*, November 29, 1942, 4.
39 Countee Cullen, review of *For My People* by Margaret Walker, *Philadelphia Tribune*, December 12, 1942, 16.
40 Laura J. Miller, *Reluctant Capitalists: Bookselling and the Culture of Consumption* (Chicago: University of Chicago Press, 2006), 30. Miller notes that there also existed "60,000 magazine outlets that carried some books" (30). Nevertheless, "industry leaders disdained newsstands, drugstores and variety stores, and even methods of distribution such as subscription publishing and direct mail," because such "distribution channels were perceived as doing little to further genteel culture." They were, in other words, "the outlets geared toward the growing mass of working-class readers" (34). This bookselling landscape would soon change. Kristin L. Matthews writes that in the postwar era, "an increase in good-quality, lower-priced hardbacks and better-quality paperbacks forced traditional booksellers to reorganize and systematize their shelves to make their stores more friendly to readers and browsers." This in turn shifted the function of bookstores themselves as well as reading habits writ large in the country: "No longer solely the domain of elite urban intellectuals, bookstores increasingly catered to the middle and lower classes, signaling a class revolution unlike any since the rise of the novel in the eighteenth century." Kristin L. Matthews, *Reading America: Citizenship, Democracy, and Cold War Literature* (Amherst: University of Massachusetts Press, 2016), 27.
41 Albon L. Hosley, "The Negro in Business," in *Negro Year Book: A Review of Events Affecting Negro Life, 1941–1946*, ed. Jessie Parkhurst Guzman (Tuskegee: Department of Records and Research, Tuskegee Institute, 1947), 184.
42 Robert Kiphuth, *How to Be Fit*, new rev. ed. (New Haven: Yale University Press, 1942), http://yalepress.yale.edu/book.asp?isbn=9780300105438.
43 "Tips from the Publisher," *Publishers' Weekly*, November 14, 1942, 2052. Yale University

Press also created a full window display for the book at the Yale Co-op, which included "cut-out and blown up figures from the book, photographs, copies of Yale's N. Y. Times ad and the store's postcard." "Shop Talk," photo of *How to Be Fit* display, *Publishers' Weekly*, November 28, 1942, 2199.

44 "Books from Yale for Fall," *Publishers' Weekly*, September 26, 1942, unpaginated. The other four books that Yale featured that fall were David J. Dallin's *Soviet Russia's Foreign Policy, 1939–1941*; A. G. Keller's *Net Impressions*; George A. Baitsell's *Science in Progress*; and *The Yale Review Anthology*, edited by Wilbur Cross.

45 Ad for *For My People*, *New York Times Book Review*, October 25, 1942, 36. The following spring Yale would run a similar ad with a more flattering blurb: "'If the Pulitzer judges had seen fit to reward a young Negro poet, Margaret Walker, for her surging rhythms in FOR MY PEOPLE, it would have been a happy choice.'—John Chamberlain in the *New York Times*." Yale University Press ad, *New York Times Book Review*, May 30, 1943, 17.

46 Stores were asked to report "their sales of the first six titles in fiction and non-fiction.... Only titles reported three or more times are charted." The survey's focus on fiction and nonfiction did not exclude poetry, however, which did occasionally appear among selections, such as Louis Untermeyer's *Treasury of Great Poems*, which was featured as a runner-up. See "What America Is Reading," *New York Herald Tribune Books*, January 10, 1943, sec. 8, 19.

47 And yet Wright's book still did not appear on the *Publishers' Weekly* or *New York Times* bestseller lists. "Not until 1946, with the career of Frank Yerby, did a black writer grace such a list," Augusta Rohrbach writes. "Aside from Frank Yerby, African American writers such as Richard Wright in 1945 and Alex Haley in 1976, only appeared on the non-fiction list. Despite the publishing phenomenon we know as the Harlem Renaissance, none of the works that appeared during that time are listed as bestsellers on the *Publishers' Weekly* list." Augusta Rohrbach, *Truth Stranger Than Fiction: Race, Realism, and the U.S. Literary Marketplace* (New York: Palgrave Macmillan, 2002), 117.

48 Cities typically featured included Chicago, Milwaukee, Peoria, Indianapolis, and several of the Quad Cities of Iowa and Illinois (Davenport, Moline, and Rock Island).

49 For instance, Kroch's Christmas feature ad for 1942 did not include *For My People*. See "Memo for Christmas! Give the Worthy Books from Kroch's This Christmas," advertisement for Kroch's bookstore, *Chicago Sunday Tribune*, December 20, 1942, 19.

50 See D. A. Bethea, comp., *Colored People's Blue-Book and Business Directory of Chicago, Ill.* (Chicago: Celerity Printing Co., 1905), 51. The 1905 volume also lists eleven entries under "Literary Societies, Concert Co's, etc." (85–86). Faulkner's still appears in 1912 (this time at 3109 State Street) under "Notions, Cigars and Tobacco, and News Stands," but not in any of the other directories mentioned in the text. See L. W. Washington, *The Chicago Negro Business Men and Women and Where They Are Located* (Chicago: Flanders Printing Co., 1912), 13.

51 Eloise Bibb Thompson, "Buy-a-Book Is New Method to Promote Culture," *Chicago Defender*, March 13, 1915, 5.

52 See Ford S. Black, *Black's Blue Book: Business and Professional Directory; A Compilation of Names, Addresses and Telephones of All Chicago's Colored Business and Professional People and Guide to Others Active in Church, State, Club and Social Life* (Chicago: Ford S. Black, 1918), 4; and *Black's Blue Book: Business and Professional Directory, a Compilation of Names, Addresses and Telephones of All Chicago's Colored Business and Professional People and Guide to Others Active in Church, State, Club and Social Life* (Chicago: Ford S. Black, 1921), 8.

53 *Black's Blue Book* (1921), 8. See also Washington, *The Chicago Negro Business Men and Women*, 13.
54 James N. Simms, *Simms' Blue Book and National Negro Business and Professional Directory* (Chicago: James N. Simms, 1923), 65 and preface [1]. Simms's count is certainly incorrect. At the time, New York City had at least two Black-owned bookstores. *The Crisis* operated its own bookshop, located at 69 Fifth Avenue, which offered "Books About Negroes," including *For My People*. There was also the Frederick Douglass Book Center, located at 141 West 125th Street, whose motto was "A Reading People Is a Rising People." The Douglass Book Center also sold and advertised *For My People* as well as other "Books on Negro History and World Relations." See the advertisements for the Crisis Book Shop, *The Crisis*, November 1943, inside front cover; and for the Frederick Douglass Book Center, *New York Amsterdam News*, March 4, 1944, 2B. The omission of the Crisis Book Shop and the Douglass Book Center in New York City illustrates the national directory's inability to tally local businesses accurately. Indeed, it is likely that the two listed for Chicago are also an undercount.
55 *Scott's Blue Book: A Classified Business and Service Directory of Greater Chicago's Colored Citizens' Commercial, Industrial, Professional, Religious and Other Activities* (Chicago: Scott's Business and Directory Service, 1947), 123–24.
56 *Scott's Blue Book*, 28.
57 "Best Buys in Books," advertisement for Negro Digest Book Shop, *Ebony*, March 1947, inside back cover. *Ebony* ran variations on this ad throughout the year.
58 *Scott's Blue Book*, 124.
59 "Honored," *Sunday Chicago Bee*, [September?] 23, 1945, 15.
60 Curiously, none of the extant Studio ads include *For My People*, though they do include *A Street in Bronzeville* and other similar selections that often appeared alongside Walker's collection in other ads. The reason the Studio would not advertise *For My People* in 1947 but the Negro Digest Book Shop would is unclear, unless this suggests uneven distribution of the book to Black booksellers by Yale University Press. Indeed, this is why, in part, Brooks chose to part ways with Harper in 1967: she felt that her books were not being adequately made available to Black businesses. See "*Black Books Bulletin* Interviews Gwen Brooks," interview by Haki Madhubuti, in *Conversations with Gwendolyn Brooks*, ed. Gloria Wade Gayles (Jackson: University Press of Mississippi, 2003), 76. It could therefore be that, with its national profile, *Negro Digest* was able to acquire the book more readily than the smaller and more local Studio bookstore.
61 Advertisement for the S. & S. bookstore, in *Scott's Blue Book*, 124. The recording studio that its proprietor, Lewis Simpkins, operated within the bookstore was affiliated with Miracle Records, a Chicago-based recording company in operation from 1946 to 1950. See Robert Pruter and Robert L. Campbell, "Miracle Records," https://campber.people.clemson.edu/miracle.html. It is possible that Simpkins's business morphed into a hotel by the end of the decade. The *Green Book* lists an S & S Hotel at 4142–48 South Parkway in 1949. See *The Negro Motorist Green Book* (New York: Victor H. Green & Co., 1949), 18.
62 Langston Hughes, "A Young Lady Lectures," "Here to Yonder," *Chicago Defender*, April 10, 1943, 14.
63 Jaime Harker, *America the Middlebrow: Women's Novels, Progressivism, and Middlebrow Authorship between the Wars* (Amherst: University of Massachusetts Press, 2007), 62, 86.
64 Liesl Olson, *Chicago Renaissance: Literature and Art in the Midwest Metropolis* (New Haven: Yale University Press, 2017), 268.
65 Langston Hughes, "Books Are Friends," "Here to Yonder," *Chicago Defender*, December

25, 1943, 10. Hughes would echo these sentiments six years later in a similar piece for the *Defender*; see Langston Hughes, "For a Gift That Lasts a Lifetime, Give a Book," *Chicago Defender*, December 10, 1949, 6.
66 Advertisement, "Have You Been Missing Something?," *Negro Story* 1, no. 6 (May–June 1945): back cover.
67 "Have You Been Missing Something?," back cover.
68 [Alice Browning], "Just to Mention That," *Negro Story* 1, no. 5 (March–April 1945): 54. Browning would also often place announcements in the *Defender* when a new issue was coming out and reminded readers, "If you cannot get Negro Story on your newsstand or at your bookstore, write Negro Story Magazine 4019 Vincennes avenue, Chicago, Ill.," assuming that readers had a favorite bookstore that they patronized. "'Negro Story' on Newsstands," *Chicago Defender*, December 16, 1944, 15, emphasis added.
69 "Have You Been Missing Something?," inside back cover.
70 Robert E. Weems Jr., *Desegregating the Dollar: African American Consumerism in the Twentieth Century* (New York: New York University Press, 1998), 37.
71 "The Negro Market: An Appraisal," *Tide*, March 7, 1947, 15, 18.
72 Cynthia Lee Henthorn, *From Submarines to Suburbs: Selling a Better America, 1939–1959* (Athens: Ohio University Press, 2006), 208.
73 Quoted in Robert E. Weems Jr. and Jason P. Chambers, introduction to *Building the Black Metropolis: African American Entrepreneurship in Chicago*, ed. Robert E. Weems Jr. and Jason P. Chambers (Urbana: University of Illinois Press, 2017), 18.
74 Elizabeth Schroeder Schlabach, *Along the Streets of Bronzeville: Black Chicago's Literary Landscape* (Urbana: University of Illinois Press, 2013), 17.
75 "More Negroes in Business: Increase in Local Commercial Enterprises of Colored People," *Black's Blue Book* (1921), 122. Credit is given to the "Chicago Daily News," but no other identifying information is offered.
76 "Book Boom for Negro Authors: Once-Hungry Writers Finally Hit Pay Dirt in Publishing Houses," *Ebony*, November 1945, 24.
77 "Washington Post Surveys Capital's Reading Habits," *Publishers' Weekly*, November 30, 1946, 2991.
78 Isidor Schneider, "Publishers' Weekly and the Book Trade since World War I," *Publishers' Weekly*, January 18, 1947, 316.
79 Norman Donaldson to Stephen Vincent Benét, June 19, 1942, Yale University Press Records (RU 554), Manuscripts and Archives, Yale University Library. The folks at Yale University Press seem to have been quite happy with Walker's selection. The editor of the press, Eugene Davidson, wrote to Benét: "I've just had a chance to read your Miss Walker's book of poetry and think it's fine. You are certainly doing a first rate job not only for the Press but for all the variety of people and talents who have come into the series since you've been running it. It's [sic] good work, my boy." Eugene Davidson to Stephen Vincent Benét, July 10, 1942, Yale University Press Records.
80 Stephen Vincent Benét, *They Burned the Books* (New York: Farrar & Rinehart, 1942), 12.

CHAPTER 4

1 [Alice Browning], "Just to Mention That," *Negro Story* 1, no. 6 (May–June 1945): 86.
2 [Browning], "Just to Mention That" (May–June 1945): 85.

3 Gayden co-edited the first three issues of *Negro Story* with Browning. In the fourth issue, Browning informed readers that "MISS FERN GAYDEN, former co-editor of *Negro Story* finds that her full time social work supervisory position and other important duties prevent her working as co-editor. But she promises to continue as a contributing editor." [Alice Browning], "Current Town Talk," *Negro Story* 1, no. 4 (December–January 1944–45): 61. Gayden was listed as a member of the magazine's staff for the rest of its run.
4 Alice Browning and Fern Gayden, "A Letter to Our Readers," *Negro Story* 1, no. 1 (May–June 1944): 1.
5 Browning and Gayden, "A Letter to Our Readers" (May–June 1944): 1.
6 Molly Guptill Manning, *When Books Went to War: The Stories That Helped Us Win World War II* (Boston: Mariner, 2015), 193.
7 Emily Miller Danton, "Victory Begins at Home," *American Library Association Bulletin* 36, no. 9 (September 1, 1942): 535.
8 Franklin Delano Roosevelt quoted in Sidney Ditzion, *Arsenals of a Democratic Culture: A Social History of the American Public Library Movement in New England and the Middle States from 1850 to 1900* (Chicago: American Library Association, 1947), v.
9 He continued, "Books must work with those who are planning the future as well as with those who are preserving the present." Frederic G. Melcher, "Editorial: Books That Are Tools," *Publishers' Weekly*, January 10, 1942, 101. Three months later he would write, "We are in the midst of a war of ideas as never before in human history, and books are not only weapons and ammunition but they supply the *best* of weapons and the *best* of ammunition." Frederic G. Melcher, "Editorial: In This War of Ideas," *Publishers' Weekly*, April 25, 1942, 1555.
10 W. W. Norton, "Wartime Trends in Reading and Publishing," *Publishers' Weekly*, May 9, 1942, 1757.
11 The VBC reached its goal by the spring of 1942. Manning, *When Books Went to War*, 52. Its final count amounted to 10,290,713 books over two years. See "V.B.C. Final Report," *ALA Bulletin* 38, no. 6 (June 1944): 217.
12 Kristin L. Matthews, *Reading America: Citizenship, Democracy, and Cold War Literature* (Amherst: University of Massachusetts Press, 2016), 21.
13 Isidor Schneider, "Publishers' Weekly and the Book Trade since World War I," *Publishers' Weekly*, January 18, 1947, 307.
14 For more on how World War II affected books and reading, see "Book Production under War Conditions," *Publishers' Weekly*, April 25, 1942, 1570–71; and "Effects of the War on Book Design," *Publishers' Weekly*, April 25, 1942, 1571–72. See also the May 9, 1942, issue for comprehensive reporting on the American Booksellers Association conference in early May, whose theme was "Books in Wartime."
15 Althea Warren, editorial, *Library Journal*, December 1, 1941, quoted in Martha Boaz, *Fervent and Full of Gifts: The Life of Althea Warren* (New York: Scarecrow Press, 1961), 96.
16 John M. Connor, "On to Victory with the Victory Book Campaign," *ALA Bulletin* 36, no. 9 (September 1, 1942): 554. On the Victory Book Campaign, see also Patti Clayton Becker, *Books and Libraries in American Society during World War II: Weapons in the War of Ideas* (New York: Routledge, 2005).
17 *The Negro Soldier* (1944), produced by the War Department Special Service Division, Army Service Forces, US National Archives, YouTube, https://www.youtube.com/watch?v=dln2dQyLNVU.
18 Enoc P. Waters Jr., "Waters Polls Soldiers on Xmas Gifts: Want Photo of Wife, Sweetie

Most," *Chicago Defender*, October 9, 1943, 1. On literacy rates of servicemen, see "Army Finds More Whites Than Negroes Can't Read," *Chicago Defender*, October 9, 1943, 6.

19 "Keeping Well-Read at Fort Benning," *Chicago Defender*, October 9, 1943, 5.
20 "How Soldiers Enjoy Camp Life at Ft. Sheridan," *Chicago Defender*, February 15, 1941, 5.
21 "Plan Book Service for Race Soldiers," *Chicago Defender*, February 20, 1943, 8.
22 "Soldiers Relax at N. Africa Red Cross Club," *Chicago Defender*, July 17, 1943, 21.
23 "2,000 Books Serve Camp Lee Soldiers," *Chicago Defender*, December 13, 1941, 8.
24 "Observes History Week at Camp Lee," *Chicago Defender*, February 14, 1942, 12.
25 Dr. Harold Kingsley, "What the People Say," letter to the *Chicago Defender*, May 31, 1941, 14. By December, a branch of the servicemen's center had opened on Chicago's South Side "to provide a recreational house for hundreds of soldiers." It included, in part, "a library partially filled with books and magazines." See "Service Men's Center Ready for Soldiers," *Chicago Defender*, December 27, 1941, 12.
26 The sorority also published its own "newsette," *The Service Man*, which "is inserted in the center of the Delta Journal and sorority members remove it from the journal and send it to their friends in the forces." "Deltas Open Campaign for 15,000 Books: Coast-to-Coast Drive for Servicemen," *Chicago Defender*, May 29, 1943, 16.
27 James G. Thompson, "Should I Sacrifice to Live 'Half-American?,'" letter to the *Pittsburgh Courier*, January 31, 1942, 3.
28 "To Our Readers," *Chicago Defender*, September 26, 1942, 3.
29 The image, and two others (one by Cortor), accompanied an article by Daniel Catton Rich, director of fine arts at the Art Institute of Chicago. See Daniel Catton Rich, "The Negro in the Art World," *Chicago Defender*, September 26, 1942, sec. 2, 33.
30 "Our Pledge of Allegiance," *Chicago Defender*, September 26, 1942, sec. 2, 20–21.
31 "To Our Readers," 3.
32 Browning almost certainly knew Reddick from her time at Columbia University, where she studied for an MA in English. From 1939 to 1949, Reddick served as curator of the Schomburg Collection at the New York Public Library; this is likely Browning's connection to Catherine Latimer, research librarian at the Schomburg Library, who is discussed in the next section of the chapter. While at Columbia, Browning studied with Vernon Loggins, an influential scholar whose 1931 volume *The Negro Author: His Development in America to 1900* concluded, "With our American social organization such as it is, much is denied [the Negro author]. But literature and the related arts are open freely to him. It is in them that he has his best opportunity to 'rise and shine,'" a message that resonates deeply with Browning's mission in *Negro Story*. Vernon Loggins, *The Negro Author: His Development in America to 1900* (New York: Columbia University Press, 1931), 366.
33 L. D. Reddick, "Propaganda and Prejudice," *Chicago Defender*, September 26, 1942, B19.
34 "Noted Authors Back Second Front," *Chicago Defender*, September 26, 1942, 13. Langston Hughes, "Klan or Gestapo? Why Take Either? Foremost Negro Author Writes of Devils, Hams, Dixie Drawls and Axis Dictators," *Chicago Defender*, September 26, 1942, sec. 2, 14.
35 Alice Browning and Fern Gayden, "A Letter to Our Readers," *Negro Story* 1, no. 2 (July–August 1944): 1.
36 Jaime Harker, *America the Middlebrow: Women's Novels, Progressivism, and Middlebrow Authorship between the Wars* (Amherst: University of Massachusetts Press, 2007), 62.
37 [Alice Browning and Fern Gayden], "Negro Story," *Negro Story* 1, no. 2 (July–August 1944): 56.
38 Browning and Gayden, "A Letter to Our Readers," (May–June 1944): 1.

39 Margaret Rodriguez, "I Had a Colored Maid," *Negro Story* 1, no. 1 (May–June 1944): 6–8.
40 Grace W. Tompkins, "Justice Wears Dark Glasses," *Negro Story* 1, no. 2 (July–August 1944): 13.
41 [Alice Browning], "Just to Mention That," *Negro Story* 2, no. 1 (August–September 1945): 56.
42 [Alice Browning and Fern Gayden], "We Recommend These Books," *Negro Story* 1, no. 2 (July–August 1944): 64.
43 Catherine Latimore [sic], comp., "A List of Books by and about the Negro," *Negro Story* 1, no. 3 (October–November 1944): 61–62. Latimer was the first African American librarian hired by the New York Public Library.
44 See "List of Books Compiled by Marcella Ricks, Oakwood Branch, Chicago Public Library," *Negro Story* 1, no. 5 (March–April 1945): inside back cover. The list continues on page 60 of issue 2, number 1. Though this second installment states that the list will be continued in the next issue, it does not appear in either of the remaining issues.
45 Browning's interest in facilitating this book drive is not surprising, given her ties to the Schomburg Collection, which she notes multiple times throughout the magazine's run. The third issue offers a profile of the Schomburg Collection, describing it for readers as "the finest collection of books and periodicals on the Negro in the World. It is housed in the beautiful Harlem Branch Library in New York City. Dr. L. D. Reddick is the capable and efficient curator who is also a professor at New York University." See [Alice Browning and Fern Gayden], "Current Town Talk," *Negro Story* 1, no. 3 (October–November 1944): 60. Meanwhile, the magazine interestingly had only a thin relationship to the Chicago Public Library system. Indeed, the list of recommended books compiled by Marcella Ricks at the Oakwood Branch is the only reference to the CPL in all of *Negro Story*; again, there is no mention anywhere in the magazine of Vivian Harsh or the Hall Branch Library.
46 [Browning and Gayden], "Current Town Talk" (October–November 1944): 60.
47 [Alice Browning], "Just to Mention That," *Negro Story* 1, no. 5 (March–April 1945): 56.
48 [Alice Browning and Fern Gayden], "Did You Know That . . . ?," *Negro Story* 1, no. 2 (July–August 1944): 61.
49 [Alice Browning and Fern Gayden], "Did You Know That . . . ?," *Negro Story* 1, no. 3 (October–November 1944): 58, 59.
50 [Browning], "Just to Mention That" (May–June 1945): 85.
51 In the beginning, Browning listed "associated editors," who included Gayden, O'Wendell Shaw, Tompkins, Sengstacke, and others; starting with issue 1, number 4, however, these names were thereafter listed as "assistants."
52 [Browning], "Just to Mention That" (May–June 1945): 87.
53 [Browning], "Just to Mention That" (August–September 1945): 56.
54 Ad for the *Sunday Chicago Bee*, *Negro Story* 1, no. 1 (May–June 1944): 64.
55 Browning notes that *The Crisis* "has aided in discovering new writers," while *Negro Digest* "is THE important Negro magazine of the times and we are proud that it is a product of Chicago." [Alice Browning], "Current Town Talk," *Negro Story* 1, no. 4 (December 1944–January 1945): 61.
56 [Browning and Gayden], "Current Town Talk" (October–November 1944): 59.
57 [Alice Browning], "Just to Mention That," *Negro Story* 2, no. 3 (April–May 1946): 59.
58 [Browning], "Just to Mention That" (March–April 1945): 54; [Browning and Gayden], "Current Town Talk" (October–November 1944): 59; [Browning], "Just to Mention That" (August–September 1945): 55.

59 [Browning], "Just to Mention That" (August–September 1945): 53, 55.
60 [Browning], "Just to Mention That" (August–September 1945): 53–54.
61 [Alice Browning], "Just to Mention That," *Negro Story* 2, no. 2 (December 1945–January 1946): 62.
62 [Browning], "Just to Mention That" (December 1945–January 1946): 62, 63.
63 [Browning and Gayden], "Current Town Talk" (October–November 1944): 60.
64 Advertisement for Great Eastern News Corp., *Negro Story* 1, no. 2 (July–August 1944): 64.
65 [Browning and Gayden], "Current Town Talk" (October–November 1944): 59; [Browning], "Just to Mention That" (May–June 1945): 86.
66 [Browning], "Just to Mention That" (May–June 1945): 86.
67 [Browning], "Just to Mention That" (May–June 1945): 85.
68 These included, in part, *Spotlighter* (represented by Leonard H. Bell), *Opportunity* (Alphonse E. Heningburg), *Color* (I. J. K. Wells), *Music Dial* (S. W. Thompson), *Expression* (Ora E. Wise), and *The African* (Rev. R. T. Brown). Browning notes that the activities of the association were first reported in "the September issue of *Spotlighter*." [Browning], "Just to Mention That" (December 1945–January 1946): 63–64.
69 Earl Conrad, "Tell Us of the Negro," "Yesterday and Today," *Chicago Defender*, August 25, 1945, 13.
70 Browning and Gayden, "A Letter to Our Readers" (May–June 1944): 1.
71 [Alice Browning], "Our Contributors," *Negro Story* 1, no. 6 (May–June 1945): 83. White writers seemed hesitant, however, to write about their own experiences. "By the way, we haven't received any recent contributions from white writers not dealing with the Negro—How about it! Our policy has been broadened to include them, you know," Browning wrote in 1945. [Browning], "Just to Mention That" (August–September 1945): 56.
72 O' Wendell Shaw, "Avers Negroes Need Magazine: But Writer Wonders about Finances," *New York Amsterdam News*, December 28, 1935, 5. O' Wendell Shaw, which was a pseudonym for Oliver W. Shaw, inhabited various editorial and publishing roles starting in 1922. For a time he was "in business as a literary manuscript revisionist" and wrote a syndicated literary column for the Black press, "Along the Literary Front." See the foreword to O' Wendell Shaw, *Writing for the Weeklies: How to Earn Sparetime Money as a Weekly Newspaper Correspondent* (Columbus, OH: Russwurm Press, 1962), 2. Shaw served as one of *Negro Story*'s "Friends to Negro Story," as listed in the first issue, meaning he contributed $5.99 or more to the magazine. He also appears first in the inaugural issue's acknowledgments and is listed as an associate editor. His story "Chief Mourner," about a forgotten actress, appears in that first issue of *Negro Story*, reprinted from the *Pittsburgh Courier*. From the beginning, he advocated for illustrations in the magazine.
73 "The Negro Market: An Appraisal," *Tide*, March 7, 1947, 17.
74 [Alice Browning and Fern Gayden], "Our Contributors," *Negro Story* 1, no. 2 (July–August 1944): 2.
75 Bill V. Mullen, *Popular Fronts: Chicago and African-American Cultural Politics, 1935–46* (Urbana: University of Illinois Press, 1999), 125.
76 [Alice Browning], "Current Town Talk," *Negro Story* 1, no. 4 (December 1944–January 1945): 61.
77 Browning and Gayden, "Letter to Our Readers" (May–June 1944): 1.
78 [Browning], "Just to Mention That" (May–June 1945): 88.

79 [Browning], "Just to Mention That" (August–September 1945): 52.
80 "Manuscript Revision," *Negro Story* 1, no. 1 (May–June 1944): 59.
81 S. I. Hayakawa, "Negro Story," "Second Thoughts," *Chicago Defender*, May 13, 1944, 13. Browning quotes Hayakawa's review in the second issue of *Negro Story*. See [Alice Browning and Fern Gayden], "People Are Writing," *Negro Story* 1, no. 2 (July–August 1944): 4.
82 Nick Aaron Ford, letter to the editor, *Negro Story* 1, no. 6 (May–June 1945): 90.
83 [Browning], "Just to Mention That" (March–April 1945): 55.
84 [Alice Browning and Fern Gayden], "Current Town Talk," *Negro Story* 1, no. 2 (July–August 1944): 62.
85 [Alice Browning and Fern Gayden], "Short Story Prize" and "Poetry Prize," *Negro Story* 1, no. 2 (July–August 1944): 63.
86 [Browning], "Just to Mention That" (August–September 1945): 51.
87 [Browning and Gayden], "People Are Writing" (July–August 1944): 4.
88 Browning and Gayden, "A Letter to Our Readers" (May–June 1944): 1.
89 [Browning], "Our Contributors" (May–June 1945): 83.
90 [Alice Browning], "Our Contributors," *Negro Story* 1, no. 5 (March–April 1945): 57.
91 "Letters from Our Readers," *Negro Story* 1, no. 6 (May–June 1945): 94–95. This section features letters from Corporal J. C. Benson, Corporal R. E. Claybrooks, and a reader using the pseudonym "Private Debunken."
92 [Browning], "Just to Mention That" (March–April 1945): 53.
93 Advertisements, *Negro Story* 1, no. 1 (May–June 1944): 50.
94 [Browning], "Just to Mention That" (May–June 1945): 84; [Browning], "Just to Mention That" (March–April 1945): 54.
95 [Browning], "Just to Mention That" (August–September 1945): 52.
96 [Browning], "Just to Mention That" (May–June 1945): 87.
97 Aldon [sic] Bland, "Let's Go Visiting," *Negro Story* 1, no. 1 (May–June 1944): 20–22. Bland would go on to publish another story in the next issue; see "Beginnings," *Negro Story* 1, no. 2 (July–August 1944): 42–44.
98 [Browning and Gayden], "Our Contributors" (July–August 1944): 2.
99 See "Poet's Baby Christened; Father Is Overseas," *Philadelphia Tribune*, April 21, 1945, 8.
100 For more on the Visionaries, see "Visionaries Set Up Poetry Prize," *Atlanta Daily World*, October 22, 1943, 3. See also Hayakawa's October 9, 1943, "Second Thoughts" column in the *Chicago Defender* (15).
101 Cpl. Robert E. Claybrook, "Chicago's Black Belt," *Negro Story* 1, no. 6 (May–June 1945): 81.
102 Margaret T. Goss, "Private Jeff Johnson, *Negro Story* 1, no. 2 (July–August 1944): 30. An important figure in Bronzeville, Goss was an artist, writer, and teacher who helped found the South Side Community Art Center and would later establish what became the DuSable Black History Museum in Chicago. In this issue of *Negro Story*, she is said to be "at present . . . rendering a most patriotic service by featuring a news letter to the men in the armed service." [Browning and Gayden], "Our Contributors" (July–August 1944): 2.
103 Nick Aaron Ford, "The Negro Soldier Speaks," *Negro Story* 1, no. 1 (May–June 1944): 60, lines 31–36.
104 Lt. William Couch, "To a Soldier," *Negro Story* 1, no. 1 (May–June 1944): 60, lines 1–11.
105 Robert A. Davis, "Sketches from the Army," *Negro Story* 1, no. 2 (July–August 1944): 55.
106 Davis, "Sketches from the Army," 56. A third piece in this same issue that documents

experiences of the war is authored by Peter Pollack (white)—art dealer, first director of the South Side Community Art Center, and member of the American Red Cross. His "Essay on Heat, by a Man Who Lived Through It," provides a second-person account of being stationed abroad. "The heat makes your impressions run together; one day is indistinguishable from the next," the narrator begins. He then takes readers inside a soldier's mindset: "'I better sleep,' you continue talking to yourself. 'Musn't think about anything. Not about how clean and cool is Lake Michigan or what you'd give for a walk in the galleries at the Art Institute.'I'm a soldier,' you say." Here, the use of second person situates readers in the experiences of soldiers abroad. Peter Pollack, "Essay on Heat, by a Man Who Lived Through It," *Negro Story* 1, no. 2 (July–August 1944): 58.

107 Davis Grubbs, "Rest Stop," *Negro Story* 1, no. 3 (October–November 1944): 27–32.
108 Edward Rutan, "Johnnie Cull," *Negro Story* 1, no. 4 (December 1944–January 1945): 49.
109 Langston Hughes, "Private Jim Crow," *Negro Story* 1, no. 6 (May–June 1945): 9.
110 Chester Himes, "A Penny for Your Thoughts," *Negro Story* 1, no. 5 (March–April 1945): 14–17; Stanley Richards, "District of Columbia: A Play," *Negro Story* 2, no. 2 (December 1945–January 1946): 58.
111 Lucia Mae Pitts, "A WAC Speaks to a Soldier," *Negro Story* 1, no. 4 (December 1944–January 1945): 63, lines 62–65.
112 Mrs. Anne M. Harper, "A Colored Soldier's Prayer," *Negro Story* 2, no. 2 (December 1945–January 1946): 38, lines 17–18 and 29–31.
113 Roberta I. Thomas, "Battle for Two," *Negro Story* 2, no. 2 (December 1945–January 1946): 34, lines 17–24.
114 Gwendolyn Brooks, "Gay Chaps at the Bar," *Negro Story* 1, no. 5 (March–April 1945): 49, lines 8, 9–14.
115 Browning would publish other pieces that meditate on soldiers' disappointing experience of returning home to conditions that were no different than when they left, illustrating in devastating detail how the nation had not lived up to its democratic promise. See, for instance, Malvin Wald, "Keys to the City," *Negro Story* 1, no. 4 (December 1944–January 1945): 19–22; Chester Himes, "A Night of New Roses," *Negro Story* 2, no. 2 (December 1945–January 1946): 10–14; and Theodore R. Hubbard, "The Negro Serviceman Returns," *Negro Story* 2, no. 3 (April–May 1946): 49.
116 [Browning], "Just to Mention That" (May–June 1945): 88.

CHAPTER 5

1 "*Black Boy*, Richard Wright, Reviewed by Clara Green at the June 1945 Meeting," "Symposium on the Activities of the Book Circle [1944–45]," compiled by Oneita Ferrell, [13], Book Circle Records, box 1, folder 3, 1940s [scrapbook], Chicago State University Archives, hereafter Book Circle Records, cited by box and folder. All Book Circle materials courtesy Chicago State University Archives.
2 Elizabeth McHenry, *Forgotten Readers: Recovering the Lost History of African American Literary Societies* (Durham, NC: Duke University Press, 2002), 3, 149, 226, 227.
3 Kevin K. Gaines, *Uplifting the Race: Black Leadership, Politics, and Culture in the Twentieth Century* (Chapel Hill: University of North Carolina Press, 1996), 2, 16.
4 Marcia Chatelain, *South Side Girls: Growing Up in the Great Migration* (Durham, NC: Duke University Press, 2015), 4, 40, 10. See also Nazera Sadiq Wright, *Black Girlhood in*

the Nineteenth Century (Urbana: University of Illinois Press, 2016), especially chap. 5 on conduct books and novels.

5 Anne Meis Knupfer, *The Chicago Black Renaissance and Women's Activism* (Urbana: University of Illinois Press, 2006), 103.

6 "Book Review Club Formed; Map Program," *Chicago Defender*, November 20, 1943, 21.

7 Ora G. Morrow to Ethel [Pritchard], December 4, 1943, Book Circle Records, box 1, folder 3, 1940s [scrapbook].

8 At this writing, the most recently dated Book Circle items in the Chicago State University Archives were a pamphlet celebrating the group's sixty-seventh anniversary in 2010 and a document laying out the group's plans and book selections for 2010–11 and 2011–12. The group has continued to meet and celebrated its eightieth anniversary in 2023. My thanks to Book Circle member Eloys Long Goon and Chicago State University archivist Kheir Fakhreldin for providing this update on the group's activities.

9 "The Book Circle," "Symposium on the Activities of the Book Circle, 1943–44," compiled by Oneita Ferrell and Mary Whitfield, [1], Book Circle Records, box 1, folder 3, 1940s [scrapbook].

10 "Financial Report of the John T. Frederick Program," Book Circle Records, box 1, folder 3, 1940s [scrapbook]. Morrow invited key community members to offer comments after Frederick's lecture. They included Vivian Harsh, Frank Marshall Davis, Sylvester Watkins (editor of the *Anthology of American Negro Literature*, with an introduction by Frederick), and Dorsey McCarthy ("formerly conductor of a column in the Chicago Sun"). "Distinguished Guest Program," "Symposium on the Activities of the Book Circle [1944–45]," [3].

11 Morrow to [Mabel], December 4, 1944, Book Circle Records, box 1, folder 3, 1940s [scrapbook].

12 Members took their reading very seriously. In the spring of 1945, for example, member Ruth Lawson wrote to Morrow and "Fellow Book Circle Members" to "regretfully beg to take leave of you for a year" because of personal changes that had left her "no opportunity to attend meetings and even less to read the books so that the most enjoyment may be obtained from the Reviews." She promised, however, to "try to keep abreast of the literature being written by being faithful to my Saturday Review of Literature" and "truly hope[d]" that the group would "be as pleased to welcome me back, as I shall be to return." Ruth T. Lawson to Ora Morrow and Fellow Book Circle Members, March 5, 1945, Book Circle Records, box 1, folder 3, 1940s [scrapbook].

13 Morrow to Ethel [Pritchard], December 4, 1943.

14 Morrow to Members, January 9, 1944, Book Circle Records, box 1, folder 3, 1940s [scrapbook].

15 Morrow to Ethel [Pritchard], December 4, 1943. The quotations that members offered ranged in topic and author. In one list that has been preserved, Morrow gave an anonymous quotation, "Next to acquiring good friends is that acquisition of good books." Ruth Lawson presented lines from Walt Whitman: "Stranger, if you passing meet me and desire to speak to me, why should you not speak to me? And why should I not speak to you?" Mary Whitfield, meanwhile, chose a more politically minded selection: "The stage of any minority in any country is a test of the degree of its civilization." "Quotations," "Symposium on the Activities of the Book Circle, 1943–44," [21].

16 [Ora G. Morrow], "Notes on How to Review a Book," [1–2], Book Circle Records, box 1, folder 3, 1940s [scrapbook].

17 Morrow to Members, August 9, 1944, Book Circle Records, box 1, folder 3, 1940s [scrapbook].
18 "A Tribute to the President and Founder of the Book Circle," "Symposium on the Activities of the Book Circle [1944–45]," [1].
19 Albertine Gray, "Dedication to the Founder," "The Chronicle: Twenty Five Years with the Book Circle, 1943–1968," inside front cover, Book Circle Records, box 1, folder 5, 1960s [scrapbook].
20 Mae to Ora Morrow, Christmas 1944, Book Circle Records, box 1, folder 3, 1940s [scrapbook].
21 Oneita Ferrell, "Book Circle Members Enjoy Busy Vacation," September 1945, "Symposium on the Activities of the Book Circle [1944–45]," [14].
22 Ferrell, "Book Circle Members Enjoy Busy Vacation."
23 John T. Frederick to Ora G. Morrow, February 24, 1945, Book Circle Records, box 1, folder 3, 1940s [scrapbook].
24 Letter from Alice Manning Dickey, October 30, 1949, Book Circle Records, box 1, folder 3, 1940s [scrapbook].
25 Alice Manning Dickey to Oneita Ferrell, April 26, 1952, Book Circle Records, box 1, folder 4, 1950s [scrapbook]. "Husbands are permitted!," Dickey added.
26 "The Book Circle," "Symposium on the Activities of the Book Circle, 1943–44," [1]. Ora Morrow's son Lucien J. Morrow passed away in 1965 at the age of fifty-three; his obituary, however, does not mention a wife. Despite this fact, and the two different spellings of Lucian/Lucien, it is unlikely that Ora Morrow knew two different Lucian/Lucien J. Morrows. See "Lucien J. Morrow," *Chicago Tribune*, July 30, 1965, 30.
27 "Satellite Groups," "The Chronicle," [20].
28 Ora Green Morrow to Lucian J. Morrow, June 5, 1944, Book Circle Records, box 1, folder 3, 1940s [scrapbook].
29 Rex Goreleigh to Ora Morrow, May 6, 1946, Book Circle Records, box 1, folder 3, 1940s [scrapbook].
30 St. Clair Drake and Horace R. Cayton, *Black Metropolis: A Study of Negro Life in a Northern City* (1945), rev. and enlarged ed. (Chicago: University of Chicago Press, 1993), 175.
31 "Book Circle Tea to Spotlight Authors," *Chicago Defender*, June 7, 1952, 6.
32 See, for instance, "Chicago's Top Social, Civic Organizations Receive High Praise from Urban League Head," *Chicago Defender*, May 18, 1963, 11.
33 See McHenry, *Forgotten Readers*, 172–73, 238–41.
34 McHenry, *Forgotten Readers*, 225.
35 Joan Shelley Rubin, *The Making of Middlebrow Culture* (Chapel Hill: University of North Carolina Press, 1992), xix.
36 Janice A. Radway, *A Feeling for Books: The Book-of-the-Month Club, Literary Taste, and Middle-Class Desire* (Chapel Hill: University of North Carolina Press, 1997), 259.
37 Beth Driscoll, *The New Literary Middlebrow: Tastemakers and Reading in the Twenty-First Century* (London: Palgrave Macmillan, 2014), 3, 6.
38 Virginia Woolf, "Middlebrow: A Letter Written but Not Sent," *Atlantic*, July 1942, https://www.theatlantic.com/magazine/archive/1942/07/middlebrow-a-letter-written-but-not-sent/654308/.
39 Elizabeth Long, *Book Clubs: Women and the Uses of Reading in Everyday Life* (Chicago: University of Chicago Press, 2003), 153–56. Further, Long notes, these effects of reading the middlebrow are heightened in group settings, such as book clubs, where "group

discussion magnifies the dynamism that can come from connecting to novelistic characters, because members must also come to terms with other participants' responses and the personal stories they elicit" (153).

40 Gordon Hutner, *What America Read: Taste, Class, and the Novel, 1920–1960* (Chapel Hill: University of North Carolina Press, 2009), 5, 4.

41 Jaime Harker, *America the Middlebrow: Women's Novels, Progressivism, and Middlebrow Authorship between the Wars* (Amherst: University of Massachusetts Press, 2007), 20.

42 Hutner, *What America Read*, 8.

43 Amy L. Blair, *Reading Up: Middle-Class Readers and the Culture of Success in the Early Twentieth-Century United States* (Philadelphia: Temple University Press, 2012), 2, 19.

44 Radway, *A Feeling for Books*, 286, 287. She adds: "The Book-of-the-Month Club judges may well have worried a good deal about what their subscribers could tolerate. In response they may have narrowed the range of literatures, experiences, and identifications that they offered to their middlebrow readers by rejecting books that depicted worlds too far outside the mainstream" (287).

45 Harker, *America the Middlebrow*, 84–85.

46 I take this information from the Book Circle's twenty-fifth anniversary program, which listed the books the group had read up to that point in 1968. I have found some discrepancies with other lists the group kept. They are, however, minimal and do not change my analysis. "Twenty-Five Years of Shared Reading," "The Chronicle," [13–14, 5–6, 17–20].

47 The three remaining volumes consisted of the Bible and two collections of poetry.

48 For bestseller and Book-of-the-Month Club data, I consulted the Books of the Century digital project, https://www.ocf.berkeley.edu/~immer/booksmain. Literary Guild selections are harder to find; I therefore relied on book reviews for this information.

49 There is, however, a record of the Book Circle reading and discussing poetry by Hughes years later at their September 1961 meeting. See "Twenty-Five Years of Shared Reading," "The Chronicle," [18].

50 See Hutner, *What America Read*, 226–32.

51 Quoted in Dorothy Curry, "The Course and Direction of the Book Circle," "The Chronicle," [3].

52 Gertrude Rogers, "Reactions to a Forced Separation," "The Chronicle," [4].

53 Esther L. Towles, "Growth through Shared Reading," "The Chronicle," [13].

54 Mabel R. Hancock to Oneita Ferrell and the Members of the Book Circle, November 12, 1978, Book Circle Records, box 1, folder 6, 1970s [scrapbook].

55 "U.S. FOREIGN POLICY: Shield of the Republic, Walter Lippman, Reviewed by Ora Morrow at the January 1944 meeting," "Symposium on the Activities of the Book Circle, 1943–44," [5].

56 "UNDERCOVER * Carlson, Reviewed by Ora G. Morrow, June 1944," "Symposium on the Activities of the Book Circle, 1943–44," [18].

57 "George Washington Carver, Rackham Holt (née Margaret Saunders), Reviewed by Beatrice Willis at the February 1944 Meeting of the Book Circle," "Symposium on the Activities of the Book Circle, 1943–44," [8].

58 "Ten Years in Japan, by Joseph Grew, Reviewed by Eloise Paris at the November 1944 meeting," "Symposium on the Activities of the Book Circle, 1943–44," [6].

59 "INDIGO, Christine Weston, Reviewed by Mary Whitfield at the March 1944 meeting," "Symposium on the Activities of the Book Circle, 1943–44," [9].

60 "THE APOSTLE, Sholem Asch, REVIEWED BY LERA HARRIS at the June 1944 meeting of the Book Circle," "Symposium on the Activities of the Book Circle, 1943–44," [17].
61 "THE PROMISE, PEARL S. BUCK, REVIEWED BY JOY BRADDAN at the May 1944 meeting of the Book Circle," "Symposium on the Activities of the Book Circle, 1943–44," [14].
62 Gray, "Dedication to the Founder."
63 Towles, "Growth through Shared Reading."
64 Gray, "Dedication to the Founder."
65 Ruth M. Williams, "Intangibles of the Book Circle," "The Chronicle," [3]; Lucille Boysaw, "Views upon Entering the Book Circle," "The Chronicle," [4].
66 Curry, "The Course and Direction of the Book Circle."
67 Mary to Ora Morrow, May 8, 1945, [2], Book Circle Records, box 1, folder 3, 1940s [scrapbook]. This Mary is most likely Mary Whitfield.
68 Hutner, *What America Read*, 4.
69 Hancock to Oneita Ferrell and the Members of the Book Circle.
70 Rubin, *The Making of Middlebrow Culture*, 22.
71 Letter from Oneita Ferrell, April 21, 1950, Book Circle Records, box 1, folder 4, 1950s [scrapbook].
72 "IN BED WE CRY, Ilka Chase, REVIEWED BY MARY WHITFIELD at the AUGUST meeting of the BOOK CIRCLE," "Symposium on the Activities of the Book Circle, 1943–44", [19].
73 Ora G. Morrow, typescript draft of review for the *Sunday Chicago Bee*, [3], Book Circle Records, box 1, folder 3, 1940s [scrapbook].
74 "Book Circle Members Disband for the Summer," "Symposium on the Activities of the Book Circle, [1944–45]," [14].
75 "NEW WORLD A COMING—INSIDE BLACK AMERICA—Roi Ottley, Reviewed by Ethel Pritchard at the December 1944 meeting," "Symposium on the Activities of the Book Circle, 1943–44," [4].
76 "Report, New World A-Comin-Roi Ottley," typescript notecards, Book Circle Records, box 1, folder 3, 1940s [scrapbook].
77 Harker, *America the Middlebrow*, 3.
78 Sean McCann, "'A Decent Life in These United States': Walker, Williams, Wright and the Problem of the Black Middlebrow," *Post45*, August 4, 2021, https://post45.org/2021/08/a-decent-life-in-these-united-states/.
79 "THE PROMISE, PEARL S. BUCK, REVIEWED BY JOY BRADDAN," [14].
80 "Lin Yutang, BETWEEN TEARS AND LAUGHTER, REVIEWED BY ONEITA FERRELL, MAY MEETING OF THE BOOK CIRCLE," "Symposium on the Activities of the Book Circle, 1943–44," [16].
81 "EARTH AND HIGH HEAVEN, GWENDOLYN GRAHAM, Reviewed by Lera Harris at the January 1945 meeting," "Symposium on the Activities of the Book Circle, [1944–45]," [9].
82 "INDIGO, Reviewed by Mary Whitfield."
83 McHenry, *Forgotten Readers*, 17.
84 Boysaw, "Views upon Entering the Book Circle."
85 Ora G. Morrow, "A Charge to the Book Circle," "The Chronicle," [1].

86 Long, *Book Clubs*, 22.
87 Jacqueline Bobo, *Black Women as Cultural Readers* (New York: Columbia University Press, 1995), 204.
88 Charlemae Rollins to Mrs. Ora G. Morrow, undated handwritten letter, Book Circle Records, box 1, folder 6, 1970s [scrapbook].
89 "Dedicated to Our Pal Charlemae Rollins," Book Circle Records, box 1, folder 3, 1940s [scrapbook].
90 Towles, "Growth through Shared Reading."
91 "NEW WORLD A COMING, Reviewed by Ethel Pritchard."
92 "U.S. FOREIGN POLICY, Reviewed by Ora Morrow."
93 "George Washington Carver, Reviewed by Beatrice Willis."
94 "INDIGO, Reviewed by Mary Whitfield."
95 Williams, "Intangibles of the Book Circle."
96 "THE PROMISE, REVIEWED BY JOY BRADDAN," [14].
97 Mary Whitfield, "Christmas with the Book Circle," "The Chronicle," [12].
98 "George Washington Carver, Reviewed by Beatrice Willis."

CONCLUSION

1 Vivian Harsh died in 1960 at the age of seventy, and Ora Morrow passed away in 1985. See Adolph J. Slaughter, "The Historian Who Never Wrote: The Vivian Harsh Story," *Daily Defender*, August 29, 1960, 9; and "Morrow," death notices, *Chicago Defender*, August 14, 1985, 21.
2 Alice Walker, "In Search of Our Mothers' Gardens," in *In Search of Our Mothers' Gardens: Womanist Prose* (Orlando: Harvest, 1983), 242, 240.
3 Combahee River Collective, "A Black Feminist Statement," in *This Bridge Called My Back: Writings by Radical Women of Color*, expanded and rev. 3rd ed., ed. Cherríe L. Moraga and Gloria E. Anzaldúa (Berkeley: Third World Press, 2002), 242.
4 Barbara Smith, "Toward a Black Feminist Criticism," in *All the Women Are White, All the Blacks Are Men, but Some of Us Are Brave: Black Women's Studies*, ed. Gloria T. Hull, Patricia Bell Scott, and Barbara Smith (New York: Feminist Press, 1982), 173.
5 Aisha Peay, "Reading Democracy: Anthologies of African American Women's Writing and the Legacy of Black Feminist Criticism, 1970–1990" (PhD diss., Duke University, 2009), 4.
6 Gloria T. Hull and Barbara Smith, "Introduction: The Politics of Black Women's Studies," in *All the Women Are White, All the Blacks Are Men, but Some of Us Are Brave*, xxx–xxxi.
7 Smith, "Toward a Black Feminist Criticism," 159.
8 The Crunk Feminist Collective, "Hip Hop Generation Feminism: A Manifesto," in *The Crunk Feminist Collection*, ed. Brittney C. Cooper, Susana M. Morris, and Robin M. Boylorn (New York: Feminist Press, 2017), xxi.
9 Mary Helen Washington, "Re(Visions): Black Women Writers—Their Texts, Their Readers, Their Critics," in *Black-Eyed Susans/Midnight Birds: Stories by and about Black Women*, ed. Mary Helen Washington (New York: Anchor, 1990), 4.
10 Alice Walker, "From an Interview," in *In Search of Our Mothers' Gardens*, 260.

11 Elizabeth McHenry, *Forgotten Readers: Recovering the Lost History of African American Literary Societies* (Durham, NC: Duke University Press, 2002), 298.
12 Patricia Hill Collins, *Black Feminist Thought: Knowledge, Consciousness, and the Politics of Empowerment* (New York: Routledge, 2009), 104.
13 Terry McMillan, *How Stella Got Her Groove Back* (New York: New American Library, 2004), 16.
14 McHenry, *Forgotten Readers*, 307.
15 Cecilia Konchar Farr, *Reading Oprah: How Oprah's Book Club Changed the Way America Reads* (Albany: SUNY Press, 2005), 14. See too Cecilia Konchar Farr and Jaime Harker, eds., *The Oprah Effect: Critical Essays on Oprah's Book Club* (Albany: SUNY Press, 2008); and Kathleen Rooney, *Reading with Oprah: The Book Club That Changed America* (Fayetteville: University of Arkansas Press, 2005). See also Jennifer Szalai, "Oprah Winfrey, Book Critic," *New Yorker* April 24, 2013. Some of these critics formed book clubs of their own in response to Winfrey's, which they perceived as either not rigorous or radical enough. In 2004, for instance, the website Feministing—which described itself as "an online community run by and for young feminists" that "offer[ed] sharp, uncompromising feminist analysis of everything from pop culture to politics, and inspir[ed] young people to make real-world feminist change, online and off"—launched its own counter–book club, the Not Oprah's Book Club. The online forum included reviews of books that were unlikely to be selected by Winfrey, primarily because of their "controversial" content, such as Kate Bornstein and S. Bear Bergman's *Gender Laws: The Next Generation* (2010). Despite accusations that it has grossly commodified the act of reading, Oprah's Book Club nevertheless has helped keep reading at the center of American popular culture into the twenty-first century. See "About," Feministing, http://feministing.com/about/.
16 Book Girl Magic, "About," https://bookgirlmagic.com/about/.
17 Alysia, "About: The Mocha Girls Read Story," Mocha Girls Read, http://www.mochagirlsread.com/contact-2/about/.
18 Glory Edim, introduction to *Well-Read Black Girl: Finding Our Stories, Discovering Ourselves*, ed. Glory Edim (New York: Penguin), xiv.
19 "About," #CiteASista, https://citeasista.com/about/.
20 #SisterPhD, https://www.sisterphd.com/ (no longer available).
21 It was unclear, however, whether the book actually needed the marketing push; indeed, Barnes and Noble reported in 2018 that "preorders of the memoir had already surpassed any other adult book published since 2015 and that the demand would likely continue to grow." Erica Armstrong Dunbar, "Michelle Obama's 'Becoming' Is Black Women's History," *Essence*, November 13, 2018, https://www.essence.com/culture/michelle-obamas-becoming-is-black-womens-history/.
22 "Michelle Obama: By the Book," *New York Times*, December 6, 2018, https://nyti.ms/2zKWoMB.

Index

Page numbers in *italics* indicate a figure.

Abbott, Beatrice, 67, 69–70, 72, 74, 76, 185n1, 188n48, 189n50
Abbott, Beatrice, publications: "Belles Lettres," 68; "Frustration," 192n116; "Good Neighbor," 68; "For Gwendolyn Brooks," 71; "Hymn of Humility," 68; "My sonnets sigh for love that's lost," 80
Abbott, Robert S., 56–57, 62–63, 65, 76, 123, 185n6
Abbott's Monthly (magazine), 19, 127
Adamic, Louis, 41
Adler, Alfred, 150
The African (magazine), 201n68
African American librarians, 43–45
"Afro-American Women, 1800–1910" (Yellin), 49
"Afro-American Women Poets of the Nineteenth Century" (Sherman), 166
Algren, Nelson, 92, 154
Allen, Annie, 52, 184n97
All the Women Are White, All the Blacks Are Men, but Some of Us Are Brave (Hull, Scott, Smith), 17, 49–50, 166
American Daughter (Thompson), 97
American Library Association, 113
Anderson, Sada J., 16
Andrews, Regina Anderson, 184n92
anthologies: *Black-Eyed Susans* (M. Washington), 166; *The Black Woman* (Bambara), 166; *Black Women Writers* (Evans), 166; *The Crunk Feminist Collection* (Cooper, Morris, Boylorn), 166; *Home Girls* (B. Smith), 166; *The Norton Anthology of African American Literature* (McKay), 166; *This Bridge Called My Back* (Moraga, Anzaldúa), 166
Anzaldúa, Gloria E., 166
archives: archive studies, 17; counterhistory, 18; research sources, 9; "from what can be found" (Lepore), 18
Associated Negro Press, 93
Association for the Study of Negro Life and History, 26, 44
Attaway, William, 41, 119, 129
Autobiography of Malcolm X, 82

Bailey, Moya, 190
Baker, Ella, 171
Baldwin, Davarian, 87
Bambara, Toni Cade, 165
Bauer, Dale, 73
Becoming (M. Obama), 170–71, 209n21
Bell, Elizabeth, 44, 47
Benét, Stephen Vincent, 86, 88, 108–9, 197n79
Benjamin, Shanna Greene, 18
Bentley, Charles, 26
best seller lists, 2, 94–95, 97, 195nn46–49

Bethune, Mary McLeod, 15, 182n68
Black America (Nearing), 24
Black Arts movement, 5, 8
Black Chicago Renaissance: bookstores and literary scene, 20, 99–100; Bronzeville and, 87, 107, 129; Brooks and, 56; commercial life in, 97; Gayden and, 1–3; Hughes and, 13; literary history of, 10, 18; *Negro Story* and, 110; reading and reception practices and, 5, 9, 11; servicemen and, 131, 134; The Sisterhood and, 17; Walker and, 102
Black feminism, 21, 49–50, 140, 162, 164–67, 172
"A Black Feminist Statement" (Combahee), 164
Black Metropolis (Drake, Cayton), 77
Black's Blue Book, 96, 106–7
"Black Women Writers" (Evans, Foster), 166
"Black Women Writers" (Hull), 49–50
Blair, Amy, 149
Blakely, Henry, 41, 132
"Blakwomen Writers of the U.S.A." (Shariat), 50
Bland, Alden, 131, 151
Bland, Edward, 41, 131–32, 202n97
Blessed Is the Man (Zara), 187n23
Bobo, Jacqueline, 159
Bond, Rebecca M., 44
Bone, Robert, 8
Bontemps, Arna, 6, 8, 33–34, 41, 92, 181n57
Book Circle: archives at Chicago State University, 204n8; Black feminist anthologies, 168; Black middle class and, 141, 158; citizen-readers, 13, 149, 154; cultural authority of members, 145; events and programs, 142; founding of, 21; Hall Branch Library and, 146; letterhead of, 143; longest lasting book club, 8, 10; middlebrow fiction and racial politics, 13, 21; middlebrow literary taste, 10, 13, 21, 140, 147, 150, 156–59, 172, 205n39; Morrow, Ora G. and, 4, 16; "Notes on How to Review a Book" (Morrow), 143–45, 156; punctuality and agendas, 142–43, 204n12, 204n15; "Qualities Which Make a Book Good Literature" (Frederick), 142; race and racism, 158; "reading up," 3, 149, 156; respectable reading policy, 139–40, 141, 146, 153; reviews, 151–52, 161, 206n46; Rollins retirement, 160; satellite groups, 146; "Short Story Hunt," 145; social benefits of, 161–62

Book Circle, titles read: *The Apostle* (Asch), 152–53, 159; *In Bed We Cry* (Chase), 154; *Black Boy* (Wright), 138, 155–56, 159; *Between Tears and Laughter* (Yutang), 157; books read and not read, 150–51; *Earth and High Heaven* (Graham), 157; *A House Divided* (Buck), 150; *Indigo* (Weston), 153, 157; *The Man with the Golden Arm* (Algren), 154; *Native Son* (Wright), 138; *New World A-Coming* (Ottley), 155–56; *The Promise* (Buck), 152, 157; *Ten Years in Japan* (Grew), 152; *Undercover* (Carlson), 152–53, 159; *Understanding Human Nature* (Adler), 150; *U.S. Foreign Policy* (Lippman), 152–53

book clubs: Black BookTock, 17; Black Girls Book Club, 17; Black writers and, 107; Home Reading Club, 107; *Negro Story* book clubs, 104; nineteenth-century reading groups, 147; Oprah's Book Club, 17, 167–68, 209n15; Sistah Girls Book Club, 17; Well-Read Black Girl project, 17; white women's book clubs, 148

Book-of-the-Month Club (BOTM), 2, 94, 141, 147, 149–50, 184n102, 193n9, 205n39, 206n44

Book Review and Lecture Forum, 42, 85, 132, 181n53, 182n69, 182n70

Book Review and Lecture Forum speakers: Gayden, Fern, 1, 6, 19; Hurston, Zora Neale, 41, 182n66

Book Review and Lecture Forum topics: *Blood on the Forge* (Attaway), 41; *Dust Tracks on a Road* (Hurston), 41; *Grapes of Wrath* (Steinbeck), 41; *The Green Years* (Cronin), 41; *Ideas are Weapons* (Lerner), 41; *Inside Latin America* (Gunther), 41; *My America* (Adamic), 41; *For My People* (M. Walker), 41; *Native Son* (Wright), 41; *The Negro and the Democratic Front* (Ford), 41; *The Robe* (Douglas), 41; *For Whom the Bell Tolls* (Hemingway), 41

Book Review Digest, 24
bookstores: Black press and, 100; in Bronzeville, 6, 20, 95–97, 103; Crisis Book Shop, 100; Faulkner's News and Book Store, 95; Hayes' Book Store, 96; Negro Digest Book Shop, 97–98, 196n60; S. & S. bookstore, 8, 83, 99–100, 102, 111, 196n61; statistics of, 93–94, 100, 194n40; Studio Bookshop, 8, 83, 196n60
Boone, Eloise M., 99
Boylorn, Robin M., 167
Boysaw, Lucille, 153
Braddan, Joy, 141–42, 152
Bradley, George, 87
Brannic, Leroy M., 125
Brawley, Benjamin, 29
Broadside Press, 82
Bromfield, Louis, 187n23
Bronze Confessions (magazine), 123
The Bronzeman (magazine), 19, 127
Bronzeville, 6, 8–9, 38–40, 106–7
Brooks, Gwendolyn: Beatrice Abbott and, 68; Black Chicago Renaissance and, 9–10; Black press and, 18; Black readership of, 111; Black woman's role, 140; Book Circle and, 145, 150; Bronzeville purchasers, 84; childhood and teenage years, 69; critical readers and, 81; early works of, 19–20, 53, 56, 70; friendships and, 70–71, 189n69; Hall Branch Library and, 24; on heterosexual romance, 77–79; Huff and, 75, 154; importance of, 163, 172; influence on literary tastes, 4; Lasers and, 53, 63, 185n1; "Lights and Shadows" column, 19, 53–55, 61–62, 65–67, 70, 72–74, 76–77, 81–83; list of goals, 69, 189n58; local influence in Bronzeville, 3; *Negro Story* and, 6; "personal is political" reception work, 21; poetry of, 16; poetry to local readers, 13–15; skin color and, 76; Special Negro Collection use, 32
Brooks, Gwendolyn, publications: *Annie Allen*, 52, 83, 87, 132, 184n102; "The Bright Star," 78–79; "Corner in a Portrait Gallery," 70, 185n2; "Count No Day Lost," 70; "Friend," 71; "Gay Chaps at the Bar," 136; "Happiness," 54–55; "Heavy resentment," 70; "Honored," 83, 190n127; "I Thank You for Your Kindness," 78; "Jingling Judy's Journal," 79; "Kismet," 79; "Life Is Too Short," 70; *Maud Martha*, 132; "To My Parents," 71–72, 77, 190n91; "Myself," 80; "An Old Apartment Building," 81; "One Little Quarrel," 70; "Plaint," 78; "Possession," 79; "Postscript to Suffering, 79; "Prayer," 78; "For Semuel H. Randolph (Ima Twin)," 70; "Shadows," 70; "A Song in the Front Yard," 81; "A Song of Thanksgiving," 70; "Sonnet," 79; "Sonnets for Beatrice," 70; *A Street in Bronzeville*, 8, 29, 83, 87, 99, 102, 122, 136, 196n60; "Two Songs for Friends," 70–71; "Wealth," 70; "You Need Not Bring Me Roses," 78
Brooks, Joanna, 18
Brown, Hallie Quinn, 29
Brown, Stephanie, 10
Brown, Sterling, 4, 14, 91, 131
Brown, William Wells, 122
Browning, Alice: Black literary magazines and, 127; Black owned distribution companies and, 125; Bronzeville connection, 13; importance of, 163; influence on literary tastes and book purchasing, 4, 103–5; legacy of, 168; lists of recommended books, 122–23; literary manifesto of, 16; little magazines and, 18; local influence in Bronzeville, 3; publications led by Black women, 124; reading and reception practices, 172; and Reddick, 199n32; on soldiers' experiences, 203n115; war effort and Black soldiers, 112, 118, 121, 129–32, 134–37; white readers and, 126. See also *Negro Story*
"Browsing with Books" (Ferrell), 145
Buck, Pearl, 150, 152, 157
Buford, Fanny, 60
Burley, Dan, 62, 75
Burns, Ben, 60, 123
Burt, Laura, 24, 52
Burton, Mary E., 91, 93
Buster, Ethel, 44
Byron, George Gordon, 78

Carver, George Washington, 33, 152
Cayton, Horace, 2–3, 6, 27, 41, 66, 77

Challenge (magazine), 127
Chambliss, Melanie, 46–47, 178n8
Chatelain, Marcia, 15, 66, 72, 79, 139
Chesnutt, Charles W., 29, 123, 151
The Chicago Afro-American Union Analytic Catalog, 27
Chicago Board of Education, 32
The Chicago Circuit (magazine), 124
Chicago Defender: advertisements, 99; anniversary of, 188n48; Black soldier literacy report, 115; Black writer support, 100; Book Circle announcement, 140; Brooks and, 53, 55, 81–82; Buy-a-Book racial uplift, 95–96; Great Migration and, 19, 57–58, 73, 185n11; Harsh obituary, 37; history of, 186n23; interest in African American history, 34; poetry columns of, 6, 10; purchase of books and, 186n18; respectable reading policy, 56–60, 73, 139, 186n12; Special Negro Collection and, 33, 37, 40; Victory Edition, 116–17; World War II and, 115–16
Chicago Defender columns: "Authors and Books," 60; "Book Chats," 60–61, 187n23; "Book Don'ts," 59–60; "Book Lover's Corner" (Junior section), 60; "Book Reviews: Read More—Learn More," 187n23; "Books" and "Off the Book Shelf," 60, 123; "Books and Those Who Write Them," 60; "The Bookshelf," 60, 186n23; column editors, 187n23; Earl Conrad's column, 125–26; "Every-Day Courtesies," 186n15; "George C. Hall Library Notes," 60; "Have a Smile, Give a Smile," 187n27; "From Here to Yonder," 60; "Here to Yonder," 103; "A Little Bit of Everything," 61–62, 187n27; "Poetry," 188n38; "This, That and T'Other," 61; "This and That," 187n25; "Two Good New Books," 59; "Verse a Day," 67. *See also* "Lights and Shadows"
Chicago History Museum, 9
Chicago Poets' Class, 132
Chicago Police Department, 2, 23, 110
Chicago Public Library (CPL): African American librarians and, 44–47, 51, 183n76, 183nn80–81; bibliographies and pamphlets, 36; cataloging and classification practices, 28–29, 178n8; 179n28; cataloging of Harsh material, 178n8; Hall Branch library 23, 33 40;; Mellon grant CPL to digitize and process documents," 181n56; Special Negro Collection renamed, 37; special research collections policy, 178n12.
Chicago State University Archives, 9
Chicago Tribune, 63, 95, 100, 145
The Chinaberry Tree (Fauset), 33
The Choice, 82
Christian, Barbara, 162
Christian Science Monitor, 92
Claybrooks, R. E., 132
Clotel (W. W. Brown), 122
clubs, African American women and, 66–67
Coffin, Ollye Marr, 41, 145, 181n53
Cofield, Ernestine, 60, 187n23
Collier, Joan, 170
Collins, Patricia Hill, 168
Color (magazine), 123, 201n68
Colored American Magazine, 48
The Colored Cadets of West Point (Flipper), 27
Colored People's Blue-Book and Business Directory of Chicago, 195n50
Combahee River Collective, 17, 164–65, 167
Connor, John M., 114
Conrad, Earl, 125
Cooper, Anna Julia, 29
Cooper, Brittney C., 15, 50–51, 74, 167
Cortor, Eldzier, 117
Couch, William, 41, 131–34, 136
Courage, Richard A., 8, 60
Craft, Ellen, 49
Crawford, Robert M., 63
The Crisis (Du Bois), 44, 67, 100, 123, 127, 182n74, 183nn80–81, 200n55
The Crisis book store, 196n54
Cronin, A. J., 41
Cullen, Countee, 62–63, 93, 109
Curry, Dorothy, 154
Curtis, Connie Nichols, 124

Dandridge, Rita B., 166
Davidson, Eugene, 197n79
Davis, Frank Marshall, 1, 6, 9, 19, 29, 34, 41, 62, 93, 131

Davis, Robert, 41, 131–32, 134–35
DeGeneres, Ellen, 170
Delaney, Sadie Peterson, 47–48, 183n84
De Priest, Oscar, 23, 44, 46, 177n1
De Vries, Peter, 65, 188n38
Dewey Decimal classification, 28–29
Dictionary Catalog of the Vivian G. Harsh Collection of Afro-American History and Literature, 179n22
Diggs, Olive, 6, 67, 123
Dodson, Owen, 132
Donoghue, Vera, 117
Douglas, Lloyd, 41
Drake, St. Clair, 6, 66, 69, 77
Driscoll, Beth, 147
Du Bois, W. E. B., 14, 29, 34, 44–48, 50–51, 117, 183n76, 183nn80–81, 183n84, 183n86
Dunbar, Erica Armstrong, 171
Dunbar, Paul Laurence, 26, 33
Dunbar-Nelson, Alice, 29, 47
The Dunbar Speaker and Entertainer, 29, 59
Dunlop, Mollie, 48, 183n84
DuSable Black History Museum, 202n102
Dust Tracks on a Road (Hurston), 41, 121–22
Dyja, Thomas, 22

Ebony, 72, 97–98, 100, 107, 124, 196n57
Edim, Glory, 17, 170
Edmonds, Randolph, 121
Ellis, Carroll, 124
Ellison, Ralph, 128–29, 150–51
Encyclopedia of the Negro (Du Bois), 47, 183n84
Essence (magazine), 171
Evans, Mari, 50, 166
Evans, Stephanie Y., 15–16, 176n34
Ewing, Eve, 22
Expression (magazine), 124, 201n68

Fagan, Benjamin, 12
"Famous Women of the Negro Race" (Hopkins), 48
"Famous WPA Writers" (Bontemps), 8
Farr, Cecilia Konchar, 169
Fast, Howard, 122
Faulkner, William, 168
Fauset, Jessie, 34, 49, 63, 151, 156

Fax, Elton, 133
Female Literary Association of Philadelphia, 11–12
Ferrell, Oneita, 140–41, 145, 154, 157
Fielder, Brigitte, 15
Fire!! (magazine), 127
Fisher, Dorothy Canfield, 149, 156
Flipper, Henry, 27
Ford, James, 41
Ford, Nick Aaron, 128, 133–34
Foreman, P. Gabrielle, 11–12
Forgotten Readers (Henry), 11
Foster, Frances Smith, 15, 49, 166
The Foxes of Harrow (Yerby), 193n9
Frazier, E. Franklin, 34, 58, 71, 186n13
Frederick, John T., 142, 145
Frederick Douglass Book Center, 196n54

Gaines, Kevin K., 139
Gallon, Kim, 56
Gardner, Eric, 11
Garner, Lonnie Richard (Mrs.), 64
Gayden, Fern: background of, 1; Black authors and, 128; Black owned distribution companies and, 124; Book Review and Lecture Forum speaker, 1, 3, 19; image of Black Americans, 119, 126; influence on literary tastes, 4; literary manifesto of, 16; reading as a civic duty, 110; recommended books, 121–22; recommended periodicals, 123; Visionaries (poetry group) and, 132; World War II and soldiers, 112, 130; Wright and, 2, 173n1. See also Negro Story
Gender, Race, and Politics in the Midwest (Hendricks), 66
"The George Cleveland Hall Branch and Its Social Environment." (Harsh), 38
George Cleveland Hall Branch Library. See Hall Branch Library
George Washington Carver (Holt), 121
Goldsby, Jacqueline, 42, 182n69
Goreleigh, Rex, 146
Goss, Margaret Taylor, 132, 202n102
Graham, Elaine, 124
Graham, Maryemma, 91
Grapes of Wrath (Steinbeck), 171
Gray, Albertine, 153

Great Eastern News Corporation, 124–25
Great Migration, 19, 57–58, 66, 71, 73, 77, 105, 139
Green, Adam, 8, 22, 71, 73, 87
Green, Clara, 138, 140–41, 155
Greene, Josiah E., 131
Grew, Joseph, 152
Gunther, John, 41

Hadley, Marian G., 26
Half-Century Magazine, 67
Hall, Delaney, 63
Hall Branch Library: African American patrons and, 19; Bentley book donation, 26; book culture of, 6; book display, 7; Bronzeville library, 1, 31; community of, 181n57; origins and violence, 23–24. *See also* Book Review and Lecture Forum; Special Negro Collection
Hall Branch Library programming: children's programming, 39; DuSable History Club, 39; Fifty and More Club (F.A.M.), 39–40; Negro History Week and, 39. *See also* Book Review and Lecture Forum
Halliday, Aria S., 67
Hamer, Fannie Lou, 171
Hancock, Mabel, 141, 151, 154
Harker, Jaime, 10, 14, 102–3, 119, 148–50, 156
Harper, Anne M., 135
Harper, Frances E. W., 12, 48, 151
Harper & Brothers, 94, 196n60
Harper and Row, 82
Harris, Lera, 141, 152, 157–58
Harris, V. Polly, 60, 187n23
Harsh, Vivian G.: at Abraham Lincoln Centre Branch, 43, 47; African American librarian lists, 45, 50–51; for Black women readers, 165; Book Review and Lecture Forum, 6, 41, 61; and Bronzeville, 3, 13, 28, 30, 38, 43, 85; circulation of special collection, 31–32; classification modifications, 28–29; and Coffin, 145; death of, 208n1; directory of Chicago African American librarians, 46, 48; event organizer, 15; Hall Branch employee list, 52, 184n92; Hall Branch and, 19, 23–24, 43–44, 177n1; "Historian Who Never Wrote," 25, 27–28, 178n8; influence on literary tastes, 4; legacy of, 169, 172; "The Negro: A List of Books," 35–36; Negro History Week and, 32–34, 37, 180n40; networking of African American librarians, 44, 47–48; at Ogden Park Branch, 46, 81; pamphlets and bibliographies by, 42, 60, 121, 182n70; "personal is political" reception work, 21; programming by, 40; public library system, 18; radio scripts and, 33; reading and reception practices of, 16–17, 24–25, 34, 37; requests for items in collection, 34; retirement of, 181n53; visits to other African American collections, 26. *See also* Special Negro Collection
Hartford Courant, 92
Hayakawa, S. I., 128, 188n38
Headlines (magazine), 124, 126
Helton, Laura, 17, 28–29, 50
Hemingway, Ernest, 41
Hendricks, Wanda A., 16, 66
Henthorn, Cynthia Lee, 106
higher education, 16, 176n34
Himes, Chester, 6, 99, 122, 127–28, 130, 135
Hine, Darlene Clark, 8, 12, 16
Hitler, Adolph, 114
Holloway, Georgia, 115
Holt, Nora Douglas, 67, 188n47
Holt, Rackham, 121
"Homely Philosophy" national column (G. D. Johnson), 67–68, 73, 189n51
Home to Harlem (McKay), 65
Hopkins, Pauline, 16, 48–50, 165
Howard University, 25, 28, 48
How Stella Got Her Groove Back (McMillan), 88, 168
How to Be Fit, 94
Huff, William Henry, 53–55, 65, 67, 74–75, 154
Huff, William Henry, publications of: "Easter Rain," 188n48; "Girls Should Neither Smoke Nor Drink!," 75; "The Girl Who Answered No," 75; "O Mother Dear," 75; "A Stitch in Time," 75; "The Ultra-Modern Wife," 75; "Womanhood Then and Now," 75

Hughes, Langston: Book Review and Lecture Forum participant, 41; Book Review column praise, 60; *Chicago Defender* and, 63, 103–4, 180n42; on Hall Branch list, 34; and Jones, 61–62; literary tradition of, 91, 93; local connections, 13; and *Negro Story*, 99, 121–22, 128; not Book Circle, 151; purchase of books and, 82; and reading, 197n65; Skyloft Players and, 6; Walker, Margaret and, 100–102; World War II and racism, 118

Hughes, Langston, publications: *The Big Sea*, 27; "Private Jim Crow," 135; *Shakespeare in Harlem*, 97, 121; *Weary Blues*, 29, 65

Hull, Gloria T., 49–50, 166

Hurston, Zora Neale, 34, 41, 63, 122, 151, 167, 182n66

Hutner, Gordon, 10, 13, 148–49, 151, 153

Illinois Federation of Colored Women's Clubs (IFCWC), 16

Illinois Library Association, 32

Incidents in the Life of a Slave Girl (Jacobs), 12

"In Search of Our Mothers' Gardens" (A. Walker), 163

Instagram, 170

Institute for the Study of the History, Life, and Culture of Black People, 163

Iola Leroy (Harper), 12

Jackson, A. L., 60, 187n23

Jacobs, Harriet, 12, 171

Jennings, Judson, 24

Jewell, Pherell, 44

Johnson, Charles S., 117, 122

Johnson, D. W., 60

Johnson, Georgia Douglas, 62, 67–70, 72, 74, 76, 80, 188n48

Johnson, James Weldon, 29, 63, 65

Johnson, John H., 24, 32, 97, 127

Johnson, William, 32

Jones, Dewey R., 53, 60–65, 67, 75–76, 185n1, 187n27, 188n46

Jones, Martha S., 15

Jordan, June, 17

Joyce, Donald Franklin, 37, 178n12, 179n22

Kaba, Mariame, 22

Keckley, Elizabeth, 49

Kemp, Marjorie, 46

Kent, George, 69, 76–77

Keys, Harriette, 162

Knupfer, Anne Meis, 8, 16, 66, 140

Kolar, Andrew J., 23–24

The Land of Cotton and Other Plays (Edmonds), 121

Latimer, Catherine, 47, 50–51, 122, 199n32, 200n43

Lawson, Ruth, 204n12

Lepore, Jill, 18

Lerner, Max, 41

Leroy, Justin, 17

Letter (magazine), 124

Levin, N. R., 183n76

Library Journal, 46

Library of Congress, 123

Library of Congress classification, 28–29, 179n28

Life of Pi (Martel), 171

"Lights and Shadows": Brooks and, 19, 54; content of, 61–65; contributors to, 67; Lasers, 19, 53, 63, 67–68, 70, 185n1; Black women stereotypes, 74–76; poetry of, 60, 62, 67–69, 74; readers' comments, 63–64; women in, 188n46. See also *Chicago Defender* columns

Lin Yutang, 157

Lippman, Walter, 152

literacy, 11–12, 105–6, 115

Literary Guild, 141, 150

literary societies: Black nineteenth century, 11–12, 42, 140; Book Circle and, 138; NAACP and, 14; in Pennsylvania, 176n34

Locke, Alain, 24, 117

Logan, Spencer, 131

Long, Elizabeth, 148, 159

Lorde, Audre, 17, 50

Louisville Courier-Journal, 91–92

Lowry, Bessie, 44

Macmillan Centenary Awards, 131

magazine publishing, 123–27

Maney, Elizabeth, 141

Manning, Molly Guptill, 112
Manuscript (newsletter), 124
The Man Who Had Everything (Bromfield), 187n23
Marshall, Nate, 22
Marshall, Russell, 41
Martel, Yann, 171
Martin, Gertrude, 60, 124, 187n23
Martin, Louis, 124
Matthews, Kristin L., 114, 194n40
Matthews, Victoria Earle, 16
McCann, Sean, 156
McCluskey, John, Jr., 8
McCormick, Ada, 124
McDowell, Essence, 22
McHenry, Elizabeth, 11–13, 139–40, 147, 150, 158, 168
McKay, Claude, 27, 62–63, 145, 151
McKay, Nellie, 166
McMillan, Terry, 5, 88, 103, 167–68
Meeker, Arthur, 145
Mein Kampf (Hitler), 112–14
Melcher, Frederic, 113, 198n9
Michaeli, Ethan, 22, 185n11
middlebrow literary taste, 4, 11, 147–50
Midwestern Writers' Conference, 142, 145
Millay, Edna St. Vincent, 63
Miller, Laura J., 93–94, 194n40
Milton, John, 109
Mishler, Max A., 17
"misogynoir," 75, 190n84
Mitchell, Koritha, 15
Monroe, Harriet, 62
Moody, Joycelyn, 11
Moore, Natalie, 22
Moorland Foundation, 28–29
Moraga, Cherríe L., 166
Morris, Edward H., 48
Morris, Susana M., 167
Morrison, Toni, 17–18, 103, 168
Morrow, Lucian J., 205n26
Morrow, Lucian (Mrs.), 146
Morrow, Ora G; Black feminism and, 172; Black youth and, 158; Book Circle and, 139–41, 143–46; Bronzeville and, 3, 13, 16, 18–19; death of, 208n1; educational value of books read, 152; Frederick's lecture comments, 204n10; influence on literary tastes, 4; middlebrow literary reading practices, 21; middlebrow literary taste, 147; "Notes on How to Review a Book," 156; praise for, 153, 161; professional identity of Book Circle, 142; Wright and, 155
Mossell, Gertrude, 48–50, 165
Motley, Willard, 8, 122, 151
Mouzon, Brunetta, 41
Mullen, Bill V., 8, 58, 127
Murray, Florence, 36, 122
The Muse in Bronzeville (Courage), 8
Music and Poetry (magazine), 67, 188n47
Music Dial (magazine), 201n68

National Association of Colored Women, 16
National Evaluative Conference on Black Studies, 163
National Negro Magazine and Publishing Association, 125
National News Service, 124
National Youth Administration (NYA), 182n68
Naylor, Gloria, 103
Nearing, Scott, 24
Negro Digest, 97, 100, 123, 127–28, 200n55
The Negro Family in Chicago (Frazier), 58, 186n13
The Negro Handbook (Murray), 36, 122
Negro History Week, 32–34, 37, 39, 115, 180n40, 182n70. *See also* Harsh, Vivian G.
"The Negro in Illinois," 27
"Negro in Our History" (Woodson), 33
Negro Peoples Theatre, 132
The Negro Soldier (film), 114, 129
Negro Story (magazine): advertisements, 104–5; associate editors, 200n51; Black servicemen authors, 131–32; boundary-pushing fiction, 111; Bronzeville book buying and, 102; Browning and Gayden and, 6; *Chicago Defender* and, 123, 197n68; *The Crisis* and, 123; Double V victory campaign, 20–21; founders, 1; "Letters from Our Readers," 202n91; "A Letter to Our Readers," 130; market for, 127–29; *Negro Digest* and, 123;

nineteenth-century Black authors in, 122–23; political and social change, 110–12; promotion of Black-owned distribution companies, 124; promotion of other periodicals, 123–25, 200n55, 201n68; promotion of talented Black women, 124; readership of, 111; reviews of books of racial pride and unity, 122; S & S Bookstore and, 100; sample page from, 133; Simkins and, 99; slave narratives in, 123; *Sunday Chicago Bee* and, 8, 123; white authors and readership, 126, 201n71, 203n106; World War II and soldiers, 118–20, 123, 129–37, 200n45; Wright and, 173n1

Negro Story (magazine), publications: "Battle for Two" (Thomas), 135–36; "Beginnings" (Bland), 202n97; "A Colored Soldier's Prayer" (Harper), 135; "District of Columbia" (Richards), 135; "Essay on Heat, by a Man Who Lived Through It" (Davis), 203n106; "Gay Chaps at the Bar" (Brooks), 136; "Ground Crewman," 134; "I Had a Colored Maid" (Rodriguez), 120; "Johnnie Cull" (Rutan), 135; "Justice Wears Dark Glasses" (Tomkins), 120–21; "Let's Go Visiting" (Bland), 131; lists of recommended books, 120, 122, 200nn44–45; "Memorial to Ed Bland" (Brooks), 132; "The Negro Soldier Speaks" (Ford), 133–34; "A Penny for Your Thoughts," 135; "Private Jeff Johnson" (Goss), 132; "Private Jim Crow" (Hughes), 135; "Rest Stop" (Grubb), 135; "Sketches from the Army" (Davis), 134–35; "To a Soldier" (Ford), 134; "A WAC Speaks to a Soldier" (Pitt), 135

Negro Year Book, 94
Newberry Library, 9
New Challenge (magazine), 127, 131
Newton, Marshall E., 130
New World A-Coming (Ottley), 122
New York Amsterdam News, 126
New York Herald, 12
New York Herald Tribune, 24, 92, 95
New York Times, 2, 95, 100, 171, 193n9, 195n47
New York Times Book Review, 94

Norton, W. W., 113
Not Without Laughter, 33

Obama, Michelle, 170–71, 173n5
Oberlin College, 16
Oliver, Homer, 115
Olson, Liesl, 13, 16, 103
online book clubs: Black BookTock, 169; Black Chick Lit, 169; Book Girl Magic (BGM), 17, 169; Go On Girl! Book Club, 169; Mocha Girls Read (MGR), 17, 169; The Sistah Girl Next Door, 169; social media and, 169
online forums: #CiteASista, 170; #CiteBlackWomen, 170; #SisterPhD, 170; Feministing, 209n15
"On the Novels Written by Selected Black Women" (Dandridge), 166
Opportunity (magazine), 127, 201n68
Orro, David, 62
Ottley, Roi, 122, 145, 151, 155
Ovington, Mary White, 187n23

Paris, Eloise, 141
Parker, Dorothy, 78
Peay, Aisha, 165
"A Penny for Your Thoughts" (Himes), 135
PEP (magazine), 124
Peterson, Carla L., 18
Petry, Ann, 122, 150–51
Pitt, Lucia Mae, 135
Pittsburgh Courier, 108, 116
Platt, Amelia, 44, 51, 182n73
Poetry (magazine), 62, 65, 85, 92, 136
Porter, Dorothy, 25, 28–30, 47–48, 50–51, 183n84
Posey Flowers Dance Group, 132
Prattis, Percival L., 61
Pritchard, Ethel, 140–42, 155, 161
The Progress of a Race, 59
Publishers' Weekly, 94–95, 107, 113, 193n12, 195n47
Pulitzer Prize, 52–53

racial uplift, 3, 15, 48, 55–57, 66, 68, 95, 140, 156, 158–59
Radway, Janice A., 10, 72, 147, 149

Randolph, A. Philip, 117
Raymond, Mildred, 183n80
reader-consumers, 14–15, 88, 102–5, 107–8, 140
reading and reception practices, 2–5, 9–12, 15–19, 21–22, 24, 56, 88, 110–12, 159–67, 171–72
Reddick, L. D., 117–19, 136, 200n45
Reed, Christopher Robert, 8, 22
Report from Iron Mountain (Lewin), 82
Rice, Frances, 47
The Rich and the Super Rich, 82
Ricks, Marcella, 122
Ridley, Florida, 48
Robinson, LaVaughn, 6, 171, 173n5
Roden, Carl, 23–24, 46, 177n1
Rodriguez, Margaret, 120
Rogers, Gertrude, 151
Rohrbach, Augusta, 195n47
Rollins, Charlemae Hill, 25–26, 32, 39, 141, 145, 159–60, 180n38
Roosevelt, Franklin D., 113
Rosenwald, Julius, 38
Rosenwald Foundation, 23–24, 26
Royster, Jacqueline Jones, 12
Rubin, Joan Shelley, 10, 147, 154
Rukeyser, Muriel, 87

Salvation Army Servicemen's Club, 130
Sanchez, Sonia, 162
Schalk, Toki, 124
Schlabach, Elizabeth Schroeder, 6, 106
Schneider, Isidor, 107
Schomburg Collection, NY Public Library, 26, 199n32, 200n45
Schomburg Library of Nineteenth-Century Black Women Writers, 166
Scott, Patricia Bell, 49, 166
Scott, William, 88
Scott's Blue Book, 96–97, 99
Second Annual Black Writers' Conference, 163
Second Black Writers' Conference (Fisk University), 82
Seeley, Samantha, 17
Senchyne, Jonathan, 15
Sengstacke, Myrtle, 123

Shakespeare, William, 42
Shange, Ntozake, 17, 50
Shariat, Fahamisha, 50
Shaw, Blanche V., 23, 44
Shaw, Emma, 44
Shaw, O'Wendell, 127–28, 201n72
Sherman, Joan R., 166
Shores, Louis, 46, 182n74
Simms' Blue Book and National Negro Business and Professional Directory, 96, 196n54
Simpkins, Lewis, 99, 196n61
Sims, W. W., 44
The Sisterhood, 17
Smith, Barbara, 49, 162, 165–66
Smith, Doris Evans, 99
Smith, Lillian, 110, 121
Song of Solomon, 171
Sojourner Truth narrative, 27
The Souls of Black Folk (Du Bois), 34
South Side Community Art Center, 132, 142, 146, 202n102, 203n106
South Side Writers Group, 1, 3, 41, 85
Special Negro Collection: bibliographies, lists and pamphlets, 34–37, 42, 181n51; cataloging and classification of, 28–29; Chicago Public Library policies and, 178n12; circulation and use of, 32; collection closed to the public, 181n53; Du Bois and, 47; expansion of, 27; grants to support and enhance, 37; Harsh and, 25–26; Harsh obituary and renaming of collection, 37; Kolar and, 24; location in library, 30–31; notable acquisitions, 27; public exhibitions of, 180n40; requests for items in collection, 33
Special Negro Collection, lists of: "Books by and Relating to the Negro," 36; *The Negro and His Achievements in America*, 36; "Negro in Our Democracy," 36; "New Books by and about the Negro," 36; "On These We Stand," 36; "We, Too, Are America," 36
Special Negro Collection, titles of: *Black Man's Verse* (Davis), 34; *Black Thunder* (Bontemps), 34; *The Dunbar Speaker and Entertainer* (Nelson), 29; *Early Negro American Writers* (Brawley), 29;

Homespun Heroines and other Women of Distinction (H. Q. Brown), 29; *House Beyond the Cedars* (Chesnutt), 29; *Negro Builders and Heroes* (Brawley), 29; *The New Negro* (Locke), 34; *Personal Recollections of the Grimke Family* (Cooper), 29; *Selected Speeches* (B. T. Washington), 28; *The Souls of Black Folk* (Du Bois), 34; *A Voice from the South* (Cooper), 29; *The Weary Blues* (Hughes), 29
Spencer, Anne, 49
Spotlighter (magazine), 201n68
Spring in New Hampshire and Other Poems (McKay), 27
Squires, Catherine, 57
Stein, Gertrude, 63
Steinbeck, John, 41
Strange Fruit (Smith), 110, 121
Sunday Chicago Bee, 6, 39, 52, 67, 83, 100–101, 123, 145, 155, 192n127
Sweeney, Shauna, 17

Teasdale, Sara, 78
Terrell, Mary Church, 15
Their Eyes Were Watching God (Hurston), 85, 167
Theory of Flight (Rukeyser), 87, 193n12
They Burned the Books (Benét), 109
Thomas, Roberta I., 135
Thompson, E. J., 44, 47
Thompson, Era Bell, 41, 62–63, 97, 122, 151
Thompson, James G., 116
Thorsson, Courtney, 17
Thurman, Wallace, 63
Tide (magazine), 105, 127
Time (magazine), 106
Tompkins, Grace W., 120–21, 123
"Toward a Black Feminist Criticism" (B. Smith), 165–66
Towles, Ester L., 151, 153, 160
Town and Stories (magazine), 123
Treasury of Great Poems (Untermeyer), 195n46
Trodd, Zoe, 59
Truth, Soujourner, 27
Twain, Mark, 109
Twin, Ima, 71

Ulrich, Laurel Thatcher, 18
Untermeyer, Louis, 195n46

Visionaries (poetry group), 132
Vivian G. Harsh Research Collection, 9, 169

Waiting to Exhale (McMillan), 167
Walker, Alice, 17, 50, 166–67
Walker, Margaret: Black Chicago Renaissance and, 9; Blacks as primary audience, 14; Book Review and Lecture Forum and, 41, 85; Bronzeville Black-owned bookstores and, 18, 99; Bronzeville connection, 3, 13; *Chicago Defender* support, 100–102; in "Famous WPA Writers," 8; Hall Branch Library and, 6, 19; influence on literary tastes, 4; legacy of, 163, 172; MFA at the University of Iowa, 86; middlebrow literary taste and, 156; obituary, 87; "personal is political" reception work, 21; poetry of, 16; reviews and popularity of, 93–95, 103; reviews of, 91–92; Richard Wright and, 85; South Side Writers Group member, 1, 85; Special Negro Collection use, 32; white readers and, 102; World War II and soldiers, 131; Yale Younger Poets prize, 20, 86, 108
Walker, Margaret, publications: "Dark Blood," 91; "Delta," 89, 91–92; *Jubilee*, 163; "Lineage," 90; *For My People*, 20, 41, 84–90, 93–95, 97, 100–103, 108–9, 111, 122, 195n45; "Our Need," 89; "People of Unrest," 89; "Since 1619," 90; "Sorrow Home," 91; "Southern Song," 91; "The Struggle Staggers Us," 89; "Today," 90
Walker, Marion, 132
Warren, Althea, 114
Washington, Booker T., 26, 28–29, 34
Washington, Mary Helen, 166–67
Washington Post, 107
Weaver, Audrey, 60, 187n23
Weems, Robert, Jr., 8, 87, 105
Well-Read Black Girl (Edim), 170
Wells, Ida B., 15, 48, 66, 171
The Welsh Review (magazine), 131
West, Dorothy, 22
West, E. James, 22

Weston, Christine, 152
Wheatley, Phillis, 48, 151, 171
Whitfield, Mary, 141, 152, 154, 157–58, 161, 204n15
Whitman, Walt, 4, 109
Williams, Brittany, 170
Williams, Fannie Barrier, 15, 43–44, 49, 66, 74
Williams, Ruth M., 153, 161
Williams-Irvin, Katherine E., 67
Williamson, Terrion L., 16
Willis, Beatrice, 141, 161
Wimp, Elizabeth, 27
Winfrey, Oprah, 168, 170–71
Woodson, Carter G., 32–33
Woolf, Virginia, 147–48
The Work of the Afro-American Woman (Mossell), 48
World War II: Armed Services Editions (ASE), 114; Black American recruitment, 114–15; Council on Books in Wartime, 109, 114; Delta Sigma Theta Victory Book Drive, 116, 199n26; Double V campaign, 108, 112, 116–17, 136; military book access, 115–16, 199n25; Ohio Negro Chamber of Commerce and, 115; "Our Pledge of Allegiance," 117; race and racism, 117–20, 198n9, 203n115; reading and war effort, 111–13; Victory Book Campaign (VBC), 109, 113–14, 198n11. See also *Negro Story* (magazine)
Wright, Richard: Black Chicago Renaissance and, 9–10; Book Circle and, 150; in "Famous WPA Writers," 8; Gayden connection, 173n1; Hall Branch Library and, 24; Margaret Wright and, 85; *Negro Story* and, 6, 99, 119; social realism of, 77; South Side Writers Group founder, 1, 3; Special Negro Collection and, 26–27, 32; white readers and, 102
Wright, Richard, publications: *12 Million Black Voices*, 29; "Almos' a Man," 173n1; "Big Boy Leaves Home," 26; *Black Boy*, 1–2, 19, 23, 97, 104, 110, 122, 138, 151, 155–56, 159; "Blueprint for Negro Literature," 27; "A Blueprint for Negro Writing," 3, 131; "Ethnographical Aspects of Chicago's Black Belt," 27; *Native Son*, 2, 33, 36, 94–95, 97, 138, 149, 193n9
Writing for the Weeklies (Shaw), 201n72

Yale Series of Younger Poets, 2, 20, 86–88, 91, 94, 108–9
Yale University Press, 86, 94, 108, 194nn43–45, 196n60, 197n79
Yale Younger Poets prize, 20, 86, 108
Yellin, Jean Fagan, 49–50
Yerby, Frank, 8, 86, 122, 151, 193n9, 195n47
Young, Frank A., 61, 187n27, 188n46, 189n50
Young, Hortense, 124
Young, Pauline A., 47

Zara, Louis, 187n23

www.ingramcontent.com/pod-product-compliance
Lightning Source LLC
Chambersburg PA
CBHW030646230426
43665CB00011B/980